Learning Needs and Evaluation

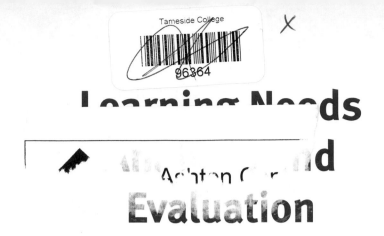

Frances and Roland Bee are personnel and learning consultants in their own business, Time for People, specialising in learning needs analysis and learning evaluation and have worked with a wide variety of public and private sector organisations. Their backgrounds, which include experience as HR professionals, finance managers and line managers, give them a unique perspective on the issues surrounding learning and development. Their other publications are *The Complete Learning Evaluation Toolkit*, *Facilitation Skills*, *Managing Information and Statistics*, *Project Management – the people challenge*, *Customer Care* and *Constructive Feedback*. They operate from a converted barn in the grounds of their late medieval/early Tudor farmhouse in Suffolk surrounded by 10 acres of newly planted woodlands and wild flower meadows.

Frances Bee read Mathematics at Oxford and Statistics at London University. Her career began in strategic planning in local government and then, following completion of her MBA, she moved into the HR area. Her next career step was into senior management with a major building society. She then moved into the retail sector, occupying several senior posts, including those of company assistant finance director and general manager of a large department store. She has worked for the CIPD for a number of years, on a consultancy basis, and currently is a member of the advisory board of experts for their portfolio of open courses.

Roland Bee began his career as an industrial chemist, then served in the RAF as a navigator. He then moved into the HR and management services fields where he has worked as a chief personnel officer in local government and held a number of senior posts in housing finance and the electricity supply industry. Roland has an MA from the Henley Management College and has taught HR and management subjects at a number of universities.

Learning Needs Analysis and Evaluation

Frances and Roland Bee

Chartered Institute of Personnel and Development

First published in 1994
This edition first published in 2003
Reprinted 2004, 2005, 2006 (twice), 2007, 2009

Design by Beacon GDT, Ruardean, Gloucestershire
Typesetting by Fakenham Photosetting Ltd, Fakenham, Norfolk
Printed in Great Britain by The Cromwell Press Group, Trowbridge, Wiltshire

British Library Cataloguing in Publication Data
A catalogue record for this book is available from the British Library

ISBN 0–85292–967–6
ISBN 13 978-0-85292-967-4

The views expressed in this book are the authors' own and
may not necessarily reflect those of the CIPD.

CIPD Enterprises Ltd has made every effort to trace and acknowledge
copyright holders. If any source has been overlooked, CIPD Enterprises
would be pleased to redress this for future versions.

cipd

Chartered Institute of Personnel and Development,
151 The Broadway, London SW19 1JQ
Tel: 020 8612 6200
E-mail: cipd@cipd.co.uk Website: www.cipd.co.uk
Incorporated by Royal Charter. Registered Charity No. 1079797.

Contents

Introduction

Our first book on this subject was called *Training Needs Analysis and Evaluation*. The change of title to *Learning Needs Analysis and Evaluation* is more than a semantic change – it acknowledges and, indeed, welcomes the very real change in approach represented by the use of the term 'learning' as opposed to 'training'. At a simple philosophical level it represents the shift in thinking away from a paradigm that suggests training is something that is done to you by other people to one that puts the emphasis on an individual taking responsibility and ownership for his or her own learning and development. As the *Change Agenda* (Schramm, 2002) referring to the work on motivation by Carl Rogers put it: 'It is only possible to facilitate learning in others, not teach them directly.'

Also, from a systems perspective the concept of learning is much *wider* than that of training and encompasses the whole range of different ways that we can develop our knowledge, skills, attitudes and behaviours. In essence, 'learning' is what it is really all about, what we are really trying to achieve – training is just one route to it. Cunningham (2000) strongly supports the use of the language of learning rather than training:

> *The error is to see training, rather than learning, as the focus. This is not a trivial distinction. Training can become a solution looking for a problem, and such a one-dimensional focus can undermine the creation of coherent learning strategies. . . . For instance, 'training needs analysis' has to go. We need 'learning needs analysis' that focuses on business-related learning needs . . .*

We have used the language of learning throughout this book – from talking about learning needs through to looking at learning evaluation. We refer to 'learning facilitators' to describe whoever is facilitating the learning – whether as a learning professional or as a line manager, or perhaps as a coach or mentor. We prefer to talk about 'learners' and 'participants' rather than 'trainees' and 'delegates', and about 'learning interventions/events/programmes' rather than 'training courses'.

We started the introduction to our first book with the statement:

> *Training Needs Analysis is one of those subjects that often makes the training professional wince. There is the feeling that it is important, that they should know something about it and – horror of horrors – perhaps should be doing some of it. . . . The term 'training evaluation' often has the same sort of effect – yes, like 'Mother's apple pie', it sounds like a good thing, but does anybody really do it, and if so, how?*

Have we moved on since then? We think the answer is a guarded 'yes'. Most organisations acknowledge the need to use some sort of process to identify and analyse learning needs and appreciate the benefits of doing some sort of evaluation of their learning interventions. How well these processes work in reality may be more debatable. Andrew Forrest, HR Director of the Industrial Society (McCurry, 1998), is quoted as saying:

> *There has been relatively little increase in the adoption of proper training needs analysis in the past five years, and organisations are wasting money by sending people on courses they may not need.*

We suspect that many learning professionals are still worried about whether the learning is really focused in the right areas – whether learning interventions actually work and deliver changes in performance in the workplace. We also suspect that many line managers remain uneasy about whether they are fulfilling their responsibilities for the development of their people, and sceptical at times of the efficacy of formal learning interventions. The role of coach and mentor has become more valued, and as a result there has been increased emphasis in ensuring that those roles are carried out in a professional way. Many senior managers still need convincing that expenditure on learning/training actually contributes to their organisation's overall performance and 'bottom line'. Guest and King (2001) quote two senior managers as saying:

> *Our investment in training is pretty impressive when you add it up, but it is a bit scattergun. It is not terribly focused and it is not very well linked to an analysis of skill gaps. . . . I think we spend a lot of 'dead' money on training, rather than determining exactly who needs what.*

This book is for all these people. We will try to demystify the whole process of Learning Needs Analysis (LNA) and Learning Evaluation (LE) and demonstrate not only their relevance to the workplace but the vital part both should play in any learning activity. However, most important of all, we will offer practical advice about how to carry out LNA and how to undertake LE.

It is important to pause a moment to consider what we mean by 'learning'. When we refer to 'training', it is much clearer what is meant – it implies some formal process intervention to change an individual's level of knowledge, skills and behaviours. Learning is a much wider and more interesting process. Learning can happen in a wide variety of different ways in the work-place:

- a formal intervention of some sort – eg a traditional 'classroom' course, an e-learning module, etc
- a semi-formal intervention – eg coaching, a secondment, working on a project, etc
- informally – ranging from an informal coaching session by a line manager, or help from a colleague, through to the learning that takes place as an almost continuous process as we experience the world and learn from it.[1]

Essentially, this book is aimed at identifying and analysing the learning needs that will be met primarily by a formal or semi-formal learning intervention of some sort. The evaluation section is similarly aimed at assessing the outcomes and worth of these types of learning interventions.

[1] See Kolb's Learning Cycle (Kolb, 1984).

Learning is a major investment both for the organisation and the individual – the Learning and Training at Work Survey (Spilsbury 2000) estimated that employers (with 10 or more employees) spent £23.5 billion on training/learning in 2000, representing an average cost per employee of £1,333. It is vital that this investment, like any other investment, is made on the basis of sound research and analysis, and delivers a worthwhile return. It highlights the importance of ensuring that the learning process is focused on providing the right learning for the right people at the right time and at the right cost. LNA and LE are vital tools in ensuring that this objective is achieved.

The first key step is to state what we actually mean by the phrases themselves. We define Learning Needs Analysis as the whole process of:

- identifying the range and extent of learning needs required to meet the business needs of the organisation
- specifying those learning needs very precisely
- analysing how best these learning needs might be met.

(This book concentrates on looking at learning needs in the organisational context. Learning needs can, of course, also exist in a personal context when an individual identifies a learning area which may be totally unrelated to his or her current job or immediate career development – eg to learn a language, learn to paint in watercolours, learn to do Tai Chi, etc.)

The definition of LNA we have set out above explains the structure of the first four sections of the book and takes us round the first half of what we have called the Learning Wheel (see Figure 1).

Section 1 sets off at the starting-point for the planning of any learning intervention – the business needs of the organisation. We have purposely called the section *Business needs – the driving force*. We would argue very strongly that it is the business needs that must drive the learning activity in organisations, and that all learning interventions must be clearly linked to identifiable business needs. We use the term 'business' in the generic sense of the word, to describe the business the organisation is in – it could apply to a private sector organisation, a public sector organisation or the not-for-profit sector. This section examines the sorts of business requirements that can give rise to the need to make a learning intervention.

Next, Section 2, *Identifying learning needs – translating the business needs into action*, looks at the link between business needs and performance, and at how the need for an intervention can be identified. It covers a range of what we describe as bridges between the business needs and the learning needs – the mechanisms that identify the range and extent of the learning intervention required. It encompasses the areas of HR planning, including succession planning, critical incidents, management information systems, and performance management systems. The section ends with a very important chapter that asks the question 'Is there (really) a learning need?' Very often the knee-jerk reaction to a gap in performance is the magic solution of a learning intervention. However, in many cases, a learning intervention may be neither the best nor even an appropriate response, and there may be other solutions that tackle the problem more effectively and possibly more cheaply. The chapter looks at the range of other options available for addressing the performance gap.

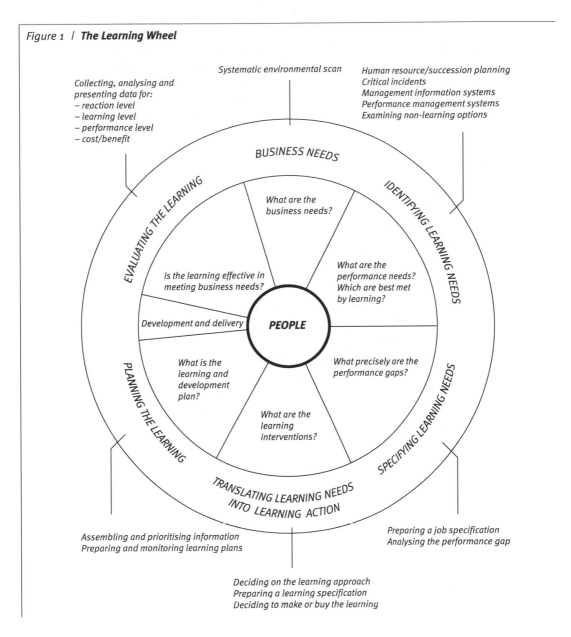

Figure 1 | **The Learning Wheel**

Section 3, *Specifying learning needs*, is about specifying the learning needs as precisely as possible. Once it is decided that the performance need is one that would benefit from a learning intervention, the next stage is to look at how to specify very precisely the learning required. The starting-point must be the requirements of the job, and so the first chapter of this section looks at how to analyse a job to provide the right sort of information for specifying the learning required to do it. The second chapter looks at ways of investigating the gap between the existing performance and the required performance.

After the learning need has been specified, Section 4, *Translating learning needs into learning action*, then moves on to analyse how this learning need can best be met. It looks at the spectrum of learning approaches available – formal, semi-formal and informal. It describes the vital step of how to prepare a learning specification – which sets out in detail the requirements for the learning. There then follows the key decision of whether to *make* – ie develop a new programme – or *buy* – ie buy an off-the-shelf programme. Or perhaps there is some option that lies between these two.

Strictly speaking, we have now completed the LNA part of the wheel. Section 5, *Planning the learning*, covers an important part of the process, but one that often gets neglected in the coverage of the learning process. It provides help and guidance on putting the information on learning needs together, prioritising the learning bids, preparing organisational learning plans and budgets, and monitoring progress.

Our remit for this book does not include the development and delivery of learning solutions and although the Learning Wheel where shown in full would include this activity, we do not deal with it.

We then move on to Section 6, *Evaluating the learning*. So what do we mean by 'evaluation'? Some detailed definitions are offered in the introduction to Section 6, but for now let's stay with the general definition that Learning Evaluation is about measuring the effectiveness of the learning. We think it would be fair to say that this is an area where much more can be done and where much more should be done than appears to be the case at present. We introduce the concept of 'evaluation that makes a difference' (Bee and Bee, 2000), arguing that there is no point in evaluating for its own sake and that evaluation must lead to a real improvement in the 'quality of learning and development and its impact on individual, team and organisational performance'.

Although we have covered LE in a separate section, the question of how you evaluate learning interventions is one that should be considered at every stage in the process, starting with the identification and analysis of learning needs, through specification and development, to the delivery of the learning solution. This section takes its main structure from a model first proposed by Kirkpatrick (in Craig and Bittel, 1967) and which has very much stood the test of time. The model looks at different levels of evaluation – the reactions of those involved, the learning achieved, the impact on the way people do their jobs, and the contribution to organisational performance – so considering learning effectiveness from four different perspectives. We also look at the difficult but crucial topic of whether, and if so how, you can actually put a monetary value on the effectiveness of a learning intervention. The final two chapters deal with the analysis, presentation and use of evaluation results. This section brings us fully round the Learning Wheel (see Figure 1), asking whether the business needs have in fact been met and whether they have been met in the most efficient and effective way.

The final section, Section 7, *Reflections*, looks back on what we have learned about the LNAE part of the learning process. It comments on how systematic and effective learning is an essential ingredient to taking organisations forward into a future which, whatever else, we know will be characterised by the need to be yet more competitive and to be able to handle a yet a greater intensity and pace of change. It will be a future where the quality of an organisation's people resource will play an even more important part, and where learning and development will be seen as a vital tool in maintaining and improving the quality of this key resource.

When we talk about learning we tend to think about its impact on the individual. However, Senge (1990) in his seminal book talks about the *learning organisation* in which learning becomes a way of a life rather than an episodic event. He defines learning organisations as ones:

> *... where people continually expand their capacity to create the results they truly desire, where new and expansive patterns are nurtured, where collective aspiration is set free, and where people are continually learning how to learn together.*

Although this book sets out to be a very practical approach to learning needs analysis and evaluation, it is salutary to remember that effective learning depends on people wanting to learn and change. In all that we do, we must nurture and encourage that desire and will to learn.

READING AND REFERENCE

BEE F. *and* BEE R. (2000), *The Complete Learning Evaluation Toolkit*, London, CIPD.

CUNNINGHAM I. (2002), 'Single-track minds', *People Management*, 28 December.

KIRKPATRICK D. L. (1967), 'Evaluation of training', in Craig R. L. and Bittel L. R. (eds) *Training and Development Handbook*, New York, McGraw-Hill.

KOLB D. A. (1984), *Experimental Learning*, New York, Prentice Hall.

GUEST D. *and* KING Z. (*2001*), 'Personnel's Paradox', People Management, 27th September.

McCURRY P. (1998), 'Surplus to requirements?', *Training*, November.

SCHRAMM J. (2002), *Change Agenda*, London, CIPD.

SENGE P. (1990), T*he Fifth Discipline: The art and practice of the learning organisation*, New York, Doubleday.

SPILSBURY D. (2001), *Learning and Training at Work 2000*, DfEE Research Report RR269.

Section 1

Business needs – the driving force

Introduction to Section 1

It perhaps seems self-evident – or, indeed, glaringly obvious – that business needs (defined as the operational needs of the organisation whether in the for-profit or not-for-profit sectors) should be the starting-point for any learning initiative. Boam and Sparrow (1992) refer to the *strategic triggers* that cause managers to take a look at the skills and competencies of the workforce. However, how many training departments still appear to be organised around the preparation and delivery of a catalogue of training courses? We have deliberately reverted to the language of training here, because it so often that 'training' departments get so bound up with the delivery of 'training' courses that the whole purpose of the exercise – helping people to learn – gets lost in the rush of activity. Increasingly, and helpfully in our view, we are finding organisations setting up 'learning' or 'learning and development' departments, making the point that learning is the objective, not training.

'Hold on one minute!' we hear the cry from those for whom this description of a catalogue-dominated approach still rings a faint bell. 'This catalogue was compiled *after* an analysis of what was required.' We would then ask several questions. How long ago was this analysis carried out? Are the learning needs still the same? Who requires the learning, and how do we know what sort of learning interventions work best? To what extent are these 'courses' related to business needs? Making the link between the business need and the relevant course might be considered the role of the line managers, but to what extent do they have the knowledge and skills to carry out this role, and how much time can they devote to this activity?

What a temptation a catalogue of courses presents – all those ready-made solutions to all those difficult performance issues. Which one would seem to fit the bill? 'Well, this one *nearly* does ...' 'Well, at least this one will be of some help, or at least it can't do any harm...' 'At least we can say we are trying to do *something*!'

We would argue that it is this approach to learning that has led to the scepticism of senior management that training/learning really is as vital as the training/learning department says it is. Why is it that when things get tough, the training/learning budget is one of the first to face the axe, viewed as a *non-productive overhead* (Kuraitis, 1981)? And why is it that 'we, in this country, still have too much of an attitude that training is a cost to be minimised rather than an investment?' as Geoff Armstrong, the CIPD's Director-General, puts it (Manocha, 2002). Perhaps one answer is that we have failed to prove that learning interventions are essential for an organisation to meet its business goals, or that they provide a good return on the investment made in them.

Learning interventions must be *driven* by the business needs of the organisation. If the link to business needs can be established, it ensures that the learning is focused on the real issues and demonstrates its relevance to the business. It also provides the vital starting-point for any evaluation of the learning.

We believe it is useful to look at the organisation as embedded in its general external environment (political/economic, etc), surrounded by the specific external environment that directly impacts on the achievement of its goals (suppliers, customers, etc), and embracing its internal environment (employees, trade unions, etc). This view illustrates the many and varied factors and stakeholders that may influence an organisation's future. The stakeholders may have a dependent role (eg as employees), a combative one (eg as competitors), or a collaborative one (eg as suppliers and/or customers). Chapter 1 looks at the way these environmental factors impact on the organisation and its needs.

We follow this up in Chapter 2 with an outline of how these factors might drive the organisation in terms of the planned business needs (the business strategy) and the unplanned business needs (the effects of unexpected and unforeseen events). These business needs then, in turn, drive the various interventions, including learning, that an organisation must adopt to ensure the success of its business strategy and cope with the buffeting winds of change.

And so we start on the first part of the journey round our Learning Wheel (see Figure 2).

READING AND REFERENCE

BOAM R. *and* SPARROW P. (1992), *Designing and Achieving Competency – A competency approach to developing people and organisations*, London, McGraw-Hill.

KURAITIS V. P. (1981), 'The personnel audit', *Personnel Administrator*, Vol 26, Part 11.

MANOCHA R. (2002), 'Leading the way', *People Management*, 26 September.

Figure 2 | *The Learning Wheel – business needs*

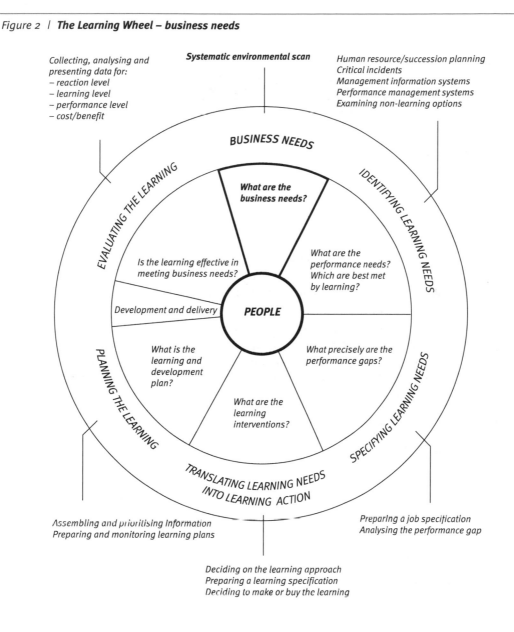

1

Factors impacting on business needs

INTRODUCTION

As students of business policy are only too aware, the external environment can pose both major threats and major opportunities to organisations and hence to the learning professional. The internal environment, or organisational culture, with its attendant strengths and weaknesses can similarly have a significant impact on what strategies organisations are able to adopt to meet those threats and opportunities. It is not intended here to give a comprehensive survey of the impact of these factors on organisations – the reader is referred to a number of good books on business strategy for this (eg Johnson and Scholes, 2001; Lynch 2003; Grant, 2001). Instead, this chapter looks briefly at some of the more common stimuli or triggers prompting changes in business needs. Our list is not meant to be exhaustive but includes:

- general external environmental factors outside the organisation and over which the organisation has no direct control – economic, technological, demographic/social/cultural, legislative and political

- specific environmental factors over which the organisation might not exercise control but might exert some influence – customers, suppliers, competitors and pressure groups

- the internal environment – employees/contractors, trade unions/staff organisations and shareholders.

GENERAL EXTERNAL ENVIRONMENTAL FACTORS

Few businesses are not directly affected by the state of the economy, either nationally or locally. Indeed, these days we are well aware that as a trading nation Britain is in a global economy, and that events on the other side of the world can soon show their effects on our businesses and our lives. Such effects may be on interest rates or oil prices or in the form of dramatic changes in markets like the opening up of Eastern Europe and Russia and the emergence of the developing countries as both major suppliers and competitors. It is not only the private sector that feels these influences – the not-for-profit sector is affected as well. Recession and its inevitable business closures will mean a reduction in the payment of business rates into the local authority, it will mean a loss of jobs, with a consequent increase in government spending on unemployment and associated benefits. On the other hand, a buoyant economy will mean the reverse – increased confidence of investors with a subsequent growth in business and trading opportunities.

Advances in technology pose both one of the greatest challenges and provide one of the greatest opportunities for most organisations. The pace of change is enormous and increasing. Today's state-of-the-art computer is tomorrow's junk. Robot assembly plants, use of lasers, transplant and genetic surgery – wherever the workplace, whatever the task, there appears to be a technological solution for everything! Technology – whether in the retail sector (with Internet shopping), in the universities (with tutorials in different countries linked by satellite), or in institutions like the police (with DNA testing and sophisticated communications networks) – is there to give the competitive edge to whoever can use (or afford) it. Changes in technology, with their impact on the numbers and skills of the workforce, pose a major challenge for most organisations and those responsible for the human resources in them. How to keep the workforce up-to-date and expert in the relevant technologies is a major issue. One thing is sure, and that is that changing technology will mean shortages in those particular skill-based areas. The non-learning solution is to recruit/poach them from elsewhere – but from where? They never seem to exist in the numbers required. Learning interventions may be the *only* solution in this case.

The ways in which we communicate have already undergone massive change and there are more changes on the horizon. The ever advancing technologies of the Internet, mobile phones, etc, have had a dramatic impact on not just the way we do our business but also the way we run our lives. They have facilitated:

- new ways of working – eg the emergence of call centres, increased working from home
- new ways of living – eg doing our banking, shopping, research while sitting at home, through the Internet
- new ways of learning – eg the e-learning revolution.

Demographic, social and cultural changes are also potentially an area of major impact for most organisations, either through the implications for the staffing of the organisation or for the demands for their products and services. Demographic changes such as the ageing population are raising issues around how long people should be expected to work, with the real likelihood that the retirement age may be raised. This in turn raises questions about how to manage people's careers, the implications for succession planning, etc. The growth in women's expectations of their work role and the increased incidence of one-parent families have led to a substantial increase in the number of women in the labour force. This in turn has impacted on issues such as equality of opportunity, flexible working practices and the work–life balance. Other social changes, such as the entry of a greater proportion of people to higher education, the influence and needs of a diverse society, will have their effect too, as well as the more business-related social and cultural changes such as the altering structures of the workforce, involving more part-time working and the use of contractors, and the move towards the learning organisation. All of these could potentially lead to the need for some sort of learning intervention.

Changing legislation has additionally resulted in major and on-going learning initiatives. We are now increasingly seeing the impact of legislation resulting from our membership of the European Union. Depending on the nature of the business, it can be a major stimulus for action which can often involve learning of some sort. A good example of this has been the legislation on data protection, health and safety, and human rights. The government can also have an influence other than through legislation, via initiatives such as NVQs/SVQs and Investors in People.

SPECIFIC ENVIRONMENTAL FACTORS

One of the factors that has a major impact on a business is its customers. To ensure that they hold on to customers in today's intensely competitive markets, many organisations make significant strategic moves to satisfy their customers' requirements. The emphasis on quality initiatives and customer care programmes are good examples.

Suppliers – ie those people or organisations from whom a business obtains its equipment, raw materials and/or services – can have a big impact on that business as well. The stability, timing and the costs of supplied goods and services can play a critical part in the success of a business. The importance of the relationship between supplier and supplied advocated by the Japanese has been highlighted by the initiatives to build strong collaborative links, such as developing common working practices and joint training schemes.

No organisation, even one in a virtual monopoly position, can afford to ignore the competition. Perhaps the classic historical example of this sin was the British motorcycle industry, previously pre-eminent on the roads of the world until the Japanese motorcycle came from nowhere to knock it into oblivion. What the competition is doing or not doing provides a major stimulus for action in most organisations.

The latter part of the twentieth century saw the growth in the pressure-group phenomenon. These range from highly organised and vocal groups such as Friends of the Earth, with their campaigns to protect the environment, and the animal protection groups with their concerns about the use and exploitation of animals, to *ad hoc* groups set up, say, to oppose the building of a bypass or new superstore, at least 'not in my back yard'. Organisations have had to become increasingly aware of and sensitive to these types of pressure, and have had to learn how to respond appropriately.

INTERNAL FACTORS

Another major stimulus to business needs comes from the necessity for the human resource of the organisation (eg managers, support staff, shopfloor workers, peripheral and core workers, contractors and consultants) to be kept up-to-date in expertise, to be motivated and focused on the business objectives. The pressures to be well managed and fairly rewarded for what they do and to be developed to their full potential, come from all categories of employee. A strategic plan that does not take into account the needs for and of a competent and motivated workforce is a plan that is doomed to failure. We demonstrate in Chapter 3 the value to the organisation of a well-conceived and executed human resource plan as an integral part of the overall corporate plan.

A further issue that has come into sharp focus over the last few years and is certain to impact on the business and human resource strategies of the future is how to harness and manage the use of 'knowledge' in the organisation. Kelleher *et al* (2001) talk in terms of a new industrial revolution taking place but state that 'this revolution is fuelled not by coal but by knowledge'. They go on to suggest:

> *In the 21st century corporate strategists will increasingly see themselves as the architects of the learning organisations and the orchestrators of knowledge management systems, harnessing this self-generating, self-multiplying, inexhaustible energy source.*

This may mean that the learning organisation will become a reality rather than a much-talked-about concept.

Another factor that can have a significant impact on the success of a business is the relationship between organisations and their employees that is often represented by the trade unions or their equivalents. In the 1970s, the power of the trade unions appeared to be a major pressure on organisations in Britain. The seemingly endless number of strikes led elsewhere to the description of industrial unrest as 'the British disease'. It seems now that the enormous growth in management training at the time did little to help cope with this particular pressure on business. Could it be that it was not focused on the real learning need? Although the power of the trade unions is much less now than it was in the 1970s, there is little doubt that relations between organisations and their employees, through their trade unions where appropriate or through EU-driven structures, is an important strategic factor and one to which there could be a substantial competitive edge in getting it right.

The influence, too, of shareholders on businesses can be very great. It can range from the financial effects on a business's strategy of providing an adequate/growing level of dividend through to influencing the whole policy and direction of the business. The growth of employee shareholders has added another dimension to their role, as has the increasing concern of shareholders over ethical issues. Very few businesses can afford to ignore the needs and views of their shareholders.

CONCLUSION

The effects of this range of external and internal factors on business needs for some organisations have been dramatic. Some have retracted to a small range of specialist products, others have diversified. Some have been able to disperse their operations, others have centralised on their core workers (Handy, 1995). Some have failed, others have survived and grown. The next chapter goes on to look at how these factors impact on the development of business strategy, and at the ability of organisations to cope with unforeseen and unplanned events.

READING AND REFERENCE

GRANT R. M. (2001), *Contemporary Strategy Analysis: Concepts, techniques and applications*, Oxford, Blackwell Publishers.

HANDY C. (1995), *The Age of Unreason*, 2nd edn, London, Business Books.

JOHNSON G. *and* SCHOLES K. (2001), *Exploring Corporate Strategy*, 6th edn, Harlow, Pearson Education.

KELLEHER M., VAN HEIJST G., KRUIZINGA E., HALDANE A., VAN DER WAL C. (2001), *KALIF: To Share is to Multiply*, Utrecht, Netherlands, CIBIT bv.

LYNCH R. (2003), *Corporate Strategy*, 3rd edn, Harlow, Pearson Education.

2

Planned and unplanned business needs

INTRODUCTION

All organisations are subject to continuous stimuli for action. At one end of the spectrum is the proactive, planned pressure of the business or corporate strategy. As Lynch (2003) describes it:

Corporate strategy is concerned with an organisation's basic direction for the future, its purpose, its ambitions, its resources and how it interacts with the world in which it operates.

At the other end is the knee-jerk reaction to unforeseen and unexpected pressures. In response to the planned pressures – internal and external – most organisations these days have mission statements, goals and objectives and some plan of how to achieve them within both long-term and short-term horizons.

These strategies in summary may be for:

- consolidation – ie strengthening the current position but essentially staying the same
- growth via:
  - market penetration – ie increasing the market for existing products
  - market development – ie moving into new markets
  - product development – ie developing new products
  - diversification which may be related – ie in some way building on the existing business such as moving up or down the supply chain – or unrelated – ie moving into completely new areas of business
- contraction, via:
  - withdrawing from markets
  - withdrawing products
  - selling off/closing down parts of the business
- closure – ie closing the whole business.

The implications of these strategies can be enormous for the human resource side of the organisation, and in particular for all those involved in the learning process. We take a look at each of these in turn and then at the effects of the unplanned business needs.

CONSOLIDATION

Strengthening the existing business can be a major strategy in its own right. We have shown in Chapter 1 how the continuous changes in the external environment mean that no organisation can afford to stand still but must continuously strive for higher levels of performance. This can be in terms of greater productivity, increased efficiency and the inevitably higher quality of goods and services. To achieve these goals puts greater pressure on the employees of the organisation. How do you achieve higher productivity, increased efficiency and higher levels of quality? What interventions do you need to make? Each of these requirements could provide the starting-point for a *needs analysis*, which *might* result in a learning intervention to, for example, carry out new processes or procedures to speed up the work flow, or improve customer care.

A good example of a major initiative aimed at improving the effectiveness and efficiency of areas of the public sector is known as Best Value. This requires local authorities, police authorities and fire authorities to review all their services using the 'five Cs' approach of Challenge, Consult, Compare, Compete and Collaborate. The very process itself has generated learning needs in how to conduct such reviews, and the outcomes often have significant implications for learning activities in these organisations.

GROWTH AND DIVERSIFICATION

This strategy opens up a potential Pandora's box of interventions. Increased market penetration could pose extra demands on the sales and marketing personnel and the distribution function. Moving into new markets may require the acquisition of new sets of skills – eg languages, if moving into new geographical areas, knowledge of clients' businesses and needs if moving into new sections of a market. Moving into completely new business areas can place even greater demands on employees than straightforward growth because it can imply the need to learn about a whole range of new products, new markets, new technologies, new legislation, etc. The learning implications of these strategies can be enormous and require detailed analysis and planning. Such a situation highlights the need for learning professionals to be involved at the earliest possible stages in the planning process. All too often they are involved after the decisions have been taken – how much better for the organisation if they were involved in the strategy-making process itself!

CONTRACTION AND CLOSURE

Sadly, many of us have experienced the pressures associated with cutback and closure. With the buoyant economy of the late twentieth century and early twenty-first, contraction has often been more associated with the need to achieve optimal efficiency in the highly competitive global markets. The strategy of contraction can result in a surprising and sometimes unexpected amount of learning needs. The remaining employees may be required to take on additional and different work and responsibilities. This may result in the need for multi-skilling, enhanced management skills, etc. Contraction may also go hand-in-hand with a radical review of the whole business to ensure that the organisation is on a stronger base for moving forward at a later date. The review may require major changes in work practice and often in the underlying culture and attitudes, with attendant requirements for learning interventions.

Most employers these days take an enlightened view of trying to ease the path of those employees that are being required to leave the business, and often provide help in developing job-seeking skills as part of the severance package. Similarly for those taking early retirement, the provision of courses – ranging from financial management to developing new interests – is becoming almost the norm.

UNPLANNED BUSINESS NEEDS

We have talked so far about the business and learning needs arising from some form of planned action by the business. At the other end of the spectrum are the business needs that arise from the myriad unforeseen events that can buffet a business. These can range from *minor* operational problems with, for example, a part of the distribution system, faults in the computer system, a flurry of customer complaints, to *major* problems such as the failure of an expensive advertising campaign, a serious defect occurring with a product, or the loss of a major customer. The characteristic of this sort of business need is that it arises usually with the label – SUPER-URGENT, SOMEBODY DO SOMETHING QUICKLY – attached to it. Some form of learning intervention often appears to fit the 'do something quickly' bill rather well. Ill-conceived poorly thought-through learning interventions are often thrown at the problem before it is even established exactly what the problem is. What are the customer complaints about? What is/are the real cause(s) of the problems? Do they affect all products/services or only some? Do they affect all staff or only some? Is it a *people* problem at all?

It is essential for learning professionals to try to avoid being catapulted into providing instant solutions of the sort that can so often be costly and, worst of all, ineffective. Analysing the exact nature of the problem may take time at the beginning but will ensure that the solution provided will actually do the trick. The chapter on *Critical incidents* (Chapter 5) discusses these issues and uses case studies to show how these problems can be approached.

Alternatively, it can be equally difficult and frustrating for the learning professional not to be involved at all in the solution of these business crises. This situation highlights the need for the learning professional and learning itself to be seen as a key part of the operation of the business, and not just as an overhead. The only way this will occur is if learning is approached in just the same way as any other intervention/activity to improve the business – as cost-effective solutions to clearly identified business problems.

It also requires the learning professionals to develop methods of keeping themselves informed about what is going on in the organisation – systems of *environmental scanning* (Robinson and Robinson, 1989), and developing their *strategic awareness* (Sloman, 1994). These methods can be formal – such as sitting on committees, being involved in project/focus teams, making sure that they are on the circulation lists of key reports, monitoring the relevant internal statistics, using the organisational intranet in a systematic way, etc. Additionally, and sometimes equally useful, are the informal approaches – having coffee/lunch with a wide range of colleagues in the business, and talking to participants of learning programmes about their work, about what business challenges and about problems they are facing.

Learning professionals must scan their external environment in exactly the same way as they scan the internal environment. The mechanisms for so doing are the same in large part, and good internal scanning also picks up many of these external stimuli. Activities such as attending conferences and seminars, in addition to reading the personnel, learning and relevant trade journals, all help this process. The use of discussion groups and chat rooms on the Internet can also be a valuable way of sharing issues and new ideas.

However, above all, it involves showing an interest in the business in the widest sense, and showing an understanding and vision of the key issues affecting the business. Geoff Armstrong, as Director-General of the CIPD responding to a question about whether HR still finds it difficult to sell itself in the business environment, comments (Manocha, 2002):

> *We specialise in the very aspect of business – the people, their learning, motivation, development, and leadership – which is the main driver of value across all functional streams. We need to be players in the team, at times leading and at times supporting the direction of the game. But at all times we need to be contributing real business value, building upon, but not confined to, our professional speciality.*

On a similar theme, Forrest comments (McCurry, 1998) that:

> *Training managers need to set up a robust dialogue with line managers and work their way into the strategic thinking of the organisation.*

CONCLUSION

This chapter has recognised that we live in an uncertain and dynamic world. Our ten-year/five-year through to one-week plans may come to nothing in the face of the organisation responding to the multitude of pressures on it. Managing rapid change, whether through consolidation, growth, contraction and/or closure, will be the stock-in-trade of managers in the future. As learning professionals we must recognise this and be able to work with it.

We chose as the title for this Section *Business needs – the driving force* because we see the business needs of organisations as not just the starting-point for any Learning Needs Analysis but the force that should be *driving* any learning interventions. Learning professionals who fail to understand this should perhaps not be too surprised when their line manager colleagues fail to support them in their work.

How does this all affect the learning professional? The word that springs to mind is *opportunity*. Change, of whatever nature, arising from planned or unplanned business needs is a golden opportunity for the learning professional to get involved. So the messages are:

- get your environmental scans going
- make sure you are at the forefront of the organisation in knowing both what is going on now and what changes are on the horizon.

In the next section we look at how these business needs might be translated into action that, where appropriate, leads to a learning solution.

READING AND REFERENCE

Lynch R. (2003), *Corporate Strategy*, 3rd edn, Harlow, Pearson Education.

Manocha R. (2002), 'Leading the way', *People Management*, 26 September.

McCurry P. (1998), 'Surplus to requirements?', *Training*, November.

Robinson D. G. *and* Robinson J. C. (1989), *Training for Impact*, San Francisco, Jossey-Bass.

Sloman M. (1994), 'Coming in from the cold: a new role for trainers', *Personnel Management*, London, IPM, January.

Section 2

Identifying learning needs – translating the business needs into action

Introduction to Section 2

In the Introduction to this book we defined Learning Needs Analysis (LNA) as the process encompassing the three stages of:

- identifying the range and extent of learning needs required to meet the business needs of the organisation
- specifying those learning needs very precisely
- analysing how best these learning needs might be met.

In Section 1 we began at the top of the Learning Wheel with the *business needs*. This section discusses the techniques that could be called the principal *tools* of the next stage of the process – which translates the business needs into the need for action to improve or add to the performance of the human resource asset of the business. That action may or may not lead to a learning intervention. So this stage in itself can be seen as having two parts:

- identifying the need for the improvement or addition to the competencies of the organisation's staff
- identifying which of these needs require a learning intervention.

It is interesting and salutary to note how learning needs appear to be identified at the present time. In the annual survey *Training and Development in Britain* (CIPD, 2000) the three methods most frequently used were: line manager requests, employee requests, and performance appraisals. It is also interesting, however, to note that when asked to rank the relative importance of the various methods listed that 'analysis of the business plan' came top. We, of course, strongly support this top ranking and advocate using a wider and more proactive range of methods for identifying learning needs.

We look at five main *tools* or, perhaps, what are better described as *bridges*, that help us make the link between the business needs of the organisation and the need for learning interventions. These are:

- human resource planning
- succession planning
- critical incidents

- management information systems
- performance management systems.

The section is structured under these headings, and the final chapter addresses the specific question of whether learning is the appropriate intervention to meet the business need. Many people see succession planning as a subset of human resource planning, but we have chosen to cover it separately because it offers such an abundant source of information on possible learning needs.

Traditionally, many books on training/learning (Boydell and Leary, 1996; Reid and Barrington, 1997) have set out to look at the different *levels* at which learning needs are assessed. Some writers use these as levels that indicate the extent of the learning intervention required, and others use them as ways to classify methods for identifying learning needs. The most common structure applied to such levels is:

- *the organisational level*: identifying learning needs which affect the whole organisation – eg the learning needed to introduce cultural change successfully across the organisation, or to introduce a procedure or process that affects the whole organisation, such as implementing a new performance management system

- *the occupational/group level*: identifying learning needs which affect particular occupations or groups – eg the learning required to implement new accounting procedures for the finance staff, or new hygiene legislation for catering staff

- *the individual level*: identifying learning needs of individuals – eg an individual's need to manage his or her time better, or to learn the skills to operate a new piece of machinery.

Most writers recognise that these do not form clear and distinct divisions but are interconnected and overlap. It is not our intention to use these levels as a method of structuring, but we refer to them as and when we feel it is helpful to use this sort of classification.

Another distinction that is sometimes used is whether learning is for present or for future needs. In very general terms:

- Present needs are seen to relate to current objectives – eg learning to support competencies required for a current job or to deal with some immediate changes in the environment.

- Future needs relate to long(er)-term objectives – eg learning for some future job, to deal with some future planned change of direction for the organisation or long(er)-term change in the environment.

In our view the distinction has its relevance in helping to prioritise and plan the timing of learning interventions. Clearly, present needs will often seem more pressing than future needs. However, the learning professional has to be careful to avoid the temptation to concentrate on the present at the expense of the future. Our view is that the rigid separation of learning into present and future needs can sometimes get in the way of the overall approach to the identification of learning needs, and again we restrict ourselves to commenting on the distinction as and when it seems helpful.

There is no one best approach to identifying performance/learning needs in a systematic way. There is no algorithm or simple flowchart that can be followed by rote. Learning professionals must be aware of *all* the sources of information or *bridges* that link into the business needs. They need to be continuously scanning their business environment with the following questions always in the forefront of their minds:

- First, what performance changes are needed to meet the business needs?
- And secondly, can those performance changes best be met by a learning intervention?

We go on now to examine these bridges that make the link with business needs, starting with a look at human resource planning. But first we take a look at our Learning Wheel in Figure 3 to see how identifying learning needs fits into the overall picture.

READING AND REFERENCE

BOYDELL T. *and* LEARY M. (1996), *Identifying Training Needs*, London, CIPD.

CIPD (2000), *Training and Development in Britain 2000*, London, CIPD.

REID M. A. *and* BARRINGTON H. (1997), *Training Interventions*, 5th edn, London, CIPD.

Figure 3 | ***The Learning Wheel – identifying learning needs***

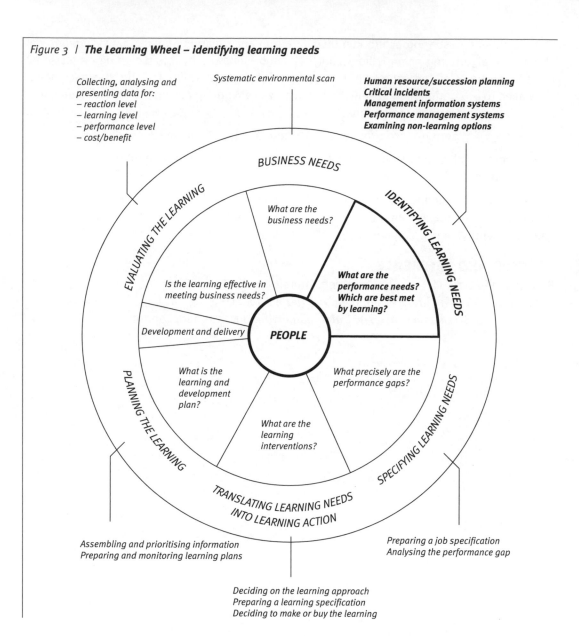

3
Human resource planning

INTRODUCTION

Armstrong (2001) describes human resource (HR) planning in terms that it:

... should be an integral part of business planning. The strategic planning process should define projected changes in the scale and types of activities carried out by the organisation. It should identify the core competencies the organisation needs to achieve its goals and therefore its skill requirements. ... In so far as there are strategic business plans, human resource planning interprets them in terms of people planning.

So the starting-point for the HR planning process is, not surprisingly, the business strategy, and HR plans provide a very potent source of information, or a very effective bridge between the business needs and the learning needs.

Marchington and Wilkinson (1996) acknowledge the debate that has taken place between what is referred to as 'hard' and 'soft' approaches to HR planning. The former covers the arena of what traditionally has been called 'manpower planning' and which essentially focuses on models (usually computerised) that answer the questions:

- How many people, with what skills, does the organisation require over a period of time – say, the next five years (based on the forecasts of activity in the organisation)? – the demand side.

- How many people is it expected that the organisation will have, over the same period (based on forecasts of factors such as wastage rates)? – the supply side.

- What is the gap in terms of numbers and skills?

Out of this analysis will come information that feeds into recruitment plans – to forecast the numbers to be recruited; and learning and development plans – to forecast the learning activity, etc.

However, there has been an increasing focus on 'soft' HR planning, which Marchington and Wilkinson (1996) describe as:

... more explicitly focused on creating and shaping the culture of the organisation so that there is a clear integration between corporate goals and employee beliefs, values and behaviours.

In essence, HR planning should cover both, and demonstrate clearly how the aims, objectives and activities of the organisation (as set out in the business strategy and underpinning plans) will be delivered through the people resource of the organisation. HR plans will consist of a mix of policies and priorities together with the quantitative analysis of numbers and skills, which together will provide the organisation with 'properly qualified, committed and competent staff in the right place at the right time' (Marchington and Wilkinson, 1996).

The calculations of the quantity and types of staff can range from a fairly simple comparison of demand for labour against supply over a short period for a small business, through to a process for large organisations involving sophisticated and complex computer models looking as far ahead as 10 or 20 years. This 'hard' component of the plan will provide direct information on potential learning needs, as is illustrated by our two case studies below.

However, the 'soft' component will also provide vital information on potential learning needs. For example, the priority given by the Police Service to the outcomes from the Stephen Lawrence Enquiry (Macpherson, 1999) on racism within the service generated a need for major diversity learning programmes. On a more positive note, a commitment in the HR plan to the development of mentoring in the organisation will have implications for the learning needs of both potential mentors and mentees.

There is little doubt that traditional 'manpower planning' had its heyday when the world markets were seen as more stable and less unpredictable. In today's world characterised by turbulence and change and the new more 'flexible' organisations it is sometimes implied that planning has no relevance. However, as Marchington and Wilkinson (2002) put it so cogently:

> Such a view misunderstands the nature and uses of the planning process and can be used to justify 'ad-hocery' and reactive management. Planning is just as important, if not more so, during turbulent times to ensure that employers have staff of the right quality and quantity available at the right time.

We strongly agree!

USING HR PLANNING FOR IDENTIFYING LEARNING NEEDS

The purpose of this chapter is not to explain how to do HR planning but to explain how human resource plans can be used as a very powerful means of identifying performance change/learning needs in order to help develop a competent workforce. It is essentially concerned with identifying needs at the organisational and occupational levels, and as the name suggests is directed towards future needs. We use two simple case studies to illustrate how human resource plans can be used to aid the learning professional in this.

The Rationalisation Company

For competitive business reasons the Rationalisation Company plans to reduce staff numbers by cutting out some levels of management and merging certain functions. The existing staffing levels and the forecast for required staffing in the next year are as set out in Table 1. What are the implications for required performance changes and possible learning needs?

Table 1 | Staffing by department

Present staffing by department			Future staffing by department		
Finance:	*Management*	*25*	*Finance:*	*Management*	*15*
	Technical	*30*		*Technical*	*30*
	Admin/clerical	*40*		*Admin/clerical*	*30*
Sales:	*Management*	*16*	*Sales:*	*Management*	*10*
	Technical	*29*		*Technical*	*30*
	Admin/clerical	*36*		*Admin/clerical*	*20*
Production:	*Management*	*16*	*Production/*	*Management*	*13*
	Technical	*24*	*Distribution:*	*Technical*	*38*
	Admin/clerical	*14*		*Admin/clerical*	*10*
	Supervisory	*130*		*Supervisory*	*71*
	Unskilled	*380*		*Unskilled*	*431*
				TOTAL	*698*
Distribution:	*Management*	*10*			
	Technical	*24*			
	Admin/clerical	*4*			
	Supervisory	*39*			
	Unskilled	*127*			
	TOTAL	*944*			

Let us look first of all at what is happening in terms of global numbers. The total numbers employed are planned to decrease by just over 26 per cent, from 944 employees down to 698 employees.

At first sight, the finance director (if he or she is expected to be still in post!) says 'Whoopee! Let's cut the learning budget by at least 26 per cent.' Seems logical – or does it? Let's look at the figures more closely. Table 2 analyses the changes by the groupings of staff.

CASE STUDY continued

Table 2 | Staff change analysis

	Present	Future	Change
Management	*67*	*38*	*−43%*
Technical	*107*	*98*	*−10%*
Administrative/ clerical	*94*	*60*	*−36%*
Supervisory	*169*	*71*	*−58%*
Unskilled	*507*	*431*	*−15%*

The big impact is in supervisory and management grades, with reductions in numbers of 58 per cent and 43 per cent respectively. Looking at the supervisory grades first, the ratio of supervisors to unskilled staff has halved, from a ratio of 1:3 (169:507) to 1:6 (71:431). This could be described as a doubling of the supervisory workload – and what is more, there could be substantial differences in the actual role of the supervisor when managing teams of about six compared to teams of about three. Also, merging the two departments, production and distribution, could mean that the supervisors are managing mixed teams from both areas. Your antennae should be well and truly buzzing – there is likely to be a need for substantial performance changes from the supervisors. A similar picture is likely to emerge for the management grades as well.

Let's take a look now at the administrative and clerical staff – a reduction of 36 per cent. So what is happening to their workload? Now it is just possible with the overall cutback of 26 per cent that there *might* be a reduction of admin/clerical work of about the same order, but the reduction in staff is even greater than this. It could well mean that the remaining staff are going to have to cover a wider area of work, and perhaps the reductions will involve the introduction of new technology and procedures. Do you see the need for some sort of performance changes? Almost certainly!

The reductions plus the merger suggest a lot of change. How is it going to be introduced? Will managers and supervisors need new skills to cope with this level of change? What about the staff who are leaving? Is the business going to offer help to ease the move, perhaps by helping to improve job-seeking skills?

The finance director is not looking so cheerful now. However, learning may not be the only or the best intervention to achieve these performance changes. The new demands on the managers/supervisors could be met by recruiting the appropriately skilled and qualified manager/supervisors or perhaps the business will hire consultants to implement the changes. But it is a fair bet that learning interventions will feature quite large. Far from cutting back on the learning budget, the learning professional may well be looking for an increase next year!

Clearly, more information and analysis is required to identify precisely the performance changes required and the appropriate solutions in the Rationalisation Company case study. However, the learning professional's scan of the environment – in this case the HR plan – has put himself/herself in the position of being ahead of the game, of being in the position to be proactive in meeting the business needs. Using the plan as a diagnostic tool, the learning professional is no longer just reacting to other people's interpretation of the business needs and, therefore, probably at too late a date for the learning intervention to be planned and implemented in the most effective way.

Let's move on to another example now aimed at the occupational level. This time there is no ready supply of the skills required from outside, so a recruitment solution is not an option and the new staff will have to learn the skills.

CASE STUDY

The Expanding Railway Company

The business plan for the Expanding Railway Company has indicated an ambitious expansion of services, and it is recognised that a key staffing requirement for this expansion is train drivers. An additional factor that has put the spotlight on to the train drivers is that it is such a specialist skill that the only reliable source is from drivers coming from the Company's own Driver Training School.

The information that has been fed into the assessment is as follows:

- The starting-point is the existing establishment of 200 drivers.
- The extra drivers required over the next five years as new lines are opened are:

Year 1	0 per cent
Year 2	+25 per cent
Year 3	+30 per cent
Year 4	+35 per cent
Year 5	0 per cent

(These percentages refer to the end of the year and indicate year-on-year changes.)
- The crude index of labour turnover forecast is:

Year 1	10 per cent
Year 2	20 per cent
Year 3	20 per cent
Year 4	20 per cent
Year 5	10 per cent

- A wastage rate of 10 per cent is forecast for new recruits failing the meet the standards required.

What are the implications of this manpower plan?

The obvious starting-point in the analysis is to produce a schedule of the flow of drivers into the organisation over the five years. It might look something like Table 3.

Table 3 |

Year	1	2	3	4	5
(a) Number of drivers needed at the start of the year	200	200	250	325	440
(b) Increase due to business needs	0	50	75	115	0
(c) Numbers of drivers needed at the end of the year (a + b)	200	250	325	440	440
(d) Labour turnover (% of average yearly figure)	20	45	58	77	44
(e) Numbers available at the end of the year if no action taken to recruit (a − d)	180	155	192	248	396
(f) Deficit (c − e)	20	95	133	192	44
(g) Learner failures	2	10	13	19	4
Total no to be recruited (f + g)	22	105	146	211	48

What do these figures tell us about the learning need? Well, the first and most obvious nugget of information is that there will be approximately a fivefold increase in the need for driver learning programmes in Year 2. Then two further large increases in Year 3 and Year 4 lead to a near doubling in requirement over those two years, before being substantially reduced in Year 5!

The main implications are these:

- Substantially more driver instructors will be needed in Year 2 and then again in Years 3 and 4. Where will they come from? Will they be a further drain on the existing driver pool, requiring further recruitment? What learning interventions will they require?
- What additional facilities will be required, such as learning accommodation, specialist simulation equipment, etc?
- The figures may also give an indication of the need to extend administrative and clerical support for the learning function, with the attendant learning needs of these staff.
- Finally, the decrease in Year 5 has also to be planned. What is to happen to the surplus instructors? It could indicate some redundancies among the instructors and others if no steps are taken to redeploy them into the workforce. There could also be some surplus learning accommodation for use on other programmes.

The essential points to come out of this exercise on drivers is that it enables the learning professional to *plan ahead* for a key performance need – in this case additional employees with driving skills – which is required to support the strategic decision for expansion. The meeting of the driver targets is almost certainly crucial to the success of the business plan. Planning well ahead will increase the probability that these targets are met, and what is more, in the most cost-effective way. It also identifies a secondary level of performance need, for qualified driver instructors. It highlights the need to look at some sort of career management route for the driver instructors, perhaps seeing a period of secondment into the learning function as the beginning of some future move into a management/supervisory role.

The computer has a lot to offer in terms of the number crunching required in human resource planning. There is a wide range of systems that have the capacity to calculate changes in numbers and types of staff from changes in business output levels. The associated model of the business allows us to play our 'What if?' games – ie if we increase (or decrease) turnover by x per cent, what are the staffing implications? Once we know the staffing changes arising from the business changes, we are well on the way to identifying the performance needs and hence the learning needs.

There is also the need for HR planning at the level above individual organisations – to identify skill gaps and skill needs across sectors of industry. This is well illustrated by the problems faced by the National Health Service in going through a period of rapid expansion after many years of contraction. The need for qualified staff across a great number of disciplines is being met in the short term by recruiting overseas and trying to encourage qualified staff to return to the profession. (This non-learning approach in itself generates learning needs – eg for language skills for foreign staff, refresher training for returnees, etc.) The longer-term solution is to increase the number of places on the professional training schemes. To aid this type of sector-wide long-term planning Sector Skills Councils are being set up to research skills needs and put forward proposals for their areas.

CONCLUSION

Human resource planning can be as sophisticated or as simple as we want to make it. However, it offers a golden opportunity for the learning professional to:

- work directly towards the organisation's strategic decisions
- be in the vanguard of the organisation's move into the future.

We next turn our attention to the specific area of succession planning, which is another very useful source of information for the learning professional.

READING AND REFERENCE

ARMSTRONG M. (2001), A *Handbook of Human Resource Management Practice*, 8th edn, London, Kogan Page.

MACPHERSON W. (1999), *The Stephen Lawrence Enquiry: Report of an inquiry by Sir William Macpherson of Cluny*, London, HMSO.

MARCHINGTON M. *and* WILKINSON A. (1996), *Core Personnel and Development*, London, CIPD.

MARCHINGTON M. *and* WILKINSON A. (2002), *People Management and Development*, 2nd edn, London, CIPD.

4

Succession planning

INTRODUCTION

In the last chapter we discussed what a powerful tool overall human resource planning can be in the identification of performance needs and hence learning needs. We turn now to a specific form of human resource planning: succession planning. As with human resource plans, succession plans are rooted in the business strategy for the organisation and provide a powerful link between the business needs and the needs for performance changes/learning needs. Again our intention is not to explain how to do succession planning but to comment on its implications for the identification of performance/learning needs. After providing some definitions we use a case study as a vehicle for demonstrating the use of succession plans as a bridge between business needs and learning needs.

Armstrong (2001) explains that the aim of succession planning:

> . . . is to ensure that, as far as possible, suitable managers are available to fill vacancies created by promotion, retirement, death, leaving or transfer. It also aims to ensure that a cadre of managers is available to fill the new appointments that may be established in the future.

The first part of this definition is quite straightforward, but the second part is very dynamic. It implies that succession planning is not simply about replacing existing managers but is about gazing into the crystal ball to determine what management skills in what quantities are required in the future. This is no mean task, and the implications for identifying performance/learning needs are potentially very considerable. Wallum (1993) develops this view beyond the manager role and into what he calls 'key future roles' by stating that succession planning, to be really effective, should encompass:

> . . . the strategic process and actions aimed at ensuring a suitable supply of suitable successors for senior or key jobs and future roles.

This definition highlights the significance of succession planning for the identification of performance/learning needs. Here we are dealing with the *key* human resources of the business, where failure to deliver the goods will almost certainly have a significant impact on business performance. Succession planning can also be a vital process for dealing with specialist jobs where there may be a limited field of suitable candidates and where long-term planning may be essential to ensure appropriate learning interventions in time to meet any gaps.

There has been considerable debate about whether the traditional approach to succession planning as set out in the case study below is still relevant 'in a world of non-stop, unpredictable organisational change' (Beeson, 2000). However, there is increasing evidence of a resurgence of interest in succession planning, including a recent survey suggesting that 'succession management [is now] the top business concern for the first time' (Simms, 2003). We believe the principles are still sound, but it must be seen as a flexible and dynamic process. Yet there are useful developments that build on and adapt the traditional approach. As the *Employee Development Bulletin* (2000) suggests:

> *Although some critical and specialist jobs will almost always require individual plans, grouping jobs together enables potential successors to be identified for a collection of posts.*

There is also the concept of setting up 'talent pools' of staff who are adaptable and can fill a number of roles. Some organisations positively set out to provide individuals with a wide range of experience across the organisation and in cross-functional roles. Byham (2000) on the same theme talks about the acceleration pool system:

> *Rather than targeting one or two people for each post, as is the case for traditional succession planning, an acceleration pool develops a group of high-potential candidates for undefined executive jobs.*

With acceleration pools and talent pools the learning needs are more generic than with traditional succession planning, and learning interventions are aimed at developing generic management competencies and wide organisational knowledge plus providing a wide range of job experiences. The use of 'blended learning' approaches (see Chapter 11) can be very useful here.

Also, there is an emphasis on using succession planning as a means of retaining what is described as the 'top talent' of the organisations. Beeson (2000) describes a survey which concluded that the expectation of career progress as provided by succession planning approaches was a key factor in the retention of those staff identified as having 'exceptional potential', and Simms (2003) talks about the importance of succession planning in nurturing 'home-grown talent'.

USING SUCCESSION PLANNING FOR IDENTIFYING LEARNING NEEDS

In terms of levels, succession planning can be used at the organisational and the occupational levels but is more likely to be used in defining individual needs, particularly for management and key specialist staff. Succession planning is to do with future needs but covers the range from the near future (simply filling the vacancies caused by labour turnover) to the far distant future (the strategic process). Here again is the opportunity for the learning professional to be involved in the strategic decisions of the business.

Let's look at a simple case study to see how succession planning can be an abundant source of learning needs.

The Planahead Organisation

Succession plans usually take as their starting-point the organisation chart. This is then annotated to show the key information required for succession planning. Figure 4 shows the succession plan for the management tiers of the Planahead Organisation over a five-year period.

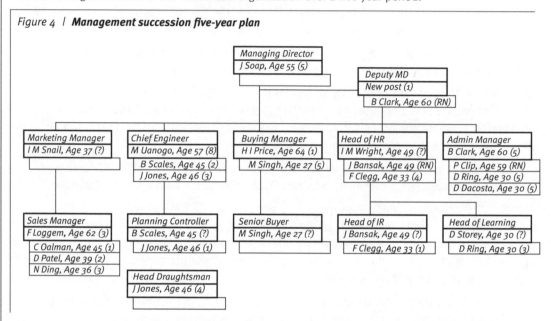

Figure 4 | *Management succession five-year plan*

The names in the boxes outlined by an emboldened border are those of the staff as they would appear on the organisation chart, but with the additional information of their age and the period of time they are expected to be in post, where known. For example, J Soap is the managing director; he or she is 55 years of age and has made it clear that he or she will retire at age 60. The box with job title deputy MD, with no name attached, indicates that this is a new post that is expected to be introduced in one year's time.

The names in the offset boxes outlined by a plain border are those of the heirs apparent, or at least of those members of staff who the organisation believes are capable of meeting the demands of the senior jobs at some stage in the future. The additional information on them is their age and the period of time before they are expected, in the normal course of events, to have the full set of competencies for the senior posts – ie before they are ready to assume the full duties and responsibilities. The letters 'RN' mean 'ready now'. Vacant offset boxes means that no one, as yet, has been identified as the possible successor for the job.

The period of time needed to acquire the full competencies for the key jobs shown assumes that some type of formal or informal learning intervention is in place or that simply experience in the current job will provide the skills and knowledge needed. This, in turn, implies that some form of learning needs analysis has been carried out already to identify the learning required to prepare those individuals for their future posts. Often this has not been done in any systematic way – which provides the first potential area for intervention for the learning professional.

The next stage is to look at the overall succession plan for gaps and weaknesses. On the basis that it might be prudent to have more than one 'crown prince/princess' for each key or senior post, the immediate response to examining the chart shows that some posts (sales manager, head of HR) are more than adequately covered, others are covered by only one possible successor, and some (MD, marketing manager, senior buyer and head draughtsman) have no cover at all. However, this is not the only problem thrown up by the chart. Other possible problems for the Planahead Organisation are:

- The buying manager is due to retire in one year, but his possible successor will not be ready for five years.
- In addition to having no nominated successor, the career intentions of the marketing manager are not known. If she leaves in the short term, the organisation would appear to be committed to external recruitment.
- The possible candidate for the new deputy managing director is the administration manager – but if the deputy MD job is seen as a staging-post for filling the MD post, is it sensible to appoint someone who will retire at about the same time that the MD is due to leave?

At this stage it is important to focus on all possible solutions to these problems – we are looking initially for how the performance needs implied by the succession plan can be met. A learning intervention may or may not provide the answers. Let's look at one or two of these problems in more detail:

- In the cases of the head draughtsman and senior buyer, for whom there are no successors identified, perhaps the next vacancy that arises in their sections should be filled by someone with supervisory skills/experience in order to provide a potential heir. In other words, the personnel specification for filling such vacancies should be modified to include some competency in supervision or managerial skills.
- So far as cover for the marketing manager is concerned, perhaps one way of postponing the problem is to secure some knowledge about Snail's plans. If you look at the age profile of the top managers, you will see that Snail is considerably younger than her colleagues. Snail is clearly no *snail* but a high flyer and might be encouraged to make a commitment to remaining with the organisation by the prospect of being groomed as a possible candidate for the new deputy managing director role. Another approach might be to expand her role and give her wider responsibilities than marketing – possibly, say, by combining marketing with buying.

If some of the solutions suggested above are not acceptable either to management or to the staff concerned, we need to look wider. For example, if the combination of marketing with buying does not secure the longer-term commitment of the marketing manager, or if I. M. Snail looks like getting the deputy MD post in a year's time, then there is a need to pencil in a possible successor. A little creative thinking might be helpful – we should ask ourselves what the competencies are that managers need at the most senior levels in organisations. Perhaps vision and strategic awareness are more important than professional knowledge and skills. While it *might* be traditional in, say, engineering to have an engineer in the top job, it is open to us to ask the questions:

- To what extent is senior management about motivating and leading people, about planning and organising, and about dealing with budgets?
- To what extent is the role of top managers about *administering* their function?

If the answers to either of these questions is 'to a large extent', we might then start to look at how we could groom, say, the head of HR to at least cover on a temporary basis for the marketing manager should she be appointed as the new deputy MD or decide to leave before a true successor is ready. The following options might be considered:

- Encourage the head of HR to acquire the full range of marketing competencies through a mix of formal and informal learning interventions – tempting, but probably impractical on a number of points such as cost and length of time taken.
- Give the head of HR some introductory overview of the marketing function if this is lacking, and also arrange for him to get involved in the marketing department/function at every opportunity, by involvement for example in the recruitment of marketing staff, in any disciplinary or performance issues, or even in a Learning Needs Analysis in the department. In these ways the head of HR could quickly gain some competence in the issues facing the function, to add to the senior management skills already gained through working at the top level.

So far we have looked at the obvious business need of the organisation to ensure that it has suitable successors to its key management posts. Another set of problems that might be identified by the eagle-eyed learning professional is what to do with those staff that are ready for promotion now, and where there is no opportunity for this promotion in the short term. For example, there is C. Oalman who is shown as a successor for the sales manager, F. Loggem who is not due to retire for another three years, and J. Bansak, if the head of HR does not move on. There is the danger of such staff becoming demotivated, with the consequent impact on their work and on the motivation of those around them, or possibly of their leaving. Solutions that may help to bridge the gap are secondments to gain wider experience of the organisation, joining project teams to hone up project management skills, or undertaking some additional professional or general management development. These staff could become part of the 'talent pool' referred to earlier.

So, as you can see, the succession plan can provide a rich source of information on performance and learning needs. It is often said, with some justification, that the learning professionals are left out of the decision-making processes and brought in only to implement the decisions of others. Let us review how proactive the learning professional in this case study is becoming. Recommendations have been made about:

- the possible combination of departments
- further development of senior managers and key staff
- changes to the personnel specifications for staff in the drawing office and in buying
- how to deal with staff who are ready to move on but where there are no opportunities for it.

Do we detect a note of panic here? Are we possibly suggesting that the learning professional might be trespassing on other professionals' territory? Yes we are, because we believe that one of the problems that has dogged the learning function is that it seems to be pigeonholed within a very narrow definition of the learning role. More than ever in today's world of rapid and major change there is a need for learning professionals to:

- take a wider view
- involve themselves as much as possible in all aspects of the business
- be seen as part of the team addressing the performance needs of the human resource assets of the organisation
- be a 'change agent'.

However, that does not mean that there is not a need for sensitivity on these issues. The message is to sell to all concerned the advantages to the organisation of the learning professional taking on this wider role and having this greater involvement.

Many organisations do not take succession planning seriously. (This is a euphemism for what we really mean, which is that they do not do it at all!) However, it only takes one situation to occur where a lack of succession planning could have serious results to persuade the organisation that it is worth doing.

The modern approach to succession planning is based around competency frameworks (see Chapter 9) which together with the appropriate software packages make the matching of people to roles relatively easy. So, for example, it is possible to search for a list of people who are the closest match to a particular role in terms of competencies. However, there will always have to be an element of judgement in identifying how readily gaps in competency fit can be bridged by some form of intervention.

CONCLUSION

So succession planning is another valuable tool to help the learning professional to respond ahead of the strategic needs of the business rather than be constantly under pressure from all those same interventions being required yesterday. In the next chapter we look at another important source of rather more immediate information on performance and learning needs: the critical incidents that occur in our organisations.

READING AND REFERENCE

ARMSTRONG M. (2001), *A Handbook of Human Resource Management Practice*, 8th edn, London, Kogan Page.

BEESON J. (2000), 'Succession planning', *Across the Board*, February.

BYHAM W. (2001), 'Pools winners', *People Management*, 24 August.

EMPLOYEE DEVELOPMENT BULLETIN 132 (2000), *Making a success of succession*, December.

SIMMS J. (2003), 'The generation game', *People Management*, 6 February.

WALLUM P. (1993), 'A broader view of succession planning', *Personnel Management*, September.

5

Critical incidents

INTRODUCTION

In Chapter 2 we made the distinction between what we called the *planned* business needs – ie arising out of the stated objectives and strategy of the business – and the *unplanned* business needs – ie those unforeseen events that buffet a business. The previous two chapters on human resource and succession planning were concerned with the planned business needs; this chapter looks at the unplanned variety. Now these unforeseen events can sometimes be of a positive nature, such as suddenly gaining a major new customer or an existing customer unexpectedly requiring new products or services. However, more often than not these unforeseen events are to do with problems, such as the major breakdown of a piece of equipment, the loss of a major customer, a poor audit result on a particular department or process, a serious customer complaint or a sudden large increase in customer complaints. Or the problem may be an unexpected event completely external to the organisation, such as a piece of legislation or a competitor initiative that demands a response. We are defining these types of occurrence as our *critical incidents*.

(A related area is the use of *critical incident technique* in analysing the learning needs for a particular job or a gap in performance for individuals. Here the critical incidents are those that occur in a particular job and include incidents in which exceptionally good performance is demonstrated as well as incidents in which poor performance is demonstrated. This technique is discussed in more detail in Chapter 10.)

USING CRITICAL INCIDENTS FOR IDENTIFYING LEARNING NEEDS

By using the word *critical* in this way we are saying that these incidents are of significant importance to the business and therefore relate most often to the organisational and occupational/group levels for the identification of learning needs. However, it is possible that the performance of one individual can give rise to a critical incident – for example, a serious accident caused by one member of staff's failure to follow safety procedures. Almost without exception critical incidents, by their very nature as problems or as failures in present performance, identify learning for present needs.

Again in Chapter 2 we described these critical incidents as business needs which usually come along with the label SUPER-URGENT, DO SOMETHING QUICKLY. Throwing some form of learning intervention at the problem is often the almost automatic response to the situation. Because the need is characterised as urgent, that intervention is then developed in a hurry without a clear understanding of the *cause(s)* of the problem. Inevitably, the resulting learning intervention will have unclear objectives and be typical of the shotgun approach to training – ie showering out a load of training pellets in the hope that some at least will hit the target and meet the need. At best this can be a costly and wasteful approach, and at worst totally ineffective.

Until the *causes* of the critical incident are clearly established it is difficult, if not impossible, to decide on the appropriate action. Has the incident been caused by a human performance problem at all, or might the cause be faulty equipment or inadequate procedures? If it is a human performance problem, is learning the appropriate solution? The first step must be to *analyse* the problem. Let's look at an example of how this is done using the following case studies.

CASE STUDY

The disturbing discrepancies incident

At the weekly management meeting of senior staff of a large department store, the accountant reports that there was a worrying level of cash discrepancies the previous month. He states firmly that this cannot be allowed to continue and requests (demands?) that immediate training be given to the cashiers on the checkout tills to improve their standards of performance. The general manager steps in and comments that this is a serious problem and the learning department must give it a high priority.

Does this sort of situation ring any bells? The learning professional's immediate response is probably to think 'Help! How on earth do I organise training for 50 cashiers at the drop of a hat?' However, stop a minute to think about what is happening – the accountant has very neatly dumped his problem on to you. Is training, or even any form of learning intervention, the best solution, or even a solution at all?

The accountant's request for an improvement in standards of cash handling is obviously an important one. A business need is clearly identifiable. But do we really know what the *causes* of this particular critical incident are? So what analysis should be carried out? The best way to approach this is to think about the questions that have to be answered:

- What is an acceptable level of discrepancies? In any operation of this nature some mistakes are inevitable, and it is only when the level exceeds the acceptable level that action is usually required. This is analogous to the concepts of quality control and use of variances in budgets – action is triggered when the level of faults/expenditure falls outside some agreed band. So first it is essential to determine the acceptable level or trigger-point. It may perhaps be expressed in terms of 'pence per thousand pounds' of takings.
- In terms of this indicator, is the level of discrepancies the same across all the tills and all the cashiers, or is it concentrated in some tills, some groups of cashiers, or individual operators?
- If it is occurring with a specific group of cashiers, is there some common denominator, such as the same learning facilitator being involved in the original programme to provide cashiers with

the skills to use the checkout tills? This could highlight the need to look at the standards of performance of the learning facilitators and to examine the systems of learning evaluation.

- Is it possibly a fault with the tills themselves? If it is, it could throw up an unexpected learning need for the service engineers of the tills!

- Are the discrepancies arising out of particular activities of the cashiers – eg in payments by cheque – which could have implications for the focus of any learning intervention?

- Could the discrepancies be occurring somewhere other than at the checkouts? For example, in the cash office where the takings are checked?

- Could the discrepancies be caused by some reason other than lack of skill? For example, could dishonesty be a cause?

As you can see, the questions, simply by being posed, have opened up a wide range of possible *causes* of the problem. Already it is becoming obvious that a learning intervention might not be the appropriate solution at all, and even if it is, it may not be necessary to train all the cashiers nor train across the whole range of cashier skills. The process:

- identifies the *exact nature* of the problem and investigates the *causes*

- ensures that non-learning solutions are considered

- if learning is a solution or part of the solution, ensures that the learning intervention is *focused* on the right people and on the right skills.

Let's look at another example.

The awful accidents

The warehouse manager has just taken over a newly built warehouse. The warehouse operatives have all been on a learning programme on how to operate the new order-pickers that are being used in the warehouse. In the first month of operation, the manager reports that there has been a worrying number of minor accidents and one more serious one which resulted in a staff injury, all involving the new order-picking vehicles. She is convinced that the original training was inadequate and wants further training given *immediately*. The learning professional, yet again, experiences that sinking feeling in the stomach – this sort of skills training is very expensive and the budget is already overspent so far this year. The warehouse manager reminds you (or threatens you?) that safety is considered a priority issue in the organisation.

However, you have learned your lesson over the cashiers – you organised a learning intervention for them all and then found out that it was a problem with the cash counting machine in the cash office! This time you are going to *analyse* the problem. Again, a good starting-point is to think of all the questions you ought to ask.

- *Who* were involved in the accidents?

CASE STUDY continued

- *What* actually happened?
- *When* did they occur?
- *Where* did they occur?

This is the basic fact-finding operation. The next stage is to consider what all the possible causes of the accidents are – this is almost a brainstorming exercise, since sometimes the cause may turn out to be very unexpected. Could it be:

- operator performance error (the hot favourite with the warehouse manager)?
- a fault with the order-picker equipment?
- a problem with the design of the warehouse?
- a weakness with the supervision of the operators?
- a problem with the way the stock is being stacked?
- vandalism of any sort?

Even if it turns out to be operator performance error, go on questioning:

Is a learning intervention the answer? For example,

- Could a rewrite of the manual or operating procedures be the answer?
- Are the staff suitable for this type of work?

If a learning intervention is the answer,

- Do *all* the operators need a further learning intervention?
- Do they need a learning intervention covering all the skills/knowledge required, or only in certain skill areas – eg reversing the order-picking vehicle?
- What was wrong with the previous learning programme? Was it poorly designed or poorly delivered – and does this have any implications for who carries out the further learning intervention?

Let's recap on what you have done. Just as with the *Disturbing discrepances incident* case study, you have:

- identified the *exact nature* of the problem and investigated the causes
- ensured that non-learning solutions are considered
- if learning is a solution or part of the solution, ensured that the learning is *focused* on the right people and on the right skills.

Monitoring that the solution has worked is usually not hard with critical incidents of this type. The business need is clearly defined – the level of cash discrepancies should return to normal, and the accidents should cease. Sometimes it will be important to continue the monitoring for a long period of time. It is possible that giving attention to the problem has in itself had a short-term effect. If dishonesty was the cause of the cash discrepancies, it is quite likely to stop for while. If the warehouse operatives have been larking about, this too may stop temporarily once an investigation is under way.

Again, do we hear a note of scepticism ('All this analysis is fine in theory, but in the real world there is simply not the time')? This chapter started out by saying these were usually business needs that came along labelled SUPER-URGENT. Is there not a danger of analysis paralysis and nothing getting done? The answer to this quite justifiable concern is fourfold:

- You must ensure that you get all the help you can from the people that can provide it – eg the accountant and the warehouse manager. It will be important to sell the idea that it is a team effort. You remember that we referred to the accountant dumping the problem on to you. Make sure that there is appropriate ownership of the problem, appropriate ownership of the analysis, and this should then lead to the appropriate ownership of the solution.

- A proper analysis of the problem and identification of the causes will help make the development of any learning solution a quicker process as well as a better one.

- The right solution may well turn out to be a quicker option than the original learning solution proposed, and the process overall may therefore turn out to be shorter.

- Can you afford to deliver the wrong answer?

This last point is a very important one – it is not only your learning budget that we are talking about, but your credibility as a learning professional, the credibility of the learning function and the credibility of learning overall.

CONCLUSION

In this chapter we have examined the identification of learning needs from what might be described as *one-off* (and, by our definition, critical) incidents. In the next chapter we look at the sorts of learning needs that can be identified from the regular, routine reporting from management information systems.

6

Management information systems

INTRODUCTION

There are many weighty tomes (Bocij *et al*, 2003; Lucey, 2001; Bee and Bee, 1999) that set out to describe the purpose of information systems and how they should be designed and implemented. The purpose of this chapter is not to cover this rather specialist ground but to examine how the learning professional might use information systems and particularly management information systems (MISs) to assist with the identification of learning needs.

However, before we begin it is important to establish what we mean by an MIS. Bocij *et al* (2003) distinguish between two broad categories of information systems:

- **Operations information systems** *are generally concerned with process control, transaction processing, communications (internal and external) and productivity.*

- **Management information systems** *provide feedback on organisational activities and help to support managerial decision-making . . .*

Lucey (2001) defines an MIS as:

A system to convert data from internal and external sources into information and to communicate that information, in an appropriate form, to managers at all levels in all functions to enable them to make timely and effective decisions for planning, directing and controlling the activities for which they are responsible.

In *Managing Information and Statistics* (Bee and Bee, 1999) we too stress that what is important is for an MIS to deliver the information that managers and specialists need to do their jobs, by defining an MIS as a system which produces:

. . . the right information in the right form at the right time, so enabling the manager or specialist effectively and efficiently to do his or her job.

All these definition rightly emphasise the *purpose* of MISs for use by managers to do their jobs – to make decisions.

We have come a long way from the early days when computers were primarily used for basic administrative data-processing activities, such as the payroll, preparing invoices, etc. Then we saw the burgeoning of a large number of separate systems within an organisation when data was held by specific functions for specific purposes. For example, the finance function would have its data on suppliers (for paying the bills) and customers (for sending out invoices). The purchasing function and the sales function might have their own data on those same suppliers or customers for their own specialist purposes. The HR department would have a system holding the data it needed on staff, and the payroll function a system holding data on staff for pay purposes. Not only was this duplication of data wasteful but because these dedicated systems had to be updated individually, data on the same customer or member of staff could – and did – vary significantly.

This multiplicity of information systems has tended to disappear with the development of corporate information systems that rely on relational databases. Here, not only can any data in the system be accessed by any authorised user, but when updating any item of data – say, salary in the employee record – the corresponding change is automatically made in other relevant files – eg the pay file and pensions file. Managers and others who are so authorised can access all the information they need from across the organisation at the appropriate level of detail, knowing that it is consistent and as up-to-date as possible. In the ideal world all the information systems operate from a common, relational database. In reality, in many organisations this may still be an aim rather than a fact.

The other dramatic change that has taken place is in the way that managers and others are able to access and analyse the information and produce reports. In the early days they would be faced with great piles of computer printout. We then moved to the situation where managers and others could access pre-designed reports from their own PCs on their desks. Now, there are sophisticated packages that enable managers and others to analyse the data in whatever form they want it and produce reports distilling out the key information they need.

USING MIS FOR IDENTIFYING LEARNING NEEDS

We talked in Section 1 about the importance of learning professionals continually scanning their environment – an MIS offers a ready-made systematic method of doing so. It can offer a ready-made window into the business needs arising out of current performance by the business. Because an MIS usually reports on aggregate performance – ie by department, factory, region, and by the organisation as a whole – this approach is geared to identifying learning needs at the occupational/group and organisational levels. Also, because an MIS reports about the past and the present, it is likely that any learning needs identified will be present ones. However, there could be occasions when the system identifies a trend for, say, growth in production and where a threshold of work is approaching that will require additional staff, plant and equipment to meet the business needs. In this situation we would be addressing future learning needs.

Learning professionals may already be familiar with accessing specific information related to the learning function through their HR information system (HRIS) (see Chapter 10). We are suggesting that they make much wider use of the information available in their organisations.

So how should learning professionals proceed? First, they must think hard about the information they require from the MIS to meet their purpose of identifying learning needs. They must decide what information they *really* want. There are no easy answers to this: it will be very dependent on the nature of the business. However, some examples of the sorts of performance measures that might be monitored include:

- levels of production output
- levels of sales
- quality indicators – eg wastage rates, defects rates, customer complaints
- productivity indices – eg output per employee, man-hours per product unit, the utilisation of machines and equipment
- accident rates
- labour turnover
- absence/sickness rates.

The second key decision is how the data should be analysed – ie the sorts of things the learning professional should be looking for. Examples include:

- trends over time
- variances from targets
- making comparisons with norms – eg particular departments with the organisation norm, the organisation with industry norms or national norms.

Let's look at some short case studies which illustrate the usefulness of an MIS as a link between the business needs of the organisation and learning needs.

CASE STUDY

The disappointing department

You have noted that over a period of time that there has been a regular shortfall against production targets in Department X. What might be the reasons for this?

- staff underperforming because of:
  - poor productivity?
  - poor motivation?
  - poor supervision?
- insufficient staff – ie high vacancy rates, vacancies taking a long time to fill?
- problems with machinery – eg high levels of downtime?
- problems getting raw materials of the right quality and quantity at the right time?
- disputes?

Some of these *could* indicate a learning need. For example:

- to improve the skills of the production operatives and hence increase productivity
- to improve the supervisory skills
- to improve the skills of staff who maintain the machines
- to improve the skills of the staff who deal with the ordering of raw materials
- to improve management skills in dealing with low motivation or the handling of disputes or the filling of vacancies.

The revolting region

You have noted that Region X has experienced above-average labour turnover rates for the last three months compared with the organisation as a whole. What might be the reasons for this?

- The labour market is particularly buoyant in that area? (Comparisons with regional norms would help here.)
- Labour is being shed for planned reasons – eg a downturn in orders?
- Staff are being dismissed at a higher-than-average rate?
- Staff are leaving of their own accord at a higher-than-average rate?

Some of these *could* indicate a learning need:

- to provide staff with recruitment skills to help cope with replacing the staff that are leaving
- to improve the quality of the recruitment process –an analysis of the leavers may indicate that the leavers were mostly relatively new recruits
- to improve performance skills to reduce the level of dismissals (if these are related to skill/knowledge deficiencies)
- to improve management and supervisory skills in dealing with poor performance issues, low morale/motivation issues, if these are diagnosed as the reason for the exodus.

Do we note some concerns with this approach:

- about the extent of the workload involved in and resulting from this process for the learning professional?
- about whether the learning professional is again going beyond the remit of his or her role?

The concern about workload is a justified one. However, it is important to remember that the process is all about identifying *exceptional* trends, variances from targets and norms. The emphasis must be on the learning professional being discriminating, using his or her judgement on what the potentially important business needs are that are being identified in this way, and prioritising his or her work and involvement accordingly.

You are not convinced. We still hear the cry 'I cannot cope with my current workload – how am I even to *begin* to do this?'

There are two encouraging developments:

- information is now usually readily available through the organisational intranet
- the advances in information systems means that it has become relatively easy for the non-expert to analyse and present information – at a press of a key (or two).

Also, if you are improving the learning needs analysis process we guarantee that there will be fewer learning interventions, but these will be focused on the right people and the right learning areas. It is important to see learning needs analysis as an *investment* – the payoff will not only be improved learning in the organisation but represent a saving in learning professionals' time previously devoted to designing and delivering ill-conceived and ineffective learning interventions.

The question whether learning professionals are perhaps going beyond their remit depends on their definition or perspective of their role, and in particular on whether they see their role as proactive or reactive. This sort of environmental scan will enable learning professionals to *demonstrate* a knowledge and understanding of the business's performance. It will enhance their credibility to perform as full members of the management team rather than as narrow functional specialists. We refer again to the quote from Geoff Armstrong (Manocha, 2002): we must 'be contributing real business value, building upon, but not confined to, our professional speciality'.

CONCLUSION

In this chapter we have discussed how MISs can provide a potent addition to our toolkit for environmental scanning. As we see it, information is the key to all business decisions, and learning professionals who choose to ignore the MIS as a provider of the information on which to base their assessment of learning needs, do so at their peril. We go on now to look at the information on performance needs that might be gleaned from a performance management system.

READING AND REFERENCE

Bee R. *and* Bee F. (1999), *Managing Information and Statistics*, London, CIPD.

Bocij P., Chaffey D., Greasley A. *and* Hickie S. (2003), *Business Information Systems*, 2nd edn, Harlow, Pearson Education.

Lucey T. (2001), *Management Information Systems*, 9th edn, Continuum International Publishing Group.

Manocha R. (2002), 'Leading the way', *People Management*, 26 September.

7

Performance management systems

INTRODUCTION

Performance management systems are generally understood to cover the whole process which 'translates the goals of strategic management into individual performance' (Anderson and Evenden, 1993). Shellabear (2002) describes performance management in more detail as:

> *... the continuous process of developing both competencies and competences to improve individual, group and organisational performance. It involves agreeing objectives, targets and standards of performance with all individuals, then supporting staff to achieve them through monitoring and development. Regular performance reviews and personal development plans (PDPs) are required if the process is to succeed.*

Marchington and Wilkinson (1996) break it down into its component parts or stages – which we have summarised in Figure 5. Typically this process is shown as a system, going through all the stages and then back around to stage 1. In reality this process is iterative – for example at all stages you may be revisiting the first stage to clarify performance requirements.

We are particularly interested in the third stage of the process – a part of which involves the formal meetings between an individual and his or her manager to review and assess the individual's performance in the job, to identify any action that is needed to improve performance, and in some cases to identify potential and future development needs. These meetings typically take place once or twice a year and consist of:

---

*Figure 5 | **Performance management process***

STAGE 1: Clarifying performance requirements

STAGE 2: Supporting performance

STAGE 3: Reviewing performance

STAGE 4: Addressing the performance gap/development needs

- a review of performance against specific objectives/targets set for the job over the review period
- a review of performance against general competencies, such as:
  - job management skills – eg planning and foresight, decision-making/problem-solving ability, resource management
  - people management skills – eg delegation, control, development/appraisal of others, resolution of people problems
  - personal skills – eg communication/interaction with others, flexibility, motivation of self and others, energy, resilience
- the identification of any gaps in performance and a discussion on any action required to improve performance, which might include the need for a learning intervention
- setting objectives for the next review period
- (sometimes) a discussion of about potential and future development.

We would emphasise that these 'formal' meetings should only form part of this stage of the process. Ideally, they should be supported by regular, more informal meetings during the year when immediate issues and feedback can be discussed.

Randell *et al* (1984) state that:

Some kind of staff appraisal activity goes on in all organisations. It ranges from intermittent, informal and often ill-informed discussion between managers about individual members of staff to highly formal appraisal procedures, based on extensive sets of forms and established times, rules and frequency of assessments.

They say that the purposes of staff review and appraisal procedures vary from *organisation-centred* to *individual-centred* and are mainly concerned with establishing controls on the behaviour of people or bringing about change in their behaviour by, among other things:

... discovering training needs – by **exposing inadequacies and deficiencies** *[our emphasis] that could be remedied by training.*

The intervening years have taken many organisations a long way from using their performance review processes for 'exposing inadequacies and deficiencies' to being more forward-looking and concentrating on performance development in the future rather than dissecting the blame-laden past. However, sadly, there are still a number of organisations where at least some of the above still holds true.

Another important development that has taken place has been the move towards a more rounded and arguably more robust approach to assessing performance with the introduction of a wider range of 'appraisers'. Often referred to as '360-degree' appraisal, such approaches may involve an individual's subordinates, their peers, internal/external customers for their services as well as the traditional immediate supervisor. The research (Fletcher, 2001) suggests that multi-source feedback works best when it is used in a review process with a more developmental context than an evaluative one.

THE RELATIONSHIP BETWEEN PERFORMANCE MANAGEMENT AND LNA

Clearly, the ability of a performance management system to deliver useful information on learning needs depends on the quality of that system. There has been a considerable amount of literature written about the problems with performance review which largely focuses on the inability of the manager to make consistent and accurate assessments. Despite these drawbacks and the pocketed nature of the existence of review systems (this is particularly so for blue-collar workers), it would appear, both from anecdotal evidence and from a survey of the training/learning needs literature, that performance review systems are often seen as a principal way of identifying training/learning needs in organisations.

Looking at performance management systems in terms of levels of learning needs, their primary purpose is usually for identifying individual learning needs, although the accumulation of individual needs can lead to the identification of occupational/group needs. Performance management systems are rarely the best source for identifying organisational needs. Since the main focus of performance management systems is on current performance, the learning needs identified are usually present ones. In as much as a performance management system looks at future development, the learning needs may be future ones.

A very interesting article by Herbert and Doverspike (1990) reviewed the US literature on the relationship between performance appraisal and learning/training needs analysis from 1961 to 1985. They concluded, among other things, that:

> *While the* needs analysis survey literature *[our emphasis] . . . seems to indicate that*
> *performance appraisal data is important for the needs analysis process, the* performance
> appraisal survey literature *[our emphasis] . . . seems to indicate that only small percentages of*
> *companies and state governments list needs analysis as an important function of their appraisal*
> *systems, and that this function ranks very low among the purposes for conducting such*
> *appraisal. This may indicate that few companies and state governments truly perform any type*
> *of needs analysis, but that when it is performed, performance appraisal data is viewed as a*
> *useful source of information.*

They went on to say that they found no reports of proper research studies addressing the use of performance appraisal as a LNA/TNA technique. They also found that although there was plenty of advice about how performance appraisals should be conducted:

> *. . . relatively little literature exists concerning how performance appraisal information should be*
> *used for needs analysis, and whether it is empirically successful. In addition, there appears to be*
> *a large number of inconsistencies and unanswered questions in the literature concerned with*
> *performance appraisal as a needs analysis technique.*

Our experience suggests that this analysis still holds good today. Also, there often still remains the potential conflict between the different purposes of the review process. In particular between the use of the process:

- to assess performance on which reward is based, whether in the form of a direct relationship with pay or through potential reward through promotion, and
- to identify learning and development needs.

The first purpose may incline the individual to hide any performance weaknesses, whereas the second purpose requires an honest and frank discussion on areas of improvement and how learning interventions might contribute.

So where does all this leave the learning professional? Perhaps with the message not to take for granted the usefulness of performance management systems nor to rely too heavily on them as a method of identifying learning needs. In the other chapters in this section we have concentrated on selling what we see as underrated methods of identifying learning needs. We find ourselves in this chapter doing the opposite, of advising caution and emphasising an awareness of the limitations of the method as practised in many organisations.

USING PERFORMANCE MANAGEMENT SYSTEMS FOR IDENTIFYING LEARNING NEEDS

To make the best use of the performance review system, the learning professional must think about the following issues:

- What is the *quality* of the review system in terms of its ability to generate accurate, relevant and useful information on the assessment of performance, the identification of areas for improvement, and the potential for development?

- What is the extent to which the *design* of any forms, procedures, etc, encourages the effective identification of learning needs? In many systems, there is a section labelled 'Learning requirements', but are managers encouraged to:
  - show clearly the link between lack of specific performance and a need for action?
  - consider non-learning solutions?
  - specify very precisely the learning *need* rather than just proposing a 'course'?
  - indicate the degree of priority and urgency of the learning needs identified?

- What is the most effective *intervention* of the learning professional in the process? Is it to:
  - simply record and action the line managers' requests?
  - discuss the requirements only when there is a problem of some sort – eg insufficient budget, unclear requirements?
  - discuss all findings with line managers to establish jointly the performance needs and the best way of meeting them?

The answers will depend on a number of factors, including the perceived role of the line manager, the learning professional's workload, the nature of the relationship between the learning professional and the line managers, and perhaps most crucial of all, the ability of the line managers to undertake what is in effect a mini-LNA on their staff. Many organisations now see learning and development as an important part of the line manager role. If this is the case and the main burden for the identification of individual learning needs is seen as the line manager's responsibility, an important issue to consider is then the learning needs of line managers in undertaking LNA.

- What *systems* should the learning professional set up to action the learning needs output from performance reviews? Potentially, this method generates a lot of information and it is vital that systems are in place to record, analyse, action and monitor the information. There is nothing worse (and how familiar does this sound) for the complaint to be made by both line managers and staff that nothing has been done as a result of their performance management report.

- How is the performance review process organised in terms of timing? There are generally two approaches:

  - The reviews take place on the anniversary of each member of staff's joining the organisation, and the appraisals are therefore spread out across the year.

  - All reviews take place over a fixed period in the year – perhaps June to September.

  The first approach spreads out the workload for line managers. The second approach makes it easier and more efficient to monitor that the reviews have been done, and helps meet a particular requirement of the learning professional – to assemble all the learning needs to feed into the learning plan (see Chapter 15).

- Finally, last but not least – how well does the system work in practice?

  - Do performance management meetings take place within the required timescale?

  - How well are the meetings handled?

  - How well are the forms and reports completed?

  - Have managers and staff received appropriate learning interventions on how to make the best use of the system?

  From our experience, many of you may be looking concerned, and indeed, some of you may actually be wincing. In one large public sector organisation with which we are involved, the answers to these questions were embarrassing. A very high proportion of reviews were more than six months overdue. The quality of the completed paperwork was poor and there was no recent evidence of any learning interventions aimed at improving the understanding and use of the performance review system.

Where there are weaknesses in the overall quality of the performance management system and/or the usefulness of the design for the identification of learning needs, it is yet another opportunity for the learning professional to take a proactive role. That is not to underestimate the difficulties of initiating a review or redesign of an existing system. This can be a large and complex task often involving negotiations with a wide range of people, including staff, managers and trade unions/staff associations. Clearly, the extent to which the learning professional presses for action must depend on the degree of inadequacy of the system. However, it is in no one's interests, nor does it contribute to the meeting of overall business needs, to have a system that is inadequately assessing performance and/or identifying learning needs.

The degree of intervention by learning professionals into the performance management process is within their control. Yet there may be sensitivity concerns if others feel in any way that their role is being usurped. In particular, the importance of developing good working relationships with line managers cannot be over-emphasised. We worked with one company to recruit a new learning and development manager, where the key competency for the job was the ability to develop productive working relationships with line managers. However, in our experience line managers usually welcome help in an area of their job where they often feel they have inadequate expertise and time to address the issues effectively.

Last but not least, ignore at your peril the need to develop systems to deal with the information! However good the process of LNA is, it will be *scuppered* if there are not effective systems in place to store, action and monitor the results from it. Although manual systems may suffice in small organisations, almost certainly for any larger organisations a computerised system is essential. There are many computer packages on the market, ranging from ones that can be used for the performance management process itself to those that can also be used as databases for the recording of learning needs information and form part of wider HR Information Systems (see Chapter 10).

In Chapter 15, where we examine the preparation of organisational learning and development plans, we investigate some of the other issues surrounding the use of information on learning needs generated from the performance management system.

CONCLUSION

Performance management systems can be generators of masses of information on the performance improvement needs and hence learning needs of staff in the organisation. The quality of the information, however, will depend on the quality of the system itself and the people operating it. This system, like the other systems and techniques in this section, identifies that there is a performance need based on a business need. In Chapter 8 we go on to examine whether or not that performance need actually translates into a learning need.

READING AND REFERENCE

ANDERSON G. *and* EVENDEN R. (1993), 'Performance management: its role and methods in human resource strategy', in R. Harrison (ed.), *Human Resource Management: Issues and strategies*, Wokingham, Addison-Wesley.

HERBERT G. R. *and* DOVERSPIKE D. (1990), 'Performance appraisal in the training needs analysis process: A review and critique', *Public Personnel Management*, Vol 19, No 3, Fall.

MARCHINGTON M. *and* WILKINSON A. (1996), *Core Personnel and Development*, London, CIPD.

RANDELL G. A., PACKARD P. M. A., SHAW R. L. *and* SLATER A. J. (1984), *Staff Appraisal*, 3rd edn, London, IPM.

SHELLABEAR S. (2002), 'Competencies in training', *Training Journal*, August.

8

Is there a learning need?

INTRODUCTION

Throughout the earlier chapters in this section we have constantly referred to the importance of *not* seeing learning as the panacea of all ills or, in this case, all business needs! In fact, we have advocated that non-learning solutions should positively be sought and examined before proceeding down the learning path. It may seem strange in a book that purports to be about learning, and is aimed at those with a particular interest in learning, to be apparently urging non-learning interventions. We are not in any way seeking to undermine the role of learning nor put the learning professional out of a job! Learning solutions often require a substantial investment of resources and do not always provide a quick answer. Also, a learning intervention may not be the *right* answer and at worst makes no impact on the business need at all.

Regalbuto (1992) supports the view that a lack of competence is only one possible cause of a performance gap, and that other possibilities include:

- problems with raw materials, equipment or work spaces
- lack of money or staff
- poorly designed work methods
- insufficient motivation.

It could be argued that the mere inclusion of the word *learning* in LNA presupposes the nature of the solution that will be proposed, and suggests that it may be better to think of the process as a *needs analysis*.

We have emphasised the necessity to:

- *analyse* each business need very carefully
- consider a *wide range* of solutions
- *assess* the potential solutions against the criteria of:
  - Will it effectively meet the business need?
  - Will it meet the business need at the lowest cost?

This is not to say that there will not be those occasions when for internal political reasons – perhaps simply to demonstrate that something is being done – a choice will be made in favour of a learning solution. There will be occasions, for a variety of reasons, where the purist will be subordinated to the pragmatist – and rightly so. It may be that the learning intervention is being used for a purpose other than to meet a performance gap. Perhaps it is being used as a morale booster or the opportunity to give staff a reward after a particularly tough period. Indeed, one of our clients actually stated this as one of its objectives for a particular learning programme. We hear the purists shudder, but this is fine – it becomes the business need or at least part of the business need. Our point is that the choice is then made knowingly, and can be defended if necessary. Any evaluation would be done against a different set of criteria – with motivation rather than performance change being the main focus of any assessment.

In the rest of this chapter we set out some alternatives to a learning solution, based in part on Boydell (1990), and in no particular order, that might be considered before the learning professional rushes off to produce a learning solution.

IMPROVING METHODS OF WORK OR PROCEDURE DOCUMENTATION

The methods of work or rate of flow of materials can seriously handicap the employees' ability to perform to the standard required. One classic story in this field is reported in *Management: Concepts and Applications* (Robbins, 1988). Here, F. W. Taylor, the so-called 'father of scientific management', is reported as noticing that every worker used the same-sized shovel, regardless of the material being moved. Taylor thought that if there was an optimum weight that would maximise the shovelling over the course of the day, the size of the shovel would vary depending on the density of the material being moved. After extensive experimentation he found that 21 pounds (9.5 kilograms) was the optimum shovel capacity. To achieve this weight when shovelling iron ore, a small shovel would be used. To achieve it when shovelling light material such as coke, a large shovel would be used. Needless to say, the result was a significant increase in worker output. Using similar approaches to other jobs, Taylor was able to define the one best way of doing each job. In other words, if the method was *wrong*, no amount of learning interventions would put it right.

Another source of problems can be the inadequate documentation of the systems and procedures in use. This, in itself, is not necessarily a problem so long as staff have time to gain the experience required to become a *qualified worker* – ie one who knows how to do all the tasks in a particular job to a defined standard of, say, accuracy or time, or both, and there is someone available to coach him or her on the job. However, where there is more than a modest level of turnover of staff, there is the danger that the knowledge of how to do the tasks in the most productive way will be lost and the availability of resources to coach become severely stretched. Staff in these situations often struggle along as best they can or resort to frequent interruptions of their supervisors when they are presented with a query. It is easy in these situations for a demand to be made for learning programmes to be set up for the new staff or poor-performing existing staff.

A highly effective alternative to a learning intervention can be to document the processes and procedures clearly, as in the requirements for the award of the various British Standards. Once the documentation is in place, the on-going costs are limited to keeping it up-to-date. Such documentation might contain:

- a *procedure narrative* – a written presentation in logical sequence of the steps and operations in the procedure. This narrative might be described in some organisations as a 'procedure record' or 'operating instruction', and although the amount of detail will depend on its purpose, it is helpful to have a standard layout for the different procedures in operation

- a *flowchart* – a diagrammatic representation of the flow of work or activities

- some form of *fault-finding* or *help manual*

- a *quick reference manual* – similar to those provided by the computer software companies to help the computer-illiterate avoid the need to delve into their weighty tomes

- *information packs* – containing details: for example, names, addresses and telephone/fax numbers of people and/or organisations who are involved in the procedure either as suppliers or customers.

Mostly, such documentation is now held on computer and usually placed on an organisation's intranet, which makes it readily accessible and quickly and easily updated.

This is not to suggest that *no* learning intervention is required for the newcomer or poor performer, but obviously the process is shortened and simplified if the procedure is clearly laid down. The learning professional can be ideally placed to commission or contribute to the systematic documentation of procedures.

Some good examples of such approach being used effectively are set out in the two case studies below.

CASE STUDY

The contract cleaning company checklist

A contract cleaning company was receiving complaints about the quality of cleaning in some of its client offices. When the management investigated the complaints in more detail, it appeared that areas were being missed out. However, there was no particular pattern in terms of areas or cleaners, and the omissions were intermittent. The problem was solved by producing a simple checklist that was attached to the cleaning box used by the cleaning staff. This checklist set out the types of areas to be cleaned in each office – eg empty waste basket, clean telephone, etc.

CASE STUDY

Rotten reports

Another interesting example related to the quality of research reports being produced in an organisation. The knee-jerk response had been to send the staff involved on a research methodology course. However, the cost and the timing (the programme only ran twice a year) caused a re-think. A guide to the research process, including specifying very precisely what information was required at each stage and the structure of the reports required, was produced. This solved the problem – it was not a learning need as such but simply that staff were not clear exactly what was required from them. We have cheated slightly with this example because it was combined with a learning intervention. However, it was not the expensive research methodology intervention but a half-day workshop to introduce the guide that did the business.

This second case study is a very useful one in that performance problems can often be caused by a lack of clarity on what is required by the job. It is always worth checking that the requirements of the job and the relevant standards are clearly set out and *understood* by those involved. You will recall that this is the first stage of the performance management system (see Chapter 7).

THE IMPACT OF TECHNOLOGY

The impact of technology on all aspects of our lives is increasing at a phenomenal pace. In our life time we have seen the development and spread of computing power from the massive mainframe computers which were the province of the computer boffins down to computers which everyone can use and some which can be held in the palm of one's hand. The Internet has revolutionised the way we communicate and the way we do business.

Sometimes a skill that has been particularly prized in the past becomes virtually redundant due to changes in technology. For example, the secretarial skill, shorthand, has been much prized in the past. However, improvements in the technology of recording and transcribing machines in the 1960s and 1970s and now the developments in voice and handwriting recognition by computers could render shorthand skills completely obsolete. The typing pool in most organisations (but not quite all yet!) has gone as most staff and managers do their own typing directly on their PCs.

We have used the example of shorthand and typing skills as examples of how new/improved technology can radically change the need for a particular skill in the workplace, but other examples abound. Machines are taking over many of the traditional skills in manufacturing, the office has been transformed by the PC and the intranet/Internet, inventory control in warehouses is governed by sophisticated computers, and the actual movement of stock has been taken over by robotic systems. Armchair shopping, whether for groceries or banking services, is with us today.

Increasingly technology is revolutionising our workplaces. The focus for that learning intervention is likely to be very different – it will be directed at helping people to use the new technology, to maintain these increasingly sophisticated machines and to manage the technological process. There can be little doubt that learning for new and changing technologies is a major growth area, and it is important that the learning professional keeps up-to-date with these developments.

COMMUNICATION BRIEFINGS

Sometimes called team briefings, communication briefings by the immediate supervisor or manager can be a very effective method for briefing and instructing staff on changes in methods of work or changes in required standards of performance. They can also be used to introduce new procedure documentation or changes to existing documentation (see the case study below). This approach may often shift the need away from the primary need – for example, running courses on the procedures – to providing learning programmes for the supervisors on how to plan and run effective communication briefings.

> **CASE STUDY**
>
> **Clever communication**
>
> A major retail company uses weekly 'Communication half-hours' as a means of informing staff of new product lines, merchandising plans and revised procedures. These are carried out in all departments of every store. They are seen both as a key means of keeping staff up-to-date and as making an important contribution to knowledge-learning in the organisation.

REDESIGNING THE JOB

Where performance in a job is not up to standard, it is always an option to change the requirements of the job rather than the person. This is not unusual, and in any dynamic organisation the job responsibilities are changing all the time. It may be something as simple as rearranging the tasks that make up the job, or it may be something more complex such as developing teamwork where previously the job had been done on a solo basis.

CHANGING PERSONNEL

The alternative to redesigning the job is to change the people doing it. This could be as dramatic as dismissing an individual if it can be shown that he or she is unwilling or incapable of gaining the competencies needed to perform the job to an appropriate standard. Actions short of dismissal could involve a transfer or redeployment to other work or a transfer temporarily to other, less demanding work while the competencies are developed.

Perhaps the staff have the skills to do the job and the change that is required is to improve their motivation. This could be linked to the immediate work environment – for example, the role, skills and attitude of the supervisor or of the peer group. Again this may highlight secondary learning needs – for the supervisor in leadership skills, or for the whole work group in developing teamworking skills.

DEALING WITH ORGANISATIONAL OBSTACLES

In addition to the job not being right for the person (redesign the job) or the person not being right for the job (change the person), it is always possible that organisational constraints might be responsible for poor performance. The insertion (or removal) of a layer of supervision, the amalgamation of sections into a department, or the separation of sections from a department are examples of organisational structural change that might be considered. Other possible organisational obstacles could be the communication systems, the financial systems and/or physical environmental factors such as noise, temperature, lighting, etc.

CONCLUSION

In any given situation there will be a range of possibilities that might be considered options capable of being tested against the business needs. We are not suggesting that non-learning solutions will always be better than learning solutions, but that other options should be considered for their cost-effectiveness and timeliness of implementation. If such an approach can be shown to be more cost-effective and timely, end the analysis there and negotiate the implementation of the non-learning solution. This means that the learning professional is then able to target his or her skills directly on those activities where there is the highest return for the investment made and not fritter away his or her resources on ineffective and costly learning events or perhaps non-events!

So, in this section we have looked at a range of sources of information that are around us – a range of approaches that provide bridges between the business needs and the learning needs. We have emphasised the importance of analysing each business need very carefully so as to identify the appropriate course of action. We have also emphasised the necessity of examining non-learning interventions to see whether they can provide a more effective solution to the business need than can a learning approach. In particular, we have advised the learning professional to keep up-to-date with the developments in IT, which undoubtedly will continue to have a profound effect on all aspects of our working lives.

In the next section we go on to look at how, having identified a learning need, we *specify* it very precisely so that the learning can be focused and directed at meeting the business need.

READING AND REFERENCE

BOYDELL T. H. (1990), *A Guide to the Identification of Training Needs*, 2nd edn, London, BACIE.

REGALBUTO G. A. (1992), 'Targeting the bottom line', *Training and Development*, April.

ROBBINS S. P. (1988), *Management: Concepts and Applications*, 2nd edn, New Jersey, Prentice-Hall.

Section 3
Specifying learning needs

Introduction to Section 3

In the Introduction to this book we defined the Learning Needs Analysis process as encompassing the three stages:

- identifying the range and extent of learning needs required to meet the business needs of the organisation
- specifying the learning needs very precisely
- analysing how best these learning needs might be met.

Section 2 has taken us around the first section of the learning wheel – translating business needs into learning needs. It described the ways in which the learning professional can take a proactive and systematic approach to identifying learning needs. It emphasised that the process was in two stages:

- identifying the need for the improvement or addition to the performance of the organisation's staff
- identifying which of these needs require a learning intervention.

Having shown that a learning intervention is required, this section is about specifying that learning need very precisely. The more precisely the learning need can be specified, the more focused can be the learning. This in turn will ensure that the learning will actually meet the original business need, and in the most cost-effective way. We suggest in Chapter 9 that the starting-point should be that the job, or relevant part(s) of the job, should be clearly defined in terms of the competencies required to carry them out. These competencies can be expressed in terms of knowledge, skills, behaviours and attitudes. We propose a format for what we call a *job specification* that sets out these competencies against their key tasks and includes the standards and measures against which performance can be assessed.

Once we have specified precisely what is required in the job we go on in Chapter 10 to look at ways in which we can establish what the gap in performance is between the required and the current performance. A clear and detailed assessment of the performance gap will provide a sound foundation for specifying the learning required both accurately and precisely.

Before we do so, let's take a look at Figure 6 to see the place that specifying learning needs takes in the Learning Wheel.

Figure 6 | *The Learning Wheel – specifying learning needs*

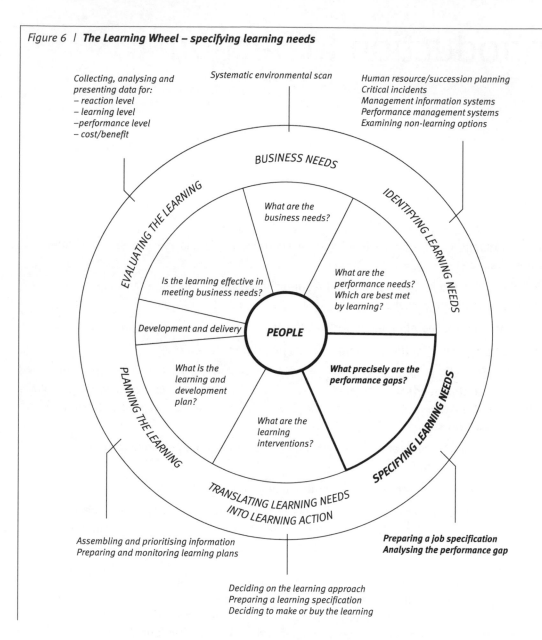

Collecting, analysing and
presenting data for:
– reaction level
– learning level
–performance level
– cost/benefit

Systematic environmental scan

Human resource/succession planning
Critical incidents
Management information systems
Performance management systems
Examining non-learning options

BUSINESS NEEDS

EVALUATING THE LEARNING

IDENTIFYING LEARNING NEEDS

*What are the
business needs?*

*Is the learning effective in
meeting business needs?*

*What are the
performance needs?
Which are best met
by learning?*

Development and delivery

PEOPLE

*What is the
learning and
development
plan?*

**What precisely are the
performance gaps?**

*What are the
learning
interventions?*

PLANNING THE LEARNING

SPECIFYING LEARNING NEEDS

TRANSLATING LEARNING NEEDS
INTO LEARNING ACTION

Assembling and prioritising information
Preparing and monitoring learning plans

**Preparing a job specification
Analysing the performance gap**

Deciding on the learning approach
Preparing a learning specification
Deciding to make or buy the learning

9

Job specifications

INTRODUCTION

Traditionally 'job analysis' has been the term used to describe the process of obtaining information about a job. Pearn and Kandola (1993) have redefined the process as job, task and role analysis, and described it as:

> ... *any systematic procedure for obtaining detailed information about a job, task or role that will be performed or is currently being performed.*

Shellabear (2002) uses the term 'competency profiling' rather than 'job analysis', which he describes as:

> *a method for identifying specified skills, knowledge, attitudes and behaviour necessary to fulfilling a task, activity or career.*

A number of documents can be produced as a result of job analysis or competency profiling. For example, Armstrong (2001) distinguishes between a *job description*, which:

> ... *sets out the purpose of a job, where it fits in the organisation structure, the context in which the job-holder functions and the principal accountabilities of job-holders, or the main tasks they have to carry out.*

and the *person specification*, which sets out:

> ... *the education, qualifications, training, experience, personal attributes and competencies a job-holder requires to perform her or his job satisfactorily.*

A *job specification* is in fact a blend of these two documents. It is specifically concerned to set out what a job-holder has to be able to do or the competencies required to carry out the job to a prescribed standard. We use the term *competencies* with some trepidation. 'Competencies' and 'competences' are words much bandied about and often with different meanings. In our view, one good definition for a competency attributed to the major insurance company Standard Life (Brown, 2001) is:

> ... *the combination of knowledge, skills, behaviours and personal attributes required to produce effective contribution.*

In preparing a job specification we will use the term *competency* to embrace both the generic behavioural dimensions and the specific knowledge and practical skills dimensions.

THE PURPOSE OF JOB SPECIFICATIONS

The job specification defines a job, or part of a job, in terms of its purpose and key function, the key tasks and the competencies required to carry them out to specified levels of performance. It is only when a job specification is available that the gap in performance (which might be the whole set of competencies if it is a new job or job-holder or a specific subset of competencies) can be identified and provide the basis for the formal specification of the learning intervention. The preparation of a job specification is a crucial step in LNA, and we neglect this phase at our peril.

While recognising that a job specification can play a role in activities other than learning (eg recruitment, job evaluation), it is the detail into which it goes that is important for LNA. It serves its purpose through cascading down the detail from an overall description of what the job is concerned with, through to the measures and standards against which the job-holder is assessed – leading to the identification of performance gaps and hence a precisely defined learning need.

HOW TO PREPARE A JOB SPECIFICATION

The most common way of preparing job specifications is to interview current job-holders and their managers. However, they can be prepared using a variety of other methods. One way is to observe qualified and experienced job operators carrying out their work. Another is actually to do the job. Some years ago the (then) Local Government Training Board, when designing a new training programme for rat-catchers, had one of their staff go through the existing training and then practise the art of rat-catching under supervision, prior to writing the job specification!

Not surprisingly, many of the methods that are used to prepare job specifications can also be used for analysing the performance gap. These methods are described in detail in Chapter 10 – so, to avoid repetition, they are not described here.

STAGES AND STRUCTURE IN WRITING A JOB SPECIFICATION

The stages and structure in writing a job specification may vary from organisation to organisation but they generally follow a format similar to the one set out below. These are:

- writing a role definition
- specifying key tasks
- specifying key competencies for each key task
- specifying performance standards and measures for each key competency.

Writing a role definition

A role definition answers the question, 'Why does this job exist?' It states the *purpose* and *main function* of the job. Examples of role definitions include:

- to ensure the provision of the highest standards of customer service, revenue control, and safety in stations (purpose) by managing operational staff; responding to public inquiries; interfacing with revenue control staff; managing contractor compliance with cleaning, maintenance, and safety standards; maintaining station equipment; and managing incidents (main function)

- to keep plant and equipment, electrical and mechanical systems in working order (purpose) by performing preventive, casual and overhaul maintenance to specified safety and quality standards (main function)

- to provide a high standard of secretarial and administrative support to the directorate (purpose) by planning and organising diaries, preparing agendas and minutes for meetings, filing and retrieving documents and word-processing documents (main function).

Specifying key tasks

Specifying the key tasks answers the question, 'What are the important parts of this job?' Although the number of key tasks will vary according to the needs of the job, these will usually be the six to eight most important tasks or functions performed in the job. It is our view that if a job has considerably more than eight key tasks, some sort of job review might be indicated. Table 4 sets out some examples of key tasks for different jobs.

*Table 4 | **Key tasks***

Key tasks		
Check tickets, passes and permits in order to detect fraud and prevent fare evasion.		
Carry out regular health and safety audits.		
Prepare minutes for all management team meetings.		

Specifying key competencies for each key task

The key competencies answer the question, 'What does the job-holder need to know or be able to do to perform each of the key tasks?' Some key tasks may have several competencies associated with them. The key competencies are listed on page 64 in the middle column immediately to the right of their associated key task. Table 5 sets out some examples of key tasks with their associated key competencies.

Table 5 | Key tasks and key competencies

Key tasks	Key competencies	
Check tickets, passes and permits in order to detect fraud and prevent fare evasion.	Question customers courteously but assertively. Identify validity of all tickets, passes and permits for travel, use of car parks and other company facilities.	
Carry out regular health and safety audits.	Demonstrate knowledge of relevant health and safety issues, including legislation. Complete health and safety checklists.	
Prepare minutes for all management team meetings.	Listen effectively and distil out key issues. Write clearly and succinctly. Liaise with members of the management team.	

Specifying performance standards and measures for each key competency

Standards and measures answer the questions, 'What is the acceptable level of performance in a key competency, and how do I know when it has been achieved?'

Standards

Two sets of standards may have to be established:

- the level of performance at the end of the learning event
- the level of performance when a person is fully competent on the job.

Sometimes these will be one and the same. Where there is a difference between the two, it is attributable to the learning that takes place on the job after the formal learning intervention has been completed.

For the purposes of a learning specification (see Chapter 12), the standards of performance expected at the end of the learning intervention are key outcomes. Clearly, the ultimate levels of performance for full competence must also be established at this stage.

Measures

The measures should be something tangible that can be observed on the job and be capable of measurement. Sometimes these will be an absolute measure (ie 100 per cent) – for example:

'Documentation completed accurately within one week of the date to which it refers.' On other occasions they will allow for some tolerance – for example: '80 per cent of queries will be resolved within 48 hours of receipt.' An interesting example used for contractors responsible for cleaning markets was the use of photographs depicting the market in the required state of cleanliness. Table 6 sets out some examples of key tasks, key competencies and associated standards and measures.

ALTERNATIVE MODELS

There are many models that can be used – often referred to as competency frameworks. We have used a specific model as an example which is straightforward, logical and easy to understand. The concepts can easily be transferred to other models and approaches. A rather different model, but fulfilling exactly the same purpose as the one we have described in detail, has

Table 6 | Key tasks, key competencies, standards and measures

Key tasks	Key competencies	Standards and measures
Check tickets, passes and permits in order to detect fraud and prevent fare evasion.	Question customers courteously but assertively.	Achieve an average score of 80% on evaluations by an observer using a checklist of courteous and assertive behaviours.
	Identify validity of all tickets, passes and permits for travel, use of car parks and other company facilities.	During spot checks by the manager, identify tickets, passes and permits in face-to-face contact with customers, with a 90% accuracy rate.
Carry out regular health and safety audits.	Demonstrate knowledge of relevant health and safety issues, including legislation.	Achieve a score of at least 80% on health and safety test conducted at regular intervals without warning.
	Complete health and safety checklists.	Documentation completed accurately within one week of the date to which it refers.
Prepare minutes for all management team meetings.	Listen effectively and distil out key issues. Write clearly and succinctly.	Draft minutes completed, requiring a maximum of 2 substantive amendments and 5 drafting amendments, within 24 hours of meetings.
	Liaise with members of the management team.	Final minutes agreed and circulated within 48 hours of meeting.

recently been established for the police service. They use the term 'role profile' rather than job specification, and describe it as 'the combination of appropriate activities, knowledge and skills and relevant behaviours' (Police Skills and Standards Organisation, 2002).

Most HR information systems incorporate flexible multi-level frameworks of competency-based job profiles which can be tailored to meet an individual organisation's needs and then used for a variety of purposes.

CONCLUSION

So we now have a very detailed description of how the job translates from its role definition through to the measures and standards that are appropriate for the effective discharge of the principal duties. This provides the yardstick against which any performance gap will be established. Some organisations are using the appropriate levels of NVQs/SVQs as a way of specifying or categorising the competencies needed in the job. These can provide the basis for identifying the performance gap between current abilities and the level of competence needed. In the next chapter we look at a range of methods and techniques for identifying and specifying the performance gap.

READING AND REFERENCE

ARMSTRONG M. (2001), *A Handbook of Human Resource Management Practice*, London, Kogan Page.

BROWN D. (2001), 'Using competencies and rewards to enhance business performance and customer service at the Standard Life Assurance Company', *Compensation and Benefits Review*, Sage Publications.

PEARN M. *and* KANDOLA R. (1993), *Job Analysis*, London, IPM.

POLICE SKILLS AND STANDARDS ORGANISATION (2002), *Competency Framework*, www.psso.co.uk

SHELLABEAR S. (2002), 'Competencies in training', *Training Journal*, August.

10

Investigating the performance gap

INTRODUCTION

So far we have identified that there is a business need requiring some form of intervention, and that a learning intervention is likely to be the best way of addressing that need. We are now at the stage of deciding what sort of learning intervention is required – ie specifying our learning requirements. The more precise and detailed we can be about the requirement, the easier it will be to develop and deliver learning that is focused and directed to meeting the business need in the most cost-effective way. This chapter discusses a range of approaches to how we set about investigating the performance gap. Many books structure these approaches under the levels of learning need – ie organisational/group/individual. However, so many of the methods can be applied to more than one level that this division does not always appear helpful to us. We prefer to present them as a portfolio of techniques, providing sufficient detail about what they are and how they can be applied to allow the reader to choose the most appropriate technique(s) to meet his or her needs.

The techniques are, of course, all different ways of gathering data on job performance. As such, they can generally be subdivided under the four major approaches to data-gathering:

- observation
- interviews
- self-complete questionnaires
- desk research.

We have chosen to group the techniques in this way as a means of helping readers to find their way through them; we are aware that some of them could be located in more than one group. Table 7 sets out the list of techniques. Each technique is then described in turn below. As we indicated in Chapter 9, many of the techniques can be used to gather data for job specifications as well as providing information on the performance gap. In the final part of this chapter we discuss the contribution of IT systems to measuring the performance gap.

Table 7 | Techniques for assessing job performance

Data-gathering approach	Technique
Observation	Direct observation
	Work samples
	Simulations
Interviews	General 1:1 interviews
	Performance review interviews
	Non-directed counselling interviews
	Critical incident interviews
	Repertory grid interviews
	Group discussions
Self-complete questionnaires/reports	Questionnaires
	Diaries/logs
	Tests
	Psychometric tests
	Self-reports/assessments
Desk research	Documents/records analysis
Combination(s)	Key person consultation
	Assessment/development centres

OBSERVATION

Direct observation

Observation of people in the workplace is perhaps the most obvious approach to gathering data on job performance. It can range from the use of detailed techniques such as the work measurement and method studies of the management services/work study officer to relatively unstructured studies of simply observing a colleague in the workplace. In the work study observation, precise recordings are made of all activities, including the times of these activities, and the tasks are rated – ie the performance is assessed against a mythical qualified worker performing at the rate of a motivated standard worker.

A distinction is sometimes made between observation that is directed towards the content of the job – eg noting the time spent answering telephones, the number and detail of activities involved in cleaning an escalator – and observation which looks at behaviours – eg the incidence of questioning behaviours, assertive behaviours. This latter approach often involves using checklists of key behaviours to record both the frequency of the behaviours and sometimes a rating of the effectiveness of the behaviour.

Observation can range from the observer being completely divorced from proceedings, the situation where the observer can intervene and question the job-holder as appropriate, to the extreme of the observer actually doing parts or all of the job. Depending on the extent to which the subject of the observation is allowed feedback on the results and the opportunity to comment on them, this method provides for the comparison of the inferences of the observer with the views of the observed.

Observation has the advantage that it is getting first-hand evidence on the job and how it is performed. It can deliver highly relevant information on learning needs at the point where the impact of well-specified learning will be best felt. Observation can be addressed at getting information on the whole job or particular elements only. For example, there may be concerns about the way retail assistants carry out stock counts or managers chair meetings. In these cases, the observation would focus on these specific activities.

The principal disadvantages of observation as a technique are:

- It can be very time-consuming and hence costly.

- It requires the use of staff who are both highly skilled in the process or system of observation being used and often having some knowledge about the content of the job. Clearly, the training of such observers is a complex and time-consuming job in itself.

- It is limited to being able to collect information only on activities that are visible (as opposed to intellectual).

- There are problems with jobs in which activities vary over a long period of time. For example, a finance assistant may only be involved in the preparation of VAT accounts once a quarter, and a senior manager's activities may be very different over the duration of a year. Observation usually works best for relatively simple jobs where the full range of activities are completed over a short timespan.

Finally, there is always the problem of the impact of the observer on job performance. The work study officer/rate fixer will at worst be seen as a *spy* in the workplace. Other observers could well corrupt the activities they are observing by their very presence in the workplace. This is often referred to as *the Hawthorne effect* after the studies carried out by Elton Mayo at the Hawthorne works of the Western Electric Company in Chicago between 1927 and 1932. Tyson and Jackson (1992) describe the Hawthorne effect as occurring when the subjects under study change their *behaviour* because they are being studied.

Work samples

The study of work samples is similar to observation of the people involved except that you are looking at the finished product rather than the way it is produced. The samples can be produced during the normal course of work. Alternatively, they can be produced specifically for the purpose of assessing performance – the old-time apprentice's masterpiece on graduation is a good example of this. Other examples might be to examine samples of word-processed documents, project reports or LNA studies. In essence you would be comparing these samples against the ideal in order to identify specific errors or areas of weakness. The equivalent for jobs where the *how* is as important as the *what* is done would be, for example, to introduce a customer satisfaction form for monitoring the performance of receptionists/telephonists. The NVQ/SVQ process uses work samples as one way of assembling evidence for assessment.

The main advantage of using work samples as a means of assessing performance is that the analysis usually relies on work that is produced during the normal operation of the job. The main disadvantage is that it can require special content analysis which can only be done by an assessor with special expertise. Clearly, work samples are more useful for assessing performance of less complex jobs or for looking at very specific parts of a job.

Simulations

A variation on observing the job activity or behaviours in the workplace is to set up assessments in simulated conditions. For example, flight simulators are used to test pilots' skills – eg to assess the ability of aircrew to handle mock emergencies. Role-plays are a form of simulation that can be used to assess, for example, performance review interview techniques. The main advantage of this approach is that role-plays can be set up to simulate situations which do not often occur in the workplace, such as emergency situations and/or where observation in the workplace may not be appropriate, such as in a real performance review interview. However, their disadvantage is cost. Simulation equipment can often be very expensive and simulation exercises very time-consuming to research and develop. There is also the costs of the time the individual spends away from the workplace.

INTERVIEWS

The interview, in one form or another, is probably the most frequently used technique for getting at the data in order to specify the required learning. Perhaps it is used too much, and sometimes without other techniques having been considered, because as a technique it appears to be familiar and relatively easy to do. In fact, using interviews to gather data on job performance requires considerable skill. However, the interview is a very flexible technique in that it can be formal or informal, be unstructured through to highly structured, be one-to-one or involve groups. It can be conducted in the workplace, in private, on- or off-the-job, face-to-face, by telephone or by video conferencing.

Interviews have the advantage that, in the hands of a skilled interviewer, they are very good at revealing vast amounts of data about deficiencies in skills, knowledge, attitudes, feelings, causes of problems *and* their solutions. They can provide the interviewees with the maximum opportunity to represent themselves spontaneously and in their own terms, especially when conducted using open and non-directive questioning techniques.

The main disadvantages are that they can be time-consuming to carry out and to analyse. The very strength of the open question and unstructured interview in obtaining a rich supply of data from the interviewees is in itself a weakness when the analysis takes place. The need to summarise the information, grouping the data into categories, means that much of the original richness can be lost. With more structured approaches you lose some of the initial richness, but this can be compensated for by easier and sometimes more productive analysis.

Also, interviewing is a skilled business requiring many hours of learning and practice. It is important to be able to establish rapport with the interviewee so that the interviewee feels confident and comfortable to respond honestly and frankly and without feelings of resentment, suspicion or embarrassment. There is also considerable skill involved in knowing what issues to probe into and how to do it. Another difficulty is one rather akin to the Hawthorne effect with observation techniques – the problem of what is called 'interviewer bias'. The way an interviewer actually asks the questions may have a significant impact on the answers. This can range from overt leading questions to the more subtle and sometimes unconscious effects of body language. It can be a particular problem when the issues being discussed are sensitive ones and where there might be perceived right or expected answers. Bias can also creep in to the recording of the answers as well. Developing good interview skills and the use of more structured approaches can help reduce this problem.

Types of interviews include:

- the *unstructured* type, where the aim is to allow the interviewees as much freedom and as little constraint as possible in providing the data. These types of interview are most helpful when trying to look at attitudes, flush out problems, etc

- what might be called *semi-structured* interviews, where the interviewer has a predetermined structure in terms of areas to cover and sometimes specific questions to ask. These can be designed for the specific purpose of the study or be standard in format – for example, using a performance review questionnaire

- the *highly structured* approaches such as using repertory grid and critical incident techniques.

A range of these types of interview are discussed below.

Performance review interviews

Performance review interviews are perhaps the most common form of interview used to generate data on the performance gap. One of their major functions is to assess past/current performance and identify where action should be taken to improve performance. The use of performance reviews for this purpose at least implies that the process is systematic, but on the whole it is only as good or as bad as the review process itself. Often performance review schemes are introduced for a particular purpose, and this purpose may not be compatible with the interviewee confessing to or accepting there are any weaknesses that may require addressing. This can be particularly so where the primary purpose of the performance review scheme is to help in the allocation of pay rises!

One advantage of the performance review interview in identifying and specifying any learning needs is that it has a degree of face validity as it arises out of a formal discussion between the individual and the supervisor or manager. It also has the advantage that the paperwork is usually designed in such a way that the identified needs are presented in a fairly standard way for aggregation by the learning professional.

Most of the problems associated with the use of performance review interviews for the *identification* of learning needs (see Chapter 7) affect their use for the *specification* of the learning required equally as much. They tend to vary between being very subjective in their assessment of performance, and being very mechanistic – measuring only the tangible. The successful assessment and specification of the performance gap depends in part on the quality of the performance review documentation and critically on the skills of the assessor. Also, the next step of specifying the action to be taken to meet the performance gap can be another weak link in the chain. As we noted earlier, in Chapter 7, managers often, through a lack of understanding, skill or time, fail to specify either accurately or precisely the action that is required. It is very tempting for them to opt for a standard training course rather than specify the particular performance need that is to be addressed. The case study below provides a fascinating example of this weakness.

CASE STUDY

Forceful communications

A director of a local authority housing department, following a number of review sessions with different members of his staff, identified that a serious problem was that staff were often subject to verbal abuse and sometimes physical abuse from members of the public with whom they were dealing. He decided that self-defence courses were needed to help his staff build confidence to deal with these situations. On opening up the discussion on the business need, and analysing the exact nature of the problem, he subsequently accepted that learning interventions related to interpersonal skills and communication skills were really the answer!

Another disadvantage of many performance review interviews as a technique for specifying learning needs is that so many schemes quickly fall into disrepute and staff and managers have little belief in the output from them – simply going through the motions once a year in order to keep the HR department off their backs!

Non-directed counselling interviews

Non-directed counselling is similar to performance review interviews in some ways (eg it is carried out in private, on a one-to-one basis, and requires similar preparation by both parties) but, as the name suggests, does not allow for any guidance from the counsellor in terms of what interventions should be prescribed. It can be very good for generating deep personal data on the learning required and is particularly valuable with problems involving interpersonal relations. However, it is very time-consuming, therefore an expensive way of generating the data, and requires highly skilled counsellors.

Critical incident interviews

An example of a highly structured interview is provided by the use of the critical incident technique. (Although similar, this is not to be confused with the critical incident approach described in Chapter 5.) As the name suggests, the interview is focused on critical incidents, which are incidents where it is felt that someone has performed particularly well or particularly badly. Having identified such an incident, the interviewee is asked to describe it – the background to the incident, where and when it occurred, and what the person actually *did* that was particularly effective or ineffective. The interviews are usually carried out with a sample of job-holders and their managers.

The advantage of the technique is that it is quite easy to undertake and only requires a minimum of development for the interviewers. The disadvantages are that it relies on the individual's memory of events and that sometimes people tend to remember more of one type of incident than another – eg the difficult ones. Also, sometimes people may be unwilling to admit to examples of poor performance, or indeed may not have identified these as such, and hence the need for another perspective from the manager.

Repertory grid interviews

Another form of a highly structured interview which is (re)gaining some popularity with practitioners is the repertory grid interview. It is based on the 'personal construct' theory developed by George Kelley in the 1950s (Stewart, Stewart and Fonda, 1981). In essence, Kelley identifies personal constructs as a mechanism for getting insights into people's view of the world. In our particular case, it is managers' and job-holders' views on what constitutes good and poor performance.

There are many variations on how to conduct a repertory grid interview. However, they are all based around the same theme. For example, a manager is asked to select, say, nine people from the target group and place their names or coded numbers on cards. These might consist of three the manager regards as effective performers, three who are regarded as ineffective, and three whose performance is variable. The nine cards are laid out as a 3 x 3 grid. Triads of cards are then selected from which the manager is asked to choose the two that are the most similar. The manager is then asked to describe the aspects of performance that distinguish the pair from the singleton. Skilful questioning is then used to probe the differences to obtain as detailed and as specific a description of the behaviours involved as possible. These differences of commission or omission are noted, and the questioning turns to another three cards, and so on. This process is continued until no new differences are being identified. Each comparison identifies the behaviours used or missing which have a significant impact on job performance that can then be used to specify the learning needed for the target group.

Repertory grid techniques can provide a vast amount of detailed data that can be analysed in a variety of ways. The technique is particularly useful in identifying the learning needed by people whose jobs are complex and/or are difficult to define (eg managers). Also, a major advantage of the technique is that it is claimed that the data obtained in this way is free of the normal interviewer bias. However, it does require great skill on the part of the interviewer in guiding the interviewee to the hidden data, and skill in analysing the mass of data to produce information that can be worked up to a learning specification. An excellent detailed description of the technique itself and its application can be found in Stewart, Stewart and Fonda (1981).

The case study on page 74 sets out a good example of the use of this technique.

Follow my leader

There were concerns that the leadership skills of managers in a large organisation were inappropriate to meet the changing needs of the business. It was thought that the nature of the business had encouraged a 'control and command' style of leadership and that a more 'transformational' style of leadership was required. Repertory grid interviews were used to explore the leadership skills of managers at all levels in the organisation. In this case a sample of staff and managers were interviewed and asked to comment either about a range of managers above them or below them or at the same level. The results were then used to develop specifically focused leadership programmes.

Repertory grid techniques can also be very useful in personal development activities. For example, a very interesting application is to help people see their future career direction by asking them to compare and contrast a range of jobs with which they are familiar. This enables them to identify the key aspects of the jobs they like and dislike, and hence build a picture of their 'ideal/dream' job.

Group discussions

Discussions in groups, often referred to as focus groups, resemble one-to-one interviews in some ways in that they can be anywhere on the spectrum of very structured to totally unstructured, formal to informal. The discussion can focus on the job or role analysis for individuals, on group issues or on any number of tasks or themes. The group discussion can use any of the familiar group facilitation techniques such as brainstorming, force-field analysis, and consensus rankings.

The main advantages of a group discussion is that it permits on-the-spot synthesis of different viewpoints while at the same time building support and ownership for the particular response that is decided upon. It decreases the client's dependence on the service provided by the expert because of their obvious involvement in the process. Another claim for this process is that it helps participants become better analysts of their own learning needs – which, if true, is a big step forward.

As with all these techniques there are downsides to its operation. By its very nature it is time-consuming, and therefore expensive, for both client and facilitator. Also, there can be difficulties in quantifying and synthesising the data, particularly where the less structured techniques are used.

An interesting example of this approach is set out in the case study opposite.

Project learning

An organisation was increasing its use of project working and was keen to ensure that this method of working was effective. Focus group discussions were used to identify the learning needs of staff working in project teams. A group of staff who had recently worked as members of a range of project teams were brought together. The session identified a surprising variety of learning needs ranging from what might be regarded as traditional project management skills, such as planning projects, to some more unexpected needs, such as creative thinking techniques and influencing skills.

SELF-COMPLETE QUESTIONNAIRES/REPORTS

An alternative to observation and interviews as a means of gathering data is the self-complete questionnaire/report. The basic and obvious difference between this approach and the other two is that it only involves the target group and there is no external intervention in the form of an observer or interviewer. The main advantages of this approach are that it is relatively inexpensive and usually quick to carry out, and therefore provides the means to survey a large number of respondents in a short time. Also, if completed anonymously, it gives the opportunity for the expression of facts and/or opinions without fear or embarrassment. Since there are no observers or interviewers involved, there can be no danger of their having an effect on the process.

The principal disadvantage is in the design of the questionnaires used. These often require substantial time and expertise to develop into effective instruments. They need piloting on a representative sample of the population to be studied. They often make little provision for the free expression of responses that the author has not anticipated, and are not very good at getting to the underlying causes of problems that arise or to possible solutions. Traditionally, questionnaires which rely on the target population completing and returning them often suffer from limited or low response rates, and it may require a considerable effort to ensure both a reasonable level of response and a representative response.

The advances in IT, particularly the use of the intranet, has facilitated the use of on-line questionnaires in a variety of situations. Respondents may find these quicker and easier to complete, which in turn will encourage greater response rates.

We shall look now at a range of techniques which have self-completion as their common theme.

Diaries and/or logs

These can be set up for individuals to record their activities in various ways. For example, they can be used to record a typical day by listing at regular intervals all the activities undertaken during that period. They can also be used to generate information on critical incidents of the sort described under the critical incident interviews. This approach is particularly useful for jobs in which the activities are not easily observable, such as cognitive activities, or where the cycle of activities is sufficiently long for observation not to be a feasible approach. The main problem with this type of approach is that those completing the logs/diaries may find the process time-consuming and boring, which can lead to incomplete and inaccurate responses. Again the advances in technology which enable the completion of diaries and logs electronically has helped, particularly if hand-held input devices are available.

Tests

Tests can be self-administered by individuals or be formally administered to large numbers of the target population, and can be used to obtain data on facts and/or attitudes. They can be practical or cognitive.

Tests can be particularly useful in determining whether a business need is caused by a specific missing knowledge or skill competency. Particularly where *objective tests* are used (ie those with a unique, non-essay type of answer) the results can be easily quantified, summarised and compared with other results. They are usually easily communicated and administered, can be highly predictive of the learning need, and can have high face-validity for those involved because of the practical nature of the test. (These are similar in nature to the types of assessment used for learning level evaluation: see Chapter 19.)

They do have certain disadvantages, however. Not the least is the availability of tests that are validated to the specific situation and measure all aspects of the competencies under review. Also, they do not indicate whether the measured competencies are actually being used back on-the-job. There is also the problem that the results are only as good as the questions that have been asked, and there is usually little opportunity for the individual to interact other than by answering the specific question. A further problem is that individuals do not always react well to being tested, and this can distort the results. Where the tests are made up of open questions and invite essay-type answers, they can be time-consuming to mark and analyse.

Psychometric tests

We have chosen to list psychometric tests separately from other tests and checklists. Because of the rigour of their design and the standardisation of their administration they are more objective and produce better feedback than many other tests. In the hands of qualified and experienced users they are easy to administer. They can be used to profile individual and group needs. However, they can be expensive in terms of the purchase of test materials and the licensing of test administrators.

Self-reports/assessments

Often, in the rush to be sophisticated and trendy in identifying and specifying the learning that is required we overlook one of the best sources of data – the individual concerned. Self-reports on learning needs can be generated in free form, against a checklist provided, or by using some form of self-appraisal questionnaire.

Self-reporting has the great advantage that there is likely to be more commitment to the results from those who are assessing themselves. Using this method it is also easy to obtain data from a wide range of sources fairly quickly and without too much expense. It relies upon the individuals having sufficient knowledge about their present and future jobs to give informed suggestions for their learning needs. Also, an individual's priorities for learning interventions may be very different from his or her manager's/organisation's priorities. Many people would love to have the opportunity of completing a company-sponsored Master of Business Administration (MBA) course, for example, when all their boss intended was for them to learn how to operate the boring old filing system!

With self-assessment the appraisee completes a self-appraisal against the key competencies required in the job. Many HR information systems include the facility for self-assessment against specific competency frameworks set up for the organisations. (The development of 360-degree feedback, of course, extends this approach to a range of different appraisers – see Chapter 7.)

With the emphasis on individuals taking more responsibility for their learning, the self-assessment approach has clearly many advantages. Individuals who have identified their own learning needs are far more likely to be motivated to take on board the learning and then apply it in their jobs. However, Tharenou (1991) suggests that although this method may be useful for the specification of technical and specialist learning required, her research has shown that staff may not perceive the management or strategic learning required as well as their managers, or peers, or customers perceive it. Perhaps this is a case of unconscious incompetence (in other words they don't know what they don't know) on their part rather than an unwillingness to specify the need.

DESK RESEARCH

This form of data gathering is basically using information that already exists and has been collected for other purposes. It is often referred to as *secondary research* and largely involves document and record analysis. It can sometimes provide a wealth of data to help specify the learning required. For example, an employee satisfaction survey, the primary purpose of which is to provide information on the morale and motivation of the workforce, can also provide invaluable insights into the quality of the management of the workforce. It can effectively constitute a form of upward appraisal and perhaps highlight skill weaknesses in communication. Another example could be that a learning need has been identified to improve the skills of managers in dealing with disciplinary issues. An examination of the records of disciplinary interviews and employment tribunal reports could furnish very useful information on the nature of the performance gap and hence the learning required.

The main advantage of this source of data is that because it already exists it can be a relatively inexpensive method of gathering information. The main disadvantage is that the data rarely comes in a standard form that can be used directly to specify learning needs. It often needs its own very careful analysis and synthesis into a usable form, and the key person consultants (see next page) can be very helpful in this process.

COMBINATION APPROACHES

These are approaches that utilise a combination of some of the above methods.

Key person consultation

Key person consultation is the process of gathering information from people who, by reason of their job and/or status, are in a good position to know what the learning needs of a particular group are. Key persons can be senior managers, internal/external customers and/or suppliers, other service providers, and individuals within the target population. Because of the way in which the key persons are selected for consultation, it is sometimes known as 'contact group analysis'. Once the key persons are identified, the data can be gathered through the use of interviews, group discussions, questionnaires, etc.

This technique has the advantage that it is relatively simple and easy to conduct. It permits an input (and ownership) and the interaction of a wide range of influential individuals each with their own perspective of the needs of the target group. Key person consultation also has the advantage of establishing and/or strengthening the lines of communication between the learners and other stakeholders in the organisation.

In part these advantages carry their own mirroring disadvantages. The use of people such as described above carries with it a built-in bias since it relies on the views of people who may see the learning needs from their own distinct individual, organisational or professional perspective. Also, the consultees must be carefully statistically selected from across the total range of possible contributors or the resulting picture will be as unrepresentative as the unrepresentativeness of the key consultant group.

A good example of the use of the key person consultation approach is shown in the case study below.

CASE STUDY

Careless with customers

A large wholesale organisation was trying to improve the quality of customer care by its front-line staff. It had used a range of traditional customer care programmes in the past and the evaluation had suggested that these had made little impact on performance. The learning department decided to take a different approach in order to try to identify the real customer care issues. It started the process by getting different perspectives on what customer care really meant, and so consulted key people such as the after-sales manager, the chief executive, a major customer, etc. Among other things, this process highlighted that a key issue was that staff did not have a detailed knowledge and understanding of each customer's needs and that any learning intervention had to focus on meeting that specific need.

Assessment/development centres

Assessment centres were originally used primarily for selection and recruitment, but increasingly they have been used for development purposes as well. They are, in a sense, the ultimate combination of measures, utilising most of the techniques set out above – psychometric tests, interviews, simulated tasks, written tests, and individual and group exercises. Woodruffe (2000) sums it up as:

> ... *one defining and common characteristic of development and assessment centres is their objective to obtain the best possible indication of people's current or potential competence to perform at the target or job level.*

Because of this they can give a very comprehensive analysis of performance measured against requirements and hence identify the performance gap and any required learning in a very detailed and precise way.

Their major disadvantage is cost. They need very careful design to ensure that the various tests and simulations accurately reflect the requirements of the job. They require a number of skilled observers who are usually external to the target group. However, during our research we came across one organisation that developed the target work group to observe their peers with support from an outside consultant – with spectacular results. Finally, the results require careful and often lengthy analysis. Apart from the costs of the observers, there is also the cost of the assessment group being away from the workplace for periods of, not unusually, a couple of days. Consequently, assessment/development centres are often restricted to key/senior posts and key groups of staff – eg staff identified for fast-track development.

An important issue is how feedback to the individuals going through the centre is handled and what follows after. It is vital that the feedback is constructive and any identified need for action is followed through. This is particularly so because the very fact that an employee is invited to an assessment/development centre can raise expectations

Assessment/development centres can combine all the best traits of the other techniques and, in the hands of the less competent designers, all the worst traits as well. As in the use of all of the most powerful tools there is a need for the practitioner to know what he or she is doing if more good than harm is to come from the process. Woodruffe (2000) provides an excellent guide to the process of setting up and managing assessment and development centres.

THE CONTRIBUTION OF IT SYSTEMS

There is a vast range of software applications on the market now that can be used to assess the performance gap and contribute to the identification of learning needs. There is nothing magical about them – in the main they are computerised versions of paper-based systems – but it is the power of IT that can make these work more efficiently and effectively. We see them as belonging to three main categories:

- *systems that are aimed at performance review* – These incorporate the organisation's competency framework and the system allows for an individual to be assessed against the specific competencies for his or her job. They normally allow and facilitate

360-degree feedback – ie assessments by a wide range of people: the individual, the manager, peers, customers, subordinates, etc. They often include an administrative element – for example, automatically sending out reminders by e-mail to encourage completion of the assessment on time. The assessments are then used in the traditional way as part of a performance review interview to identify gaps in performance and learning needs. Where 360-degree feedback is used, differences in the results, particularly between job-holder and manager, often provide fertile ground for discussing performance at the interview. The systems usually include personal development plans on-line which can then be updated and amended as needed.

The great advantage of these systems is that they make the whole process more efficient. However, they are only as good as the underlying competency framework and of course the people doing the assessments! Sometimes these systems stand alone and sometimes they form part of an overall HR information system.

- *systems that are directed particularly at identifying learning needs* – One example is NVQ-based but can be customised to meet the requirements of the organisation. The user is asked a set of questions about tasks relating to a particular job/skill area. If the system is being used for self-assessment, each user is asked to rate himself or herself on a five-point rating scale about his or her level of confidence in carrying out that task and also on a five-point scale about how important that task is to the job. Again the assessment can be carried out by a range of people. The software application then prioritises the learning needs based on the answers to these two questions. The results can be used to analyse individual learning needs and combined to provide group and even organisational learning needs priorities – all at a press of a button (or two). Such systems are easy to use and can generate large amounts of data on learning needs. Once more the caveat is on the quality and relevance of the underlying framework, and how it is used.

- *what we call 'diagnostic systems'* – As the description suggests, these are mainly used to diagnose issues or behaviours affecting the way an individual, group or organisation is working. The best-known are the traditional personality tests. An interesting example uses an electronic questionnaire based on 400 behaviours to provide an assessment of the effectiveness of managers' behaviours and categorise them into those that accelerate, those that sustain and those that block momentum in the business. These can be used as an individual diagnostic tool, although their real power can be seen in diagnosing group and organisational behaviours and then identifying learning interventions to move the group or organisation towards more effective performance. They can be particularly useful as part of team-building and cultural change initiatives.

CONCLUSION

Above we have listed many of the techniques and methods of getting at the data to specify the learning needed to bridge the gap between present performance and required performance. Most of the learning professionals we consulted in researching this book use only one of the techniques on a regular basis – the performance review system, with all its known faults. We are strongly of the view that the specification of learning needs can be made much more scientific and more systematic at the same time by widening the range of techniques used in the LNA process. The best results are often achieved through a combination of the different approaches – using the concept of 'triangulation' that is drawn from research methodology. The development of the wide range of IT applications offers the learning professional yet another tool in the toolbox, but they are only as good as the frameworks and systems that underpin them.

READING AND REFERENCE

PEARN M. *and* KANDOLA R. (1993), *Job Analysis*, London, IPM.

STEWART V., STEWART A. *and* FONDA N. (1981), *Business Applications of the Repertory Grid*, Maidenhead, McGraw-Hill.

THARENOU P. (1991), 'Managers' training needs and preferred training strategies', *Journal of Management Development*, Vol 10, No 5, MCB University Press.

TYSON S. *and* JACKSON T. (1992), *The Essence of Organisational Behaviour*, London, Prentice-Hall.

WOODRUFFE C. (2000), *Development and Assessment Centres*, 3rd edn, London, CIPD.

Section 4

Translating learning needs into learning action

Introduction to Section 4

You will recall that in the Introduction to this book we defined Learning Needs Analysis as the whole process of:

- identifying the range and extent of learning needs required to meet the business needs of the organisation
- specifying the learning needs very precisely
- analysing how best these learning needs might be met.

Sections 1 and 2 have covered the first stage of the process – identifying the range and extent of learning needs from business needs. Section 3 has covered the second stage of the process – developing a precise specification of the job and investigating the performance gap. By establishing a very clear picture of what the relevant job requirements are, through the job specification, and a very clear picture of what the gap in performance is, we now have a very precise picture or description of what the learning intervention is intended to achieve. The more precise the specification, the easier it is to move on to the final section of the LNA process – looking at what is the best approach to providing that learning solution.

At last – you might say – we are about to see some action! Yes, this chapter is about translating those learning needs into action. However, do not be tempted to try to skip over the earlier stages. The better the analysis of the need, the easier it will be to turn it into action and, what is more, action that will actually meet the business need in a cost-effective way. It will also provide the foundation for assessing the effectiveness of the learning intervention in meeting that business need. The more comprehensive and complete the analysis, the more secure the foundations for building your learning provision.

Enough of this polemic. What next? The first basic decision you will face is whether some form of formal learning intervention is required or whether some other approach is merited. Chapter 11 looks at the spectrum of learning approaches from formal to informal. Chapter 12 is the heart of the process, or perhaps – for those of you we have convinced that feelings and intuition have been cast out and who prefer to continue with the more concrete building analogy – provides the framework for the (learning) building. This chapter covers the preparation of the *learning specification*, the vital document that provides the blueprint for how the learning is to be carried out *and evaluated*. The learning specification, then, provides the basis for the next key decision in Chapter 13 – the *make or buy* decision: whether to develop a learning intervention specifically to meet the learning need, or whether to buy an existing one, or perhaps to opt for some combination of these options.

As in previous sections we see where these activities fit into the whole process by looking again at our Learning Wheel – see Figure 7.

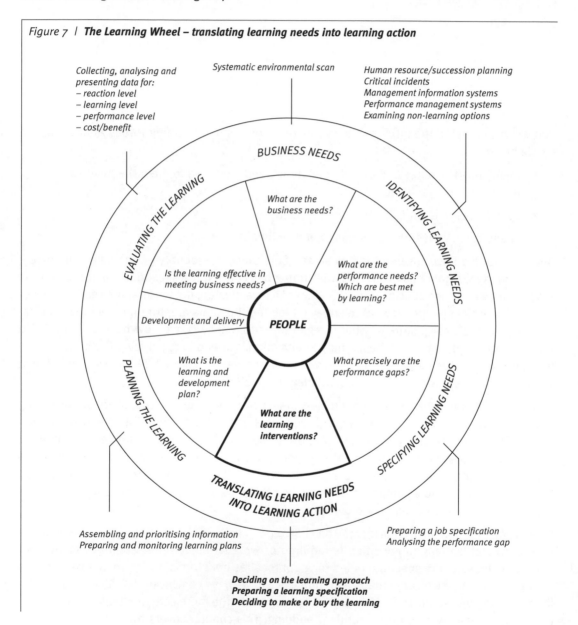

Figure 7 | **The Learning Wheel – translating learning needs into learning action**

Collecting, analysing and
presenting data for:
– reaction level
– learning level
– performance level
– cost/benefit

Systematic environmental scan

Human resource/succession planning
Critical incidents
Management information systems
Performance management systems
Examining non-learning options

BUSINESS NEEDS

EVALUATING THE LEARNING

IDENTIFYING LEARNING NEEDS

What are the
business needs?

Is the learning effective in
meeting business needs?

What are the
performance needs?
Which are best met
by learning?

Development and delivery

PEOPLE

What is the
learning and
development
plan?

What precisely are the
performance gaps?

**What are the
learning
interventions?**

PLANNING THE LEARNING

SPECIFYING LEARNING NEEDS

TRANSLATING LEARNING NEEDS
INTO LEARNING ACTION

Assembling and prioritising information
Preparing and monitoring learning plans

Preparing a job specification
Analysing the performance gap

**Deciding on the learning approach
Preparing a learning specification
Deciding to make or buy the learning**

11

The spectrum of learning – from formal to informal

INTRODUCTION

It is not the intention of this book to enter into the debate of what constitutes formal learning and what does not. As we set out in the Introduction to this book, learning can happen in a wide variety of different ways in the workplace:

- through a formal intervention of some sort – eg a traditional 'classroom' course, an e-learning module, etc

- through a semi-formal intervention – eg coaching, a secondment, working on a project, etc

- informally – ranging from an informal coaching session by a line manager, help from a colleague, through to the learning that takes place as an almost continuous process as we experience the world and learn from it.[1]

This book generally – and this section specifically – is aimed at the first two areas of formal and semi-formal interventions. In a sense an informal learning intervention can almost be defined as one which has not been subject to the disciplines proposed in this book. It has not been the subject of rigorous analysis nor been specified very precisely. It is often the sort of spontaneous intervention that happens every day in the workplace, either when someone seeks help from a colleague or manager or when a colleague or manager perceives the need to give some help. It also covers the sort of learning that takes place when we look up a process in a manual or use the help facility on our computer.

At the far end of the spectrum is the almost continuous learning we are undergoing as we simply do our jobs or live our lives. It may be that we note that on reflection we might have drafted a set of minutes better or handled a discussion with a colleague differently. Kolb's Learning Cycle provides a deceptively simple but very useful model for understanding this process (see Figure 8).

---

[1] See Kolb's Learning Cycle (Kolb, 1984)

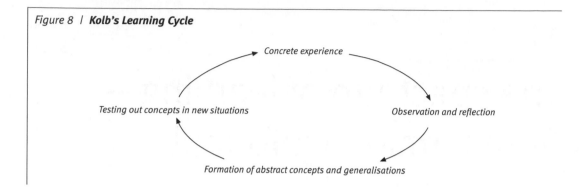

Figure 8 | *Kolb's Learning Cycle*

If we take one of the simple examples mentioned above:

- The first stage is the concrete experience – you have a drafted a set of minutes of a meeting you attended, but it has been returned with lots of additions by your colleagues at the meeting.

- The second stage is you observe and reflect on what has happened – you observe that your colleagues have added more information and reflect that the minutes did not meet their needs as a record of the meeting.

- The third stage is that you try to make sense of what has happened and formulate some idea of how to deal with it – you decide that the minutes should be more detailed.

- The fourth stage is to test the new approach in a new situation – you draft a more detailed set of minutes for the next meeting, and so generate a new experience.

Hopefully, this time the minutes come back with fewer changes!

This sort of experiential learning is happening all the time and can be a very powerful way to learn. This book is not addressed at this type of learning, which by its nature is unplanned.

FORMAL LEARNING

In the last few years there has been something of a revolution in how formal learning interventions take place. Traditionally, we have usually thought of it in terms of the 'classroom' approach, involving inputs of information by the 'trainer/instructor' combined with a variety of participative elements such as case studies, exercises, role-plays, etc. However, there has been a considerable movement away from the traditional classroom approach, and the learning professional now has a much wider range of choices available for a formal learning intervention. These include:

- *technology-based training* (TBT) – The 1990s saw the growth in TBT which harnesses the use of computers to deliver learning solutions. These involve learners working their way through a predesigned programme delivered by disk or CD-ROM and often incorporating multimedia inputs, such as video clips, etc. Primarily used for knowledge competencies – eg learning an administrative procedure or using a computer package

– they can also provide the knowledge input of a skill – eg creative thinking. Where the skill can be practised on the computer, this type of approach also can be used very successfully for skills training, the obvious example being learning keyboard skills. The advantage of this type of learning intervention is that people can learn at their own pace, with self-assessments built in, and in their own time. The limitations are that there is often no interaction with tutors/facilitators nor inter-learner interaction, so the opportunities and stimulus of learning with others can be lost.

- *e-learning*, arguably one of the major developments in learning technology of the late twentieth and early twenty-first centuries – This takes TBT a step further and harnesses the power of the Internet and intranet. Sloman (2001a) defines e-learning as 'learning and training that takes advantage of connectivity'. E-learning can operate on several levels. At its most basic it is very similar to technology-based learning but with the facility for the learner to access the package through the intranet or Internet. It allows for packages to be updated easily and regularly. However, the real power and potential of e-learning comes from the ability for learners to interact with on-line tutors and other learners. This can happen asynchronously (ie not in real time) and involve the use of discussion groups, question-and-answer tutoring by e-mail, etc, or synchronously (ie the learner and tutor on-line at the same time) and involve virtual classrooms, audio-video conferencing, etc.

- *blended learning*, which has developed from the realisation that e-learning will be 'most effective when it forms part of an overall strategy involving the classroom and on-the-job learning' (Sloman, 2001b) – Merrick and Pickard (2002) describe a 12-month management development programme at the House of Fraser as:

  ... the epitome of blended learning. ... It combines workshops, workbooks, seminars and on-line learning with every type of on-the-job development from 'sitting by Nellie' to assignments, coaching, job rotation and shadowing.

  Blended learning makes the best use of a range of different learning methods.

- *out-of-doors learning events* – These can range from carrying out practically based exercises out-of-doors (but in a normal environment such as the local streets or coun-tryside) to adventure training in rugged and testing environments of mountains and the sea. Such events are typically used to inculcate leadership and team-building skills.

- *a wide range of distance/flexible learning programmes* where the focus is on the learners working on their own, in their own time, through a package of material which will include inputs of information and exercises – The material will often be a mix of paper-based and technology-based inputs. These programmes may also involve some tutor sessions and sometimes include injections of classroom learning for developing the softer skills. They can range from very straightforward, focused learning – for example, some organisations use this approach to inform staff about the implications of new legislation – to learning aimed at long-term development, such as a professional qualifications – eg for membership of the CIPD, or a degree.

SEMI-FORMAL LEARNING

This is a growing but probably still under-utilised learning arena. Perhaps the most common type of semi-formal learning intervention is coaching.

So when is coaching an appropriate intervention? It is used:

- *usually* for the development of a skill (rather than for learning a new skill)
- when there is a need for the learning to be tailored to specific work environments
- when the individual responds better to this form of learning – some people are more comfortable in the less formal situation
- when there are no suitable formal learning solutions available
- when there is a limited learning budget
- when timescale is a problem – either the learning is required more quickly than a formal solution can deliver or it sometimes happens that the phasing requirements can be more readily met by the flexible approach of informal learning.

Coaching is sometimes seen as a cheap solution. This may appear to be true, in that often it does not come with a readily identifiable cost or cannot be readily allocated to some form of cost/budget centre. However, properly planned and executed coaching can be very demanding of the time of line managers or whoever is doing the coaching. Also, although we are describing it as semi-formal learning, successful coaching requires considerable skills, and itself may give rise to learning needs for the *coaches*. Despite these points, on the plus side coaching can have a number of spin-off benefits because:

- it can develop manager/staff relationships
- it can develop managers'/coaches' skills
- it can provide great job satisfaction for the coaches
- it can help teamworking
- it can promote a learning environment.

Coaching, although described as a semi-formal learning solution, benefits considerably from an element of formality. Clear objectives and a plan for achieving those objectives within a timescale are the ingredients for successful coaching. Coaching can encompass a wide range of different approaches – from the traditional 'sitting next to Nellie/Norman' to the planned involvement of individuals in areas outside their normal work.

Semi-formal learning can also involve such activities as:

- *job rotation programmes*, where the learning is provided by a planned sequence of different job experiences and often supplemented by more traditional or formal learning interventions. The classic example of this form of learning is the type of programmes used for graduate or management trainees. An interesting instance of this type of approach is provided by a major retailer who recruits potential senior managers from non-retail sectors. These new recruits then spend up to a year working their way through many of the different retail jobs, starting as a retail assistant on the shop floor and working through the roles of section manager, department manager, merchandise manager, etc, before taking on their senior job in the organisation.

Another variation is provided by a manufacturer who uses a planned sequence of 'stretch assignments' defined as 'those that build new skills and abilities by taking the individual out of his [sic] "comfort zone" to develop future senior executives' (Beeson, 2000).

As more and more organisations streamline their management structures by removing layers and the opportunity for development through progression up the ladder is curtailed, forms of job rotation are being used increasingly to develop staff who have become 'plateaued' – ie who have reached their peak performance in their current job and now have no opportunity for upward progression.

- *secondments*, where the learning is provided by a planned short-term move into another job. These are often used as a way of providing experience and learning in areas that are not covered by the individual's job and that have been identified as useful for developmental purposes. So, for example, it might be used for a head office manager to gain experiences at the front line of the business, perhaps in a call centre or working in a factory.

- *project working*, which provides the opportunity for an individual to work either part-time or full-time on a 'project'. There may be an opportunity for learning in the project subject area, perhaps while introducing a new IT system, and/or for learning in project management skills.

- *job shadowing*, often used as part of a range of learning interventions, which involves learners observing or working alongside relevant job-holders to gain experience of particular tasks or skills where the opportunity for learning the skill first-hand is limited. Examples are shadowing a manager dealing with a disciplinary issue or preparing a budget.

For each of the above to qualify as a semi-formal learning intervention (rather than as a convenient means of dealing with a problem) the following should have occurred:

- the business need and associated learning needs must be identified

- the competencies to be addressed by the activity must be clearly set out

- the learning must be supported by some form of learning facilitator, perhaps the individual's line manager, a mentor, or an appointed coach

- the learning must be monitored and assessed.

Sometimes the interventions listed above are not seen as learning opportunities, or if they are, they are perceived as some sort of general opportunity for development or learning. Sadly, in these cases the full potential of the learning opportunity is unlikely to be realised. As with more formal interventions, they need planning – in fact, they must be subject to exactly the same sorts of Learning Needs Analysis as for the more formal learning interventions.

Semi-formal learning approaches can play a particularly valuable role in meeting the learning needs that arise out of succession planning (see Chapter 4).

Finally, we come to the area of mentoring. The use of mentors as part of both formal and semi-formal learning interventions is becoming increasingly popular. These 'trusted advisors' (*New Oxford Dictionary*, 2001) can play a wide variety of roles from a 'listening ear' or 'acting as a sounding board', to taking a proactive role in the development of the individual. Eric Parsloe (in Clutterbuck, 1999) describes the purpose of developmental mentoring as:

> *To help and support people to manage their own learning to maximise their potential, develop their skills, improve their performance, and become the person they want to be.*

Mentors can be line managers but more often are outside the line management function and chosen for their abilities to act as role models and nurture and develop staff. Often mentors, particularly for more senior staff, come from outside the organisation, and organisations tend increasingly to use professional mentors or coaches. Being a mentor can in itself be a developmental process. Clutterbuck (1999) provides a straightforward and practical guide to the mentoring process.

CONCLUSION

Consideration of the full range of learning solutions should always form part of the learning professional's systematic approach to analysing how the learning need should be met. However, it is vital that if the decision is made to use a semi-informal approach, perhaps that coaching or a secondment should be adopted, you should not be tempted to withdraw gracefully with a sigh of a relief, thinking 'Another problem solved!' Hopefully it is, but hope is not good enough – there must be some mechanism for establishing that the learning need has been met and in turn the business need that gave rise to it successfully addressed. The key to this is the learning objectives covered in the next chapter, and the techniques and approaches discussed in Section 6 on evaluation.

READING AND REFERENCE

BEESON J. (2000), 'Succession planning', *Across the Board*, February.

CLUTTERBUCK D. (1999), *Everyone Needs a Mentor*, 2nd edn, London, CIPD.

KOLB D. A. (1984), *Experiential Learning*, New York, Prentice-Hall.

MERRICK N. *and* PICKARD J. (2002), 'Whistles and bells', *People Management*, 7 Februrary.

SLOMAN M. (2001a), *The e-learning revolution*, London, CIPD.

SLOMAN M. (2001b), 'All plug and no play', *People Management*, 13 September.

12

The learning specification

INTRODUCTION

Without doubt, preparation of a learning specification is an essential requirement for the implementation of all formal learning solutions and, we would argue, in a modified form, of all semi-formal approaches. We define the *learning specification* as:

> *a* blueprint *or* detailed plan *for the learning required to meet the gap in performance and measure its effectiveness.*

The exact form or structure may vary, but we would suggest that every learning specification should include the following information:

- background details of the business need that has given rise to the learning need
- description of the target learning population – ie the staff that require the learning intervention
- overall aim of the learning intervention – a key section, which should contain the criteria for assessing that the business need has been met
- learning objectives – another really key section, which sets out specifically what the learning intervention is intended to achieve
- learning methods to be used
- skills required by the learning facilitator(s)
- how the learning is to be evaluated (do *not* be tempted to miss this out)
- time-scale for the delivery of the learning
- venue, if relevant
- any other constraints that have to be taken into account.

We will describe each of these areas in turn and provide two examples of learning specifications at the end of the chapter as Appendices 12.1 and 12.2. Again, the amount of information and degree of detail provided is a matter of judgement – the main guideline is that it should provide:

- a learning supplier, either internal or external, with sufficient information to design and develop the learning intervention
- the basis against which the learning can be evaluated.

BACKGROUND TO THE BUSINESS NEED

This part of the learning specification should provide a good description of the business need with as much detail as possible of what stimulated the requirement for a learning intervention. Its purpose is to make sure there is a clear link between the proposed learning and an identifiable business need.

For example, the business need could be to address the large number of customer complaints, which highlighted the poor level of knowledge that the sales staff had of the products they were selling. Alternatively, the business need could be to tackle a high level of wastage of new recruits, which on investigation was shown to be a result of poor interview techniques. More detail may be helpful in these cases – for example, did staff display poor product knowledge across the whole range of products, or was it only some products that caused the problems? Had the analysis of the learning need shown what particular aspect of the interviewing technique was causing the problem? The business need could be to provide staff with the knowledge and skills to meet new legislative requirements – eg on health and safety – or to implement new accounting procedures. It could be to prepare staff to sell a new product or to handle a new machine.

It may also be helpful to provide some background information on the local context – eg a department or organisational unit – giving details of:

- the function or principal activity of the unit
- how the unit fits into the overall organisational structure
- the structure of the unit itself
- its size and geographic location(s).

A DESCRIPTION OF THE TARGET LEARNING POPULATION

It may perhaps seem a statement of the obvious to say that the learning intervention must be targeted at the people that require it. However, it is surprising how often people participate in learning interventions that they do not need, and equally, how often some of the people who really do need the learning slip through the net. This can mean that the intervention is both wasteful and ineffective – a deadly combination. So the name of the game here is to identify as precisely as possible the target audience. If the business need has been investigated and analysed fully, this information should be readily available.

Next it is important to describe or provide a profile of the population. The key information is:

- the projected number of learners
- the jobs/grades and locations
- the current levels of knowledge/skill and experience in the area of proposed learning.

Sometimes it may be useful to provide additional information – for example:

- an age profile
- the gender mix

- an ethnic origin profile
- the educational level/qualifications
- previous learning undertaken
- lengths of service
- likely attitudes towards the learning.

This last category can be very useful if there are possible morale or motivational problems. Anybody who has carried out learning interventions in the midst of major organisational change will be aware how much that can affect the quality of the learning experience. If attitudes are known in advance, sometimes the event can be designed to allow time to address such issues.

THE AIM OF THE LEARNING INTERVENTION

As you will have gathered, this part has a twofold purpose. It is to provide:

- the desired outcome(s) of the learning stated in terms of the business need – for example, to reduce the customer complaints by x per cent or cut the level of wastage in new recruits to y per cent within z months following the completion of the learning programme. Sometimes it may prove difficult to provide precise quantitative measures. If it is not possible, provide as detailed a description of what the business (or that specific area of the business) will look like after completion of the learning intervention. It is surprising how often this very process will reveal measurable indicators. In *Goal Analysis*, Mager (1991a) provides an excellent and straightforward account of how to turn *fuzzy goal* statements into well-defined statements of performance
- a clear statement of the change required or the standard to be achieved in workplace behaviour – eg to provide a high quality of customer care (as measured against a customer-care checklist), or to manage an emergency situation according to company procedures.

This, in turn, provides an essential:

- starting-point for developing the detailed learning objectives
- benchmark for one of the key stages of the evaluation process – measuring the effect on organisational performance.

LEARNING OBJECTIVES

Learning objectives are descriptions of the performance and/or behaviours that you want participants to exhibit at the end of the learning intervention. They are concerned with the *results* of the learning, not the learning process itself. They are a vital stage in the LNA process because if you are not clear where you are going, it is very hard to plan how you are going to get there! The learning objectives should follow easily and logically from specification of the business need and aims of the learning. It is essential that learning objectives are correctly specified because:

- the development and delivery of the learning will be based on them

- they will form the basis of one of the key stages of learning evaluation – measuring whether the learning has taken place

- their clear and full specification will help ensure that the right people undertake the learning intervention

- they enable learners, their managers and the organisation to prepare for and make the best use of the learning.

Learning objectives must have the following key attributes:

- focus specifically on the gap between current and required performance

- be expressed in behavioural terms which allow them to be measurable in some way

- be achievable and realistic, but challenging.

Types of learning objectives

The usual outcome of a learning intervention is that learners gain the ability to do something they could not do before or to do something better. Most learning objectives therefore deal with skills competencies and will begin with an action word which reflects a behaviour. Examples of some commonly used action words for skill objectives include:

build	exhibit	perform	test
carry out	make	present	train
design	measure	select	use
drive	operate	set	write

Examples of learning objectives for skills include:

- operate a telephone switchboard

- write a business report

- build a project network

- carry out a selection interview.

In learning interventions, knowledge often supports skill, and so some learning objectives will deal with knowledge competencies. For example, in a programme on recruitment interviewing the participants will probably require knowledge of relevant employment law and knowledge of the content and use of job descriptions and person specifications. They will also need to know the possible ways to structure the interview and arrange the interview room. Sometimes learning events may be solely concerned with knowledge – for example, where the learning is about new legislation or new office procedures. Knowledge-based objectives must also begin with action words that reflect measurable behaviours. These are sometimes harder to find.

Examples of useful action words for knowledge objectives include:

calculate	explain
classify	identify
compare	list
define	name
describe	state

Avoid words that are difficult to establish measures for, such as 'appreciate', 'know' or 'understand'. What do we mean by an objective such as 'To appreciate the role of the HR director'? How do we know or how can we measure whether someone has an *appreciation* of the role of the HR director? A better alternative objective would be 'To state the main functions of the HR director'.

Very often knowledge objectives are expressed in terms of *understanding* – for example: 'To understand the performance review process'. However, what does it mean, and how do you measure this concept of understanding? It is essential for you to go that one step further and be specific about what you mean – perhaps to list the main purposes of the performance review process and/or describe the stages in the process.

Examples of learning objectives for knowledge competencies include:

- to list the steps in the procedure for handling a grievance
- to state four benefits of learning evaluation
- to identify well-formed (ie that meet the criteria) learning objectives
- to calculate the duration of a project from a project network using critical path analysis.

Attitudinal change is often a part of a learning programme and sometimes an end in itself. It is notoriously difficult to measure, and therefore requires sophisticated measurement tools. Often it may be better to target and measure the behaviours that result from particular attitudes. For example, if encouraging staff to adopt the equal opportunities policy is the required outcome, then defining objectives such as 'To conduct a recruitment interview according to the principles of the equal opportunities policy/without gender or race bias', may be the best approach. Mager (1991a) gives a detailed account of how to turn attitudinal objectives into measurable behaviours.

Well-formed learning objectives

In another excellent book, *Preparing Instructional Objectives*, Mager (1991b) describes the characteristics of a well-formed objective as:

Performance – *describing what the learners will be able to do.*

Conditions – *setting out the conditions (if any) under which the performance will occur.*

Criterion – *describing, wherever possible, the criteria or standards for acceptable performance – this may be in terms of speed, accuracy or quality.*

So far, we have concentrated on the performance element. Let's look at some objectives that incorporate all three elements:

- diagnose the fault (*performance*) in Coldpoint Dishwasher Models 1/2/3 (*condition*) within 15 minutes (*criterion*)

- without reference material (*condition*), state the actions to be taken in the event of a fire (*performance*) according to the company health and safety policy (*criterion*)

- make a presentation (*performance)* to a group of superiors, colleagues or subordinates (*condition*) lasting 15 minutes (*condition)* on a work-based topic (*condition*), achieving an 80 per cent or better score on a checklist (*criterion*).

How much detail to include in the objectives must be a matter of judgement – it must be sufficient to set out *clearly* to everyone concerned the purpose of the learning intervention in terms of what is expected from the learner at the end of it.

LEARNING METHODS

Learning methods usually depend on:

- the learning objectives
- the content of the learning material
- the target audience.

How much detail is included here is a matter of choice. It may be that as a result of your detailed knowledge and understanding of the three areas above, you will have a very clear idea about how the learning solution should be delivered – at least in terms of the first level of choice – for example, as to whether it will involve formal classroom instruction, use e-learning, distance learning, or perhaps a blended learning approach, etc. On the other hand, it may be that you are not clear as to what might be the most effective approach and want to leave it up to the learning supplier to come up with proposals – in which case your learning specification should state this.

Sometimes even greater detail is provided, such as specifying the use of case studies or role-plays. It may be that a very tight specification is required. However, this loses the opportunity of finding out what the learning suppliers actually think are the most appropriate methods. This is one area of the specification where there are benefits to not being too precise at this stage. If the learning objectives and target audience have been well specified these should provide sufficient information for the development of the event by experienced and professional learning suppliers. Their proposals for the learning methods can be a valuable indication of the quality of their 'product' and particularly their approach to learning – do they see themselves as trainer/instructors or learning facilitators?

LEARNING FACILITATORS: SKILLS AND EXPERIENCE

This is frequently, and surprisingly, a neglected area. Sometimes no skills are specified and often only very general requirements are made. Depending on the nature of the learning intervention, consider specifying:

- precise skills and qualifications – this is often important for technical courses and where a nationally recognised qualification is awarded at the end of the course

- experience in providing learning interventions in the subject area

- experience in facilitating learning with similar types of staff – there is a world of difference between working with front-line supervisors and working with senior managers!

- experience in working with similar types of organisations, in terms of sector and size – there can be considerable advantages in having facilitators who are familiar with the issues involved with working in perhaps a small organisation or one in the charity sector.

METHODS OF EVALUATING THE LEARNING

This part is the one that most frequently gets left out – for two main reasons:

- Many organisations do not evaluate their learning either at all, or in any systematic way.

- Many organisations (dare we say most) do not think about evaluation until the stage when the learning programme is about to take place or even until after it has happened.

For evaluation to be most effective it is essential that the evaluation methods are designed as part of the development stage of the learning intervention. It is therefore important to include in the specification what evaluation is to be undertaken and who is to carry out any design work. Section 6 sets out details of the approaches to evaluation and the techniques that can be used.

TIME-SCALE

It is important to indicate the projected time-scale for the delivery of the learning intervention and achievement of the objectives. This will be based on:

- the urgency of the business need – Sometimes there will be a requirement to provide the learning as quickly as possible in order to deal with a current and important performance gap. Sometimes the business need will not require such urgent attention, and sometimes the learning will actually be to meet a future need and will require to be phased in at the appropriate time

- practical constraints, such as the availability of the learners, venue, etc

- budgetary constraints – when there is money available to provide the learning.

The benefits of providing a time-scale are:

- It forces the learning specifier to think through the above issues and *plan* accordingly.

- It enables all those involved to be aware of the time-scale and to comment if it will not meet their needs.

- It allows learning suppliers to consider whether they can keep to the time-scale and prepare a project plan (a plan of how they will meet the specification within the time-scale).

VENUE

This is an optional section because specifying a venue may or may not be important at this stage. If you intend to make use of internal facilities, they may need to be booked. If the programme is required to take place in particular locations – eg in regional centres – then specifying so is helpful. Depending on the imminence of the learning event, the venue may become a higher priority.

OTHER CONSTRAINTS

This is an opportunity to include any other limiting factors not already covered – for example:

- the maximum number of participants who can be released at a time
- specific requirements for participants with disabilities, with caring responsibilities, or any other special needs
- the maximum duration of the learning event
- the maximum length of learning days
- any cost limitations.

Think carefully about whether and what time and cost limitations are included. As with learning methods, there is a lot to be gained from seeing what the suppliers come up with. On the other hand, indicating maximum daily rates can sometimes be helpful in targeting appropriate learning providers. However, bear in mind the total costs – sometimes suppliers with high daily charges may be able to offer learning interventions which require very little development work and therefore lower overall charges.

Having completed your draft learning specification, make sure it fully and accurately sets out the requirements for the learning by ensuring that *everyone* involved has an opportunity to comment – the learning sponsor if one exists, prospective learners, their managers, subject specialists, etc. This not only ensures that the specification is *right* but also gives a sense of ownership to those that have been involved in its development.

CONCLUSION

'Do you always need a learning specification? It seems an awful lot of work . . .' I hear the cry from the hard-pressed learning professional. There are two particular situations in which this comment tends to arise.

Some people argue that there is no point in preparing a detailed learning specification if there is an obvious learning programme available that will meet the need. However, it is surprising how often the learning specification, when compared with the details of the existing programme, highlights significant differences. Now it may be that the existing programme can still be used, but if so, it will then be used in the knowledge of how far it meets the actual need, and allows for consideration of how the areas of unmet need can perhaps be addressed, perhaps by tweaking the programme or supplementing it with coaching or additional handouts.

Another argument sometimes used against preparing learning specifications is that it is not worth the effort if there are only one or two staff involved or when the learning is to be delivered through semi-formal approaches. Clearly, this is a matter of judgement and depends to a large extent on the type and level of staff concerned. For certain management positions or highly specialised jobs it will almost certainly be worthwhile preparing a detailed learning specification even if only one member of staff is involved. In other situations a shorter, simpler specification may be sufficient. However, we would argue that preparing a specification of some sort is very useful in *all* circumstances, and is a vital step in ensuring that the learning solution provides a close fit with the learning need. So far as semi-formal approaches are concerned, we would argue that, in fact, these types of learning intervention can benefit as much as formal ones from having a learning specification. The discipline of having to describe the business need, the aims and objectives of the coaching or secondment, etc, and how it will be evaluated, etc, will help to ensure that the business need is met.

So what next? We are now ready to consider the choice of whether to *make or buy* the learning intervention. Read on.

READING AND REFERENCE

MAGER R. F. (1991a), *Goal Analysis*, 2nd edn, California, Pitman Learning.

MAGER R. F. (1991b), *Preparing Instructional Objectives*, 2nd edn, London, Kogan Page.

LEARNING SPECIFICATION
(Customer care programme for cashiers)

Background to the business need

Backland Trading Company Ltd (BTCL) has recently taken over another company, Substandard Ltd. A number of problems have been identified at Substandard Ltd – one of which is that there have been problems between customers and cashiers, resulting in customer complaints and grievances from the staff. In the first three months of the trading year there have been 10 customer complaints concerning the poor service offered by the cashiers. Of these only two were concerned with poor technical skills, the remainder concerned the cashiers' ability to relate positively to customers and handle queries and difficulties. The branch manager believes that the poor level of customer service is responsible for sales not reaching expected levels for the time of year. These appear to be running at about 5 per cent below target.

The cashiers are managed by the duty checkout supervisor, who in turn reports to the branch manager of each outlet.

As a result of the takeover by BTCL, morale in Substandard Ltd is quite low.

Target population

The cashiers operate checkout tills in five separate retail outlets distributed across the London area. There are 100 cashiers in total – mostly female staff, all on the same hourly rates of pay – 75 per cent are part-time on contracts varying between 15 and 30 hours per week, the remainder are full-time staff allocated to specific shifts. At any one time there are about 10 temporary staff. Most of the cashiers have been with the company for more than two years and have limited experience of other jobs. Most have only basic educational qualifications. The temporary staff are usually students doing vacation work.

All cashiers have received training on the use of the checkout tills – however, none of them has been trained in customer care. Their attitude to this training is unknown but because their morale is known to be low, time should be allowed in the programme to address the possibility of an attitude issue.

Aims of the learning

To provide the cashiers with the necessary knowledge, skills, attitudes and behaviours to provide a high quality of customer care, so that:

- customer complaints regarding poor service are eliminated
- customer satisfaction reaches company standards
- sales are on target.

Because poor morale as a result of the takeover is considered a contributory factor, the learning event will be expected to address this issue.

Learning objectives

By the end of the event, participants will be able to:

- describe the benefits of the merger to staff at Substandard Ltd
- explain why customer care is important to BTCL
- greet and acknowledge customers at the checkout tills in a welcoming manner (achieving a minimum score of 80 per cent on Part A of the customer-care checklist)
- deal with queries from and difficulties with customers at the checkout tills in a professional and friendly manner (achieving a minimum score of 80 per cent on Part B of the customer-care checklist)
- close the customer transaction at the checkout tills in a positive way (achieving a minimum score of 80 per cent on Part C of the customer-care checklist).

Learning methods

The programme should be very participative and practical.

Of necessity the learning event will take place away from the sales floor.

Facilitator skills

Facilitators will be expected to have had practical experience of dealing with customers in a high-pressure retail environment and to have a track record of carrying out customer care learning programmes. Also, it will be helpful if facilitators have had experience of carrying out learning programmes against a background of change and low morale.

Evaluation

A reaction level questionnaire will be used, which will be provided by BTCL. The supplier is expected to undertake the learning level evaluation.

A specialist consultant will be used to design a performance level evaluation for implementation by BCTL to assess performance on the job. The programme will be evaluated in terms of organisational performance through monitoring the level of customer complaints, customer satisfaction surveys and sales performance.

Time-scale

The need is considered to be urgent. It is intended that a decision on the appointment of suppliers will be made by the end of January, and it is a requirement that the learning is completed by the end of March.

Venue

The learning event will be undertaken at the well-equipped BTCL Learning Centre at Welwyn.

Constraints

A two-day course is envisaged, giving a maximum of 16 hours' learning. A maximum of 10 participants can be released at any one time.

LEARNING SPECIFICATION
(Time management programme)

Background to the business need

The Rationalisation Co Ltd (RCL) is involved in the design, manufacture and maintenance of scientific equipment. There is a total workforce of about 400, of which about 70 staff have management responsibilities. RCL has recently identified a significant loss of business due to late delivery on commercial contracts. It was estimated that £300,000 (5 per cent of turnover) was lost over a six-month period due to late penalty clauses being invoked by customers. In addition, two customers withdrew their business as a result of poor performance on delivery times. An outside organisation was invited in to research the cause of this and, if appropriate, to carry out a learning needs analysis (LNA) to specify the learning needed to redress the business needs.

The learning needs analysis identified that the main causes of the problem were:

- interruptions, unplanned meetings, queries and emergencies
- lack of systematic planning
- shifting priorities
- lack of, or inadequate, delegation
- poor systems for reviewing progress on contracts.

As a result, one of the recommendations is a learning programme in time management for all managers in the company.

Target population

There are about 70 staff on management grades, all located at the company offices in Dover. It has been agreed that they will attend within their section/team (finance, sales, production/distribution) where possible, subject to appropriate cover on the job.

None of the staff has attended formal time management programmes although some of them will have covered some of the issues as part of other management and/or professional learning programmes. Some may consider the requirement for them to attend a learning event in time management an insult, and may therefore be resistant to new ideas.

The age profile is skewed towards the older age-groups. 45 per cent of the managers are female, and these tend to be among the younger age-groups.

Aims of the learning

To provide managers with the knowledge, skills, attitudes and behaviours required to discharge their duties to appropriate standards in an efficient and timely manner, in order that:

- the cost of late penalty clauses is reduced to a maximum of 1 per cent of turnover in any six-month period
- no customers are lost through poor performance on delivery times.

Learning objectives

By the end of the programme participants will be able to:

- identify their current use of time by using time-logs, distinguishing between proactive and reactive activities
- select/prioritise daily the *right* tasks in the *right* order
- schedule personal planning time on a regular basis
- demonstrate flexibility in their personal plan to respond to changing circumstances
- delegate effectively, achieving a minimum score of 75 per cent on the delegation checklist
- explain the relationship between good time management and good communication
- select and use appropriate time management techniques
- set up effective systems to review progress on contracts.

Learning methods

The course should have a ratio of about 1:3 in the philosophical grounding in time management as against practical exercises which demonstrate to the learners the strengths of good time management practice.

It should be a balance of case studies, individual exercises and group exercises, and provide some means of assessing current time management practice.

An output should be a personal action plan which sets out the changes in time management that the learners intend to introduce over the next six months.

Facilitator skills

In order to be credible with the learners it is essential that the facilitators have had substantial experience of management, preferably in a scientific, engineering and/or production environment. They should have a track record in carrying out time management learning events at middle manager level and above.

The facilitators should have good interpersonal skills, be able to role-model good time management practice, and be able to involve themselves in fairly *robust* learning sessions.

Evaluation

The supplier will be required to provide a reaction level questionnaire and make proposals for learning level evaluation. Performance level evaluation will take place as a part of the formal performance review scheme between the learners and their managers, when progress against their personal action plans produced on the event will be reviewed.

Performance evaluation at the organisational level will be based on the two indicators included under *Aims*.

Time-scale

It is important that the learning intervention is concentrated into a fairly short period of time and that all 70 managers should have completed the programme by July of this year.

Venue

The programme will take place in an appropriate venue in or around Dover.

Constraints

Because of the domestic commitments of many of the participants, the programme cannot be held on a residential basis and must be completed in normal working time.

13

Make or buy decisions

INTRODUCTION

We have now reached the stage of having a very clear and comprehensive specification of what learning is required to meet the particular business need identified. Next we need to consider the options of how the learning is to be provided.

The first stage is the decision on the type of learning intervention being considered. Is it:

- a 'classroom' programme?
- an e-learning or a TBT-type intervention?
- a distance or flexible learning approach?
- a semi-formal approach – eg coaching, secondments, etc?
- a combination of some or all of these – a blended learning approach?

Within each of the formal learning options there is usually a further choice – traditionally called the 'make or buy' option. Taking the first type of learning intervention as an example,

- the *make* option involves designing and developing a new programme
- the *buy* option involves using an 'off-the shelf' programme, either
  - purchased from an 'inside' supplier, or
  - purchased from an 'outside' supplier.

Clearly, there may be solutions that lie between these, such as adapting an existing programme or developing a new programme made up of parts of existing programmes.

The choice of whether to go for the make or buy solution hinges to a large extent on four factors:

- the size of the population requiring the learning
- the nature of the competencies to be learned
- the timing of the learning
- the type of learning experience required.

Table 8 sets out how some of these factors tend to influence the choice between the make or buy solution.

Table 8 | Choosing the make or buy solution

Factors	Make solution is most appropriate when:	Buy solution is most appropriate when:
Size of learning population	*the learning population is large and the costs of developing and delivering a programme are less than the recurring per learner or per programme costs of a bought programme.*	*the learning population is small and the per learner or per programme costs incurred are less than the costs of developing and delivering a new programme.*
Nature of competencies	*most of the competencies involved in the learning are company- or job-specific.*	*most of the competencies involved in the learning are generic.*
Timing of learning	*the timing is important – because there is more control over timing. (However, generally needs greater planning and longer lead times.)*	*the learning is needed quickly.* *a greater flexibility of dates is required (assuming a widely available course).* *coverage at work is a problem and participants can only be released in small numbers.*
Type of learning experience	*there is a need for/advantage in staff learning together, eg for teamworking, sharing knowledge or experience.*	*participants will benefit from learning with people from other organisations (for an external course) to give a wider perspective, or from other parts of the organisation (for an internal course), or when the mix simply does not matter.* *participants will benefit from being away from their own organisation or colleagues – eg dealing with sensitive issues such as interpersonal skills.*

The first of these factors involves a trade-off between the costs of developing and delivering a new programme and the recurring per learner or per programme costs of buying the learning event. The subject of costs is quite a complex one and the following is intended only as a starting-point. Learning professionals who want to arrive at a comprehensive assessment of the costs may wish to consult their finance colleagues for advice. So, with this caveat, let's look at the costs of *buying* and the costs of *making* a new programme.

THE COSTS OF BUYING A PROGRAMME

The cost of the *buy* solution to meeting learning needs is quite straightforward to assess. It is either the per person cost of sending learners away on external open programmes, or the cost of bringing in a learning consultant to deliver a predesigned package to a group of employees. Sometimes it is possible to arrive at a hybrid solution. An external learning provider who runs open programmes may be prepared to bring their open course into your organisation and negotiate a fee that is significantly cheaper than the normal charges per learner. Sometimes the programme can be tailored to the organisation's requirements so that you have many of the benefits of a made course but without heavy development costs. To the cost of the external programme would be added the costs of travel and subsistence; to the costs of the bought-in programme would be added any accommodation, food and beverage costs and such items as hiring equipment – for example, for showing videos.

THE COSTS OF DEVELOPING AND DELIVERING A NEW PROGRAMME

It is easiest to consider the costs for the two elements, development and delivery, separately because the first is a one-off cost and the second is a recurring cost which will depend on the number of learners who attend the programme.

Development costs

These are the costs associated with taking the learning specification and turning it into an effective learning event that is ready for delivery, and includes the following activities:

- designing the form and structure of the learning to meet the learning objectives
- designing the learning materials – eg PowerPoint presentations, case studies, role-plays, learning logs and sometimes videos and CBT material where relevant
- preparing pre-course material where necessary
- preparing handouts
- preparing evaluation tools.

This work is sometimes carried out by external consultants who will charge a consultancy fee, and the costs are therefore clear-cut. However, sometimes it will be tackled by internal staff, often joint teams of learning professionals and specialist managers in the area, and in these cases it is important that the development costs are fully logged and recorded. The best way is to institute time-sheets and log the time spent by all involved. Usually your finance department will be able to let you have person hour/day costs that will reflect the actual costs, including any relevant overheads, of using those staff. Many organisations choose the internal route and are then horrified – if they actually do the calculation – at how expensive it turns out to be. Consultants are often experienced in development work, may have similar programmes already within their portfolios, and are therefore likely to be able to provide a cost-efficient service.

The next and vital stage in the development process is piloting the programme. This is properly a development cost, although if the pilot is successful, you have the benefit of having a group of learners who have completed the programme! Now the costs for a pilot are very similar to the final delivery costs, so let's look at these next.

Delivery costs

These are the costs associated with delivering a developed programme and are compiled on a per programme basis. They include:

- costs of the facilitator(s) – these may be fees for external facilitators or guest speakers, or the costs of using internal staff
- costs of the venue:
  - learning rooms
  - equipment
  - accommodation, if relevant
  - catering.

  These may be readily identifiable charges from a hotel or learning centre or may involve assessing the costs for using internal facilities – again seek help from your finance department
- costs of duplicating/printing learning materials and handouts, and licence fees for the use of copyright materials
- administrative costs involved with making the arrangements for the programme and the learners.

To be added to any development and delivery costs are the costs that are common to both bought and made programmes:

- the costs of the learners' time away from work
- travel costs.

On some occasions, temporary staff may be brought in to cover for the learner, or payments made for overtime worked. When this happens the costs are relatively easily identified. In many situations, the costs correspond to the loss of productive work. Again your finance department may be able to help. Otherwise, such costs are usually estimated as follows:

$$\text{Cost per day} = \frac{\text{salary}}{\text{number of working days*}} + \text{overheads}$$

*often taken as 225 days

Once more, your finance department will usually be able to help on the overheads. As a common rule of thumb, overheads are often calculated as between 30 per cent and 50 per cent of salary costs, but can be higher. For example, in one organisation we worked with overheads were estimated at 67 per cent of salary. (In some cases organisations add in a loss of profit as well, but this is a more complex calculation.)

The cost of learners' time away from work will not usually enter into any calculations for comparing different types of learning intervention unless the options are of different durations, but should always form part of any assessment of the overall cost of a learning event – for example, as part of an evaluation study.

So let's look at a simple case study.

The fundamental finance programme

Suppose there are a group of 35 managers for whom a learning need has been identified in the areas of budgeting and interpreting management accounts (excuse this woolly language – we do have, of course, a detailed learning specification!). The options are to send the participants on a well-established and reputable two-day open programme run by Super Training Courses Ltd at a cost of £700 per delegate, or alternatively to develop your own two-day programme. You have had a proposal from a small learning consultancy who will develop the course for £4,000. Because the numbers are relatively few you are going to regard the first programme run as a pilot. You have estimated the costs of delivering the course as follows:

For a programme of 10 learners:

Facilitator costs (using a learning consultant)	2 days @ £800 per day	£1,600
Venue costs:		
room hire (main learning room + 1 syndicate)	2 days @ £150 per day	£300
equipment (a video machine)	2 days @ £50 per day	£100
catering (coffees/teas/lunch)	10 learners @ £15/delegate/day	£300
Costs of materials/handouts	10 learners @ £10 per delegate	£100
Administration costs	10 hours @ £15 per hour	£150
TOTAL COSTS		**£2,550**

Take the cost of the pilot as the delivery cost of one programme for five learners – ie £2,350 (the total costs less the reduction for learner-related costs – ie £150 for catering and £50 for materials). If the pilot is successful, this part of the cost can be set off against the delivery cost.

See Table 9 for a comparison between the two approaches.

Table 9 | *Example of a make or buy decision*

	Make solution	**Buy solution**
Costs	*Development costs:* 　　= £4,000 + £2,350 　　= £6,350 *Delivery costs:* *3 programmes @ £2,550 per programme* 　　= £7,650 *Total = £14,000*	*35 learners @ £700 per delegate = £24,500*
Nature of competencies	*Although mostly general competencies, programme can be tailored to use the organisation's own finance documents/systems.*	*General competencies with the advantages of some coverage of different approaches.*
Timing of learning	*Learning can be delivered 3 months after need identified – due to development time and agreeing suitable dates with learners.*	*Learning can be delivered 2 months after need identified – learners may appreciate flexibility of dates.*
Type of learning experience	*Learners are able to discuss in-depth problems with current budgetary system.*	*Learners get a broader appreciation of different systems/approaches and their problems, by interaction with participants from other organisations.*

The decision will be based on looking at the advantages and disadvantages of each option. Clearly, in this case the 'make' option has come out considerably cheaper – £14,000, as against £24,500 for the 'buy' solution. However, what is the learning experience that is required – understanding a range of different systems or obtaining a detailed knowledge of the organisation's own system? How important is the issue of timing and flexibility of dates? The learning specification should provide the answer to these questions, and cost will be only one factor in the decision-making process.

CONCLUSIONS

The costing principles underlying the choice between the make or buy options for the traditional learning programme described above can equally be applied to the full range of learning interventions. It is important to take into account all the costs, including that of learners' time, when the different options are of different durations. This is often of particular importance when comparing e-learning and TBT learning approaches with other approaches because one of the features of this type of intervention is reduced learner time away from work. We would also advocate that semi-formal learning interventions – such as coaching, secondments, etc – are costed in exactly the same way.

An identical approach to calculating the costs of the learning intervention can be used for evaluation purposes – but remember always to include learners' time: see Chapter 21.

We now move on to looking at how we plan our learning activities.

Section 5
Planning the learning

Introduction to Section 5

In terms of the learning wheel, see Figure 9, we have gone around the stages of:

- identifying the range and extent of learning needs required to meet the business needs of the organisation (Sections 1 and 2)
- specifying those learning needs very precisely (Section 3)
- analysing how best these learning needs can be met (Section 4).

Having been very hard-working, professional and systematic, the learning professional is now in possession of a vast amount of data/information on business needs and the associated learning needs at the organisational, group and individual levels. The problem now is how to plan and organise to meet those needs!

This section looks at this very important, but sometimes neglected, stage in the learning process. Strictly speaking, purists might argue that this is not part of the Learning Needs Analysis stage. However, equally it tends not to be addressed in books on the development and delivery of learning, which concentrate more on the development, planning and delivery of specific individual learning events. It is not an easy part of the process to examine, largely because the preceding stages – ie getting at the learning needs – can be very different in different organisations and rarely fit the ideal of a well-ordered approach. Also, we live in a business world characterised by an ever-increasing pace of change.

It is rare for the learning professional to be able to assemble all the information on learning needs during a specific period preceding the planning year, then formulate a learning strategy/plan and budget. With limited resources it is likely that once the learning professional has brought together all the *bids* for learning, there will be the need for some considerable adjustment. It may even be as dramatic as revisiting the LNA process as a whole and re-asking all the questions previously posed. Through the iterative (and reiterative) process a final balance of what learning needs can be met within the resources available will be arrived at. However, the process does not stop there. Learning needs are often generated at short notice, and needs and priorities can change all the time. So it is important to be flexible and develop the ability to be able to respond and revise plans. Any learning plan must be viewed as a living document that may have to be revisited regularly and adjusted.

However, this does not obviate the need for planning. Rather, it means that the learning professional has to be both skilled in the planning process and willing and able to react to change. This section looks at:

- assembling and prioritising the information on learning needs (Chapter 14)
- the preparation and use of learning strategies and plans (Chapter 15).

It does not purport to offer all the answers on this complex subject but tries to provide the basis for learning professionals to develop an approach that best meets the needs and challenges of their own organisations.

Figure 9 | **The Learning Wheel – planning the learning**

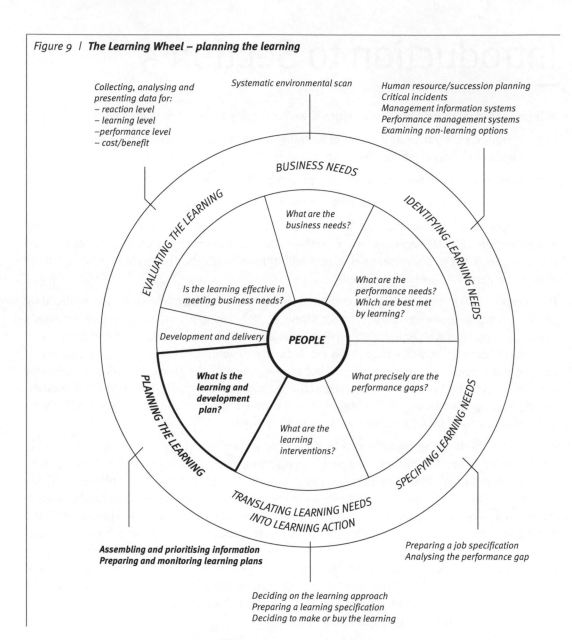

14

Assembling and prioritising the information

INTRODUCTION

In this chapter we look at how we assemble the information that has been so painstakingly gathered as part of the LNA process, and how we prioritise it. It is the crucial first step in the preparation of the learning plan and budget.

ASSEMBLING THE INFORMATION

The LNA process will have generated needs from a number of sources. In Section 2 we set out a range of what we described as *bridges* between the business needs and the learning need. These were:

- human resource planning
- succession planning
- critical incidents
- management information systems
- performance management systems.

These basically generate information on the need for some sort of performance change in the human resources of the organisation – which might be for new skills and knowledge or an improvement in the existing knowledge and skills being used. Having considered a range of ways that these performance changes can be achieved, a learning intervention may be identified as the best approach in some cases. In those cases, the next stage will be to specify the learning need very precisely to ensure that the learning is focused and targeted to meet the business need in a cost-effective way (examined in Section 3).

Then each learning need will be analysed to decide the best approach to meeting that need, choosing semi-formal or formal learning, the appropriate learning methods, etc. We suggested that the final output of this process should be some form of written statement detailing the learning required – what we call a learning specification.

At its simplest and at one end of a spectrum, the LNA process can be seen to generate a mass of learning specifications all posing demands on the learning resources of the organisation. At the other end of the spectrum, at its most chaotic, the LNA process can be seen to generate a mass of demands that are for the large part badly researched and poorly specified. Clearly, the closer you are to the ordered end of the spectrum, the easier life becomes at the planning stage. Most people who live in the real world will know that they are unable to do all the things they might want to do. For the learning professional the limiting factor is usually the availability (or rather, the lack) of money to finance the learning activities. Other factors may be the lack of suitably qualified facilitators or learning accommodation, or the operational constraints on the release of learners. Whatever the reason, it is clear that some prioritising will be necessary in the development of most learning plans.

SETTING PRIORITIES

Setting priorities will help you to decide:

- which learning interventions should be included
- in what order these learning interventions should be carried out
- which learning interventions might be put on a waiting list to be carried out in the event that some other learning intervention is cancelled or postponed
- which learning interventions might not be undertaken, with an assessment of the cost/effect of this decision.

Key information

The assembled data/information on learning needs represents the shopping list for the learning professional to work on. The key elements of the information that will aid the decision-making process are:

- details of the business need that the learning intervention is meeting
- the resources required in terms of finance, facilitator time, learner time, accommodation, etc
- the time-scale(s) over which the learning must take place.

All the above data/information should be contained in the learning specification (see Chapter 12) and in the analysis of the make or buy decision (see Chapter 13) for each learning intervention required. This documentation really comes into its own at this stage – it is a key source of data for feeding into the prioritisation process.

The first stage is for the information on requirements to be compared with the resources that are available. For example, in financial terms, if the learning budget is set at a given figure and the anticipated total cost of meeting all the proposed learning needs is double that figure, then something has to give! Either the budget is increased to take account of all the specified learning or some of the learning bids have to be cut out or postponed. In reality, the latter is more likely to be the case. However, we would argue that a well-thought-out case for learning to meet a specific business need should stand its ground against any other business proposal requiring budgeted funds.

Next, some sort of assessment should be made against the other resources – eg accommodation and learning facilitators' availability. Both of these items lend themselves to being set out diagramatically using PERT and Gantt charts. Examples of the use of these are given in Chapter 15, which looks at learning plans. These techniques help to schedule the timing of the learning events in order to get the most from the limited resources. As with many such tasks, there is a range of computer programs to help with the donkey work if the process is large or complex.

Key factors in prioritising

The key factors that might be considered when prioritising are:

- *importance* – How big an impact will the completed learning intervention have on organisational performance – ie how important is the business need? The degree of importance could be affected by operational constraints, by legal/safety implications or by the return demonstrated in your cost/benefit analysis (see Chapter 21). Alternatively, it could be the high visibility of the learning or political factors that dictate decisions about 'relative' importance. It may be helpful to give a *high importance*, *medium importance* or *low importance* ranking to the learning bids.

  For example, in our second human resource planning case study, the Expanding Railway Company (see Chapter 3), there is a substantial increased demand for drivers in particular years. Because there is no means of increasing supply other than by providing learning interventions internally, and because the drivers' availability is crucial to the planned expansion, this would merit a high ranking. It is essential to remember that ranking is a largely subjective process and might best be carried out by the learning professional in conjunction with line manager colleagues. It is important also to note that the resultant rankings are relative. Giving a bid a low-importance ranking is not to say that it is unimportant but that it is less important than the other bids against which it is being judged.

- *urgency* – How quickly must you act? A learning intervention is urgent if failure to complete it within a short time-scale will have a highly negative impact on the organisation and/or reduce or cancel the benefit of doing it.

  It may be helpful to use a concept drawn from the project planning arena, critical path analysis, which identifies the window of time over which the learning must take place. With this technique, the earliest date that the learning can be undertaken is identified – for example, if it is learning to use a new computer system, it would be ineffective to carry out the learning too early. Then the latest date for the learning is identified – for example, the learning must be completed before the new computer system becomes operational. In the case of the drivers in the Expanding Railway Company, there will certainly be a latest date by which learning must have been completed to meet the operational requirements of the expansion. There may be some flexibility in the earliest date if the additional drivers can regularly practise their skills before taking up their jobs, perhaps by covering for illness or double running.

  Some learning interventions may just come labelled 'highly urgent' – for example, the learning needs relating to health and safety, such as those arising out of the case study, the *Awful Accidents* (see Chapter 5). Some learning interventions, too, are highly constrained in terms of time-scales for operational reasons. For example, retailers would not consider providing learning events for any of their shopfloor staff in the run-up to Christmas, universities might elect to provide learning events for their lecturing staff only in the student vacation periods.

- *trend* – What happens if you do nothing? Will the business need stay the same or become greater? Or is it possible that the business need will reduce or actually go away, perhaps as staff learn on-the-job?

Your learning plan (examined in detail in Chapter 15) will now depend on the prioritising process of weighing up all the items on your list of learning bids. If several learning issues are of *high* importance, deciding which to put in the schedule first will depend on their relative urgency and trend. Thus the highly important, highly urgent learning issues with a high trend for the business need to get greater without the learning intervention, would be prioritised first in the plan, while others take up their relative position. However, there is no easy way or simple algorithm to use. In general, bids labelled 'high importance' take precedence over bids ranked 'medium' and 'low', but it may be a matter of judgement to weigh up a medium-importance bid with a high-urgency rating against a high-importance bid but where there is some flexibility in the time-scale. For example, where the introduction of a new computer system could be delayed a couple of months, the learning need could be pushed into the following budget year.

Life is made a good deal easier if the planning can take place over a time-scale longer than a year, even if it is accepted that for the later years the plan is tentative rather than firm.

Many organisations use a working group of managers representing all parts of the organisation to decide on the priorities. It is always helpful to have carried out some form of pre-analysis as described above as a basis for the discussions, but involving managers helps in two ways. Firstly, they can provide a cross-organisation perspective, and secondly, there will be far greater ownership of the final priority listing and of the learning plan into which they will feed.

CONCLUSION

In most organisations there will almost always be more bids for learning interventions than the financial and/or physical resources will allow. Following a systematic process such as that outlined above will help ensure that limited learning resources are prioritised into those areas where they can have the biggest impact.

The process described above is not meant to be prescriptive for all organisations. Clearly, local factors will be important in prioritising which learning activities get the first call on resources. It is the setting up of the process – ie starting to think about the issues involved – that is important, not what the prioritisation process actually contains. Prioritising the learning interventions is, in our view, an essential step in the process and one that is often given scant attention, which means that it sometimes happens by default and is sometimes approached in a haphazard manner.

Who knows? At some stage in the future (or possibly in enlightened organisations even now) setting the learning budget will be based on the learning plan that is identified as delivering business success. This would be a significant improvement over the present situation in many organisations where the learning budget is a fixed sum (seen as an overhead rather than as an investment) to be worked within . . .

More about this vital subject in the next chapter.

15

The learning and development strategy and plan

INTRODUCTION

As we have found so often in previous sections, it is important to start off by defining our terms. The term *learning* or *training plan* is probably the most commonly used and is employed in many different ways to describe many different entities. It is interesting that the government survey *Learning and Training at Work 2001* (DfES 2002) found that 60 per cent of organisations (with five or more employees) claimed they had what they called learning/training plans, but only 38 per cent of organisations had learning budgets!

There is often confusion about the terms *strategy* and *plan*. We define:

- the learning and development *strategy* as the high-level document which sets out the overall approach that the organisation takes to learning and development
- the learning and development *plan* as the document that sets out how the strategy is to be implemented over the plan period.

The learning and development strategy and plan will be part of the hierarchy of strategies and plans:

business strategy and plans

human resource strategy and plans

learning and development strategy and plan

It is now generally accepted that any sensible organisation – ie one that wants to survive and grow – will have a business strategy (which we describe in Chapter 2). Those organisations, and we would hope that it is all these days, which see people as key to their success will then have a human resource (HR) strategy. The HR strategy and plans will be based on the business strategy and plans, and will usually consist of:

- a set of value statements about how people will be treated in the organisation; these will generally include key statements on the issues of diversity and equal opportunities

- an HR plan and a succession plan – see Chapters 3 and 4

- a recruitment strategy and plan

- a performance management strategy and plan

- *a learning and development strategy and plan.*

This book of course concentrates on the last of these components.

THE LEARNING AND DEVELOPMENT STRATEGY

The learning and development strategy will set out the fundamental principles that will drive the learning and development processes in the organisation. It will generally include some or all of the following:

- statements about the value that the organisation places on the learning and development of all its staff

- the key philosophical approaches that underpin learning and development in the organisation – for example, being learner-centred and learner-driven, an emphasis on continuous and lifelong learning, the kind of learning culture envisaged

- the key policy approaches to delivering learning – for example, a move to e-learning or action-based learning, partnerships with other organisations (colleges, customers, sector consortiums), the approach to qualifications (NVQs, professional/academic qualifications)

- the overall approach to how learning needs will be identified, analysed and prioritised

- an evaluation strategy for assessing the effectiveness of learning interventions (see Chapter 16)

- roles and responsibilities for all those involved in the learning and development process – including the chief executive, HR director, line managers, learning professionals, individual members of staff, etc.

It is likely that the learning and development strategy once formulated will not change very much each year. It will be reviewed and refreshed in line with the business strategy, but essentially provides a bedrock for the long-term planning of learning and development in the organisation.

THE LEARNING AND DEVELOPMENT PLAN

The learning and development plan is essentially an implementation plan for the strategy over a set period of time. Traditionally, learning/training plans cover a period of one year. However, as we commented in the previous section, it can be very useful to plan over a longer period. The business plan is likely to be over at least a three-year period, and many of the methods of identifying learning needs – eg HR and succession plans – by their very nature will throw up needs over a considerably longer time-scale than a year. Also, during the prioritising process, having the flexibility to plan further ahead can ease the situation where constraints are biting hard. A common complaint made about British management is the tendency towards short-termism. Investing in the human resource asset of a business must be a long-term strategy, so it makes sense to reflect this in the learning and development planning process.

Clearly, if the plan covers a longer period, perhaps three years, the level of detail will be greatest in the first year, with the later years perhaps highlighting on-going or major learning initiatives only.

There are usually three main parts to the learning and development plan:

- context and objectives
- learning costs and budget
- the operational plan.

Context and objectives

This section sets out the context for the plan and the key themes for the plan period, and would generally include:

- trends in expenditure, the number of learning days, the distribution by department, type of learning, etc
- performance against last year's plan/part of the plan including evaluation results
- the key objectives and the business plan priorities driving the plan
- how the learning and development plan contributes towards the business objectives
- major learning initiatives – eg the training of all supervisors in leadership skills or an organisation-wide customer-care initiative
- any major policy themes for that period – eg a move towards the use of NVQs, greater use of external providers
- an evaluation plan.

Costs and budgets

It may be surprising to those learning professionals who are used to working with learning/training budgets to find that currently overall only 38 per cent of organisations actually budget for their learning activities (see earlier survey, DfES, 2002). This same survey shows that the proportion is strongly related to organisational size – only 30 per cent of small organisations (of fewer than 25 employees) have a learning/training budget, rising to 92 per cent of very large organisations (of more than 500 employees). There are clearly considerable advantages to having an identified and dedicated source of funding for learning activities. It implies a commitment to learning and *guarantees* a certain level of learning activity.

The learning plan will set out the cost of the planned learning activities. In an ideal world the plan will then be used as the basis for agreeing a budget. In the less ideal and perhaps more realistic world, the plan is often based on a preset budget or budget estimate!

A very important issue is the need to include a contingency allowance for learning needs which could not be foreseen during the preparation of the plan. We would suggest that learning activities focused on business needs have as much right to contingency funds as any other part of the organisation. The alternative, when a previously unforeseen need occurs, is to carry out a re-run of the prioritising exercise described in Chapter 14. Perhaps only when it can be demonstrated that no further slack can be shaken out of the budget should any contingency or additional funds be made available.

The budget may take many forms these days. There has been a proliferation in the ways that organisations fund their learning activities often in response to a general policy of tightening the controls on the use of resources and increasing accountability for expenditure.

Who funds the learning?

Newby (1992) debates whether learning costs are best charged as an overhead across all other functions, according to some indicator such as the number of staff employed, or whether it should be re-charged according to the take-up of learning days by each function, so that the learning function operates as a form of profit centre. He suggests that there are advantages and disadvantages with both methods.

Newby argues that an *overhead systems* approach encourages a longer-term view of learning with less emphasis on short-term fire-fighting, and allows for more corporate direction and control. However, such approaches can tend to encourage the inertia of running a standard menu of courses from year to year with little attempt to review learning provision against business needs. Also, they do not encourage line management to take an interest in the systematic identification of learning needs, based on business needs, with the associated analysis and evaluation.

Re-charging systems, on the other hand, do have the virtue of concentrating line management interest on selecting the right people for the right learning because they are being *charged* for the learning provided. Newby comments that this alone is sufficient, in his view, to come down in favour of re-charging as opposed to overhead systems, which leave line managers largely indifferent to the costs (and therefore benefits) of learning. We strongly concur with this view.

In our research for this book we have found that there is no single trend of moving to one system or the other. Some organisations are moving towards re-charging while others are moving back to the overhead system. An example of this is a major financial institution which, prior to its takeover by another major financial organisation, used the re-charging system. The new owners have a policy that all the work and costs associated with internal re-charging is simply not worth the effort, so they have moved back to the overhead system of charging. Some organisations have taken re-charging one stage further, so their separate business units hold their own learning budgets. The learning function has been set up as a self-financing business unit with a profit target. Each business unit – eg a particular factory, department store or functional unit – sets its own budget and is able to *purchase* its learning from any source, using resources internal to the business, from the internal learning business unit or from any external supplier.

Another disadvantage of the overhead system is that it often leads to the learning budget being determined by adding (or subtracting) a percentage to (or from) the actual spend on learning in the previous financial period. This, in part, is responsible for the spurt in learning activity in these organisations in the final quarter of their financial year! However, Newby comments that some organisations have overcome this by combining an overhead system with a system of zero-based budgeting. Here, in theory, each budget-setting exercise starts effectively with a clean piece of paper, no expenditure, and is built up from justified proposals.

The monitoring and control of budgets

The monitoring and control of the learning budget is an important activity. It is usually carried out at regular intervals, often monthly or in some cases quarterly. A comparison is made between the budget – ie the planned level of income and expenditure – and what has actually occurred. The key is to look for what are referred to as variances between the budget and the actual. Generally, small differences are not of concern, and quite often a form of tolerance limit is specified – perhaps around 5 per cent of the budget – and only variances outside this tolerance level are highlighted.

Most commonly the focus will be on expenditure. If there is a variance, it will be essential to find out what the cause is – is it a question of timing, has some learning activity been brought forward or delayed, or has there been a worrying increase in costs? If income is involved, for example, where the learning function has been set up as a business unit, it will be essential to know whether sales are on target, and if not, what action is required. Is it a timing problem – has the need for the learning intervention perhaps been delayed, so that the income will arrive in a later period? Or has the income been lost – in which case, what effect will it have on the final outcome in terms of profit or loss for the budget period?

Another aspect of budgeting is for cash flow. Cash flow analysis is critical in running a commercial learning enterprise where a shortfall of income against outgoings will require financing. Many businesses that are basically sound and profitable fail because of cash flow problems.

Costing and budgeting is often an area in which the average learning professional feels a little uncomfortable. The mechanics and approaches used will vary considerably between organisations. However, there are considerable benefits to understanding the concepts and systems involved. Our advice is not to be embarrassed to seek help and explanations from your financial colleagues. Setting up the learning and development budget and monitoring it in a professional way will not only ensure that the learning provision is securely and soundly based but will also ensure your credibility with both your financial and your line manager colleagues. You will be demonstrating that you appreciate the requirements for sound financial planning and stewardship!

Operational plans

The learning and development budget is an excellent tool for planning and controlling the financial side of learning activities. However, there is also a need for operational plans that schedule the learning in terms of time-scale and non-financial resources. There will probably be two levels of operational plan:

- The first level, which will usually form part of the formal learning and development plan, will set out for the main learning interventions:
  - a schedule of dates
  - total learning days per intervention.

- The second level, which will be used as a planning tool for the learning department, will set out:
  - the time-scales for each stage of every learning event, from preparation of the learning specification if this is not already available, through the development stages of the learning programme, its delivery, and finally to the evaluation of the programme
  - the resources required at all stages – for example, your time, that of other facilitators, accommodation, learning materials, the learners' time (to ensure practicality of release).

The method most commonly used for the second more detailed level of planning is probably still the Gantt chart. Named after Henry Gantt, who first used horizontal bar charts for this purpose in the early 1900s, the Gantt chart offers a method for setting out learning activities in a straightforward, logical, diagrammatic form that is easy to understand. It can be used to plan and monitor the overall learning programme or to plan and monitor a specific activity such as the development of a new learning event to meet a specific business need. It can be used to show the learning activities against a number of parameters, although elapsed or calendar time is usually displayed along the base. Additional information, such as key dates, review meetings, etc, can be shown with a variety of symbols and colours.

A number of manual systems are used, such as pegboards and white boards, which enable the plan to be updated and modified relatively easily. There are also many computer packages (see below) which make the original drawing and any subsequent modification a quick and simple process. These also allow for the scheduling of resources for a number of learning events to be carried out fairly effortlessly, whereas with manual systems it can be a laborious exercise. Such packages also enable the monitoring of the plan to be undertaken very simply and easily.

Gantt charts are not without their limitations. In particular, it is not easy to show the relationship between the various learning activities and therefore the knock-on effect of activities – for example, the effect on other activities if the development of a learning programme is accelerated or delayed. Two techniques, critical path analysis (CPA) and the programme evaluation and review technique (PERT), were developed in the late 1950s to overcome this problem. The differences between these two project management techniques in practice has largely disappeared, and the best features of both have been merged in modern computer packages. Not only do they enable the planning and scheduling process to take place effortlessly, but they will auto-matically adjust the whole programme for any changes made. These systems can provide the scheduling information in a wide variety of ways, including Gantt-type charts.

An example of a simple Gantt chart is shown as Figure 10. It sets out the schedule of learning programmes to be undertaken over a particular period of time. You will see from Figure 10 that the chart has already taken into account the scheduling of the facilitator resource in that there is no double-booking (hopefully!) of any facilitator. Symbols can be used to show key dates, but care should be taken to ensure that the chart does not become so cluttered that the detail is impossible to see. In our case we have limited ourselves to showing the timing and duration of the delivery of the programmes, the team progress meeting (♥) following shortly after a short programme has taken place (and also midway through a long programme), and the timing for the evaluation (♠) of those learning programmes which are to be formally evaluated. We have used the term 'team progress meeting' to cover whatever you want it to cover. For some organisations this will be the time when the learner(s) get together with their line manager(s) to discuss how the learning event went, and how the results will be applied. In other organisations it might mean a meeting of the facilitators, with or without the line manager(s), to review how the learning programmes have gone and to make such adjustments as might be necessary to achieve the learning objectives.

This is a very versatile planning tool. We could have a Gantt chart showing the planning of one learning programme right through from the identification of the business need to the final evaluation, or showing the activities/workload of a particular facilitator, or the use of a particular learning facility, and so on. Monitoring the learning activity on the chart in Figure 10 can be shown by shading the bars on the chart to indicate activities that have been completed or by

---

Figure 10 | **Example of a Gantt chart – learning programme planning chart**

LEARNING PROGRAMME PLANNING CHART

Quarter: Apr to Jun   Sheet 1 of 1   Drawn by: NPD   Approved by: KBG

LEARNING ACTIVITY	FACILITATOR	1	2	3	4	5	6	7	8	9	10	11	12	13
Senior mgt programme (3 × 1 week)	J Able		▥	♥			☐	♥			☐	♥		
Supervisor programme (10 × 2-day modules)	A Baker	▥		▥	☐		☐	♠	☐		☐			☐
Customer care (4 × 1 week)	J Singh	▤		▤		☐		☐		♠				
Induction (3 days)	A Baker		▥			☐								
H&S programme (1 × 2 weeks)	External				▨	☐	♠				☐			
Teambuilding (weekend)	J Able								☐					
Time management (2 days)	External		▥			☐				♠	☐			

WEEK/PROJECT TIME

KEY: Estimated duration: ☐ Completed: ▥ Performance level evaluation: ♠ Team progress meeting: ♥

Original issue date: 22 December   Date of revision: Revision number:

drawing bars to represent the actual timing of activities underneath the planned activities to show any adjustment to the planned learning or slippage from the plan.

For those of you that would like to find out more about the project planning techniques described in this chapter try Young (1993) for a simple introduction, and Burke (1999) for a more in-depth approach.

CONCLUSION

We have looked at what constitutes a learning and development strategy and at the three elements of a learning and development plan. The plan will not and should not be *written on tablets of stone* but will be a working document against which decisions will be taken during the period, and against which progress will be monitored. It will almost certainly change over the period of its life, possibly many times. Any plan must be monitored regularly, asking:

- Are you on plan and within budget?
- If not, what action is required – eg should learning events be rescheduled?
- Has anything new happened that might affect the plan – eg an urgent, high-priority new business initiative?
- If so, how can the need be accommodated – eg any spare capacity, any possibility of additional budget, what existing learning events planned might be postponed?

Planning the learning is a vital stage in ensuring that all the hard work that has gone into the LNA process is translated into effective action to meet the business needs. The old adage 'To fail to plan is to plan to fail' could not be more true in the learning and development context.

We now pass through the stage in the Learning Wheel which deals with the detailed development and delivery of the learning which is outside the scope of this book and come to the final crucial stage of evaluating the learning.

READING AND REFERENCE

Burke R. (1999), *Project Management – Planning and Control Techniques*, London, John Wiley & Sons.

Learning and Training at Work 2001 (2002), Sheffield, DfES.

Newby A. C. (1992), *Training Evaluation Handbook*, Aldershot, Gower.

Young T. L. (1993), *Planning Projects*, London, The Industrial Society.

Section 6
Evaluating the learning

Introduction to Section 6

There is a saying among pilots that a landing is not complete until you have walked away from the aircraft. The meaning of this is that following the very demanding process of landing an aeroplane, it is all too easy for a pilot to relax and so, during the relatively simple process of taxiing to a vacant space and parking the plane, to commit some enormous blunder. Something similar applies in the learning field.

The learning professional has taken a systematic approach to the identification and analysis of the learning needs and the planning of the learning. The learning has been delivered to meet these needs and according to plan. It is very tempting at this stage to breathe a sigh of relief and file the papers away. However, we would argue that you have not yet walked away from the aircraft until you have evaluated the learning.

The starting-point for this section must be to establish what in fact we mean by the 'evaluation' of learning. It is one of those phrases much bandied around and equally much misunderstood. Or rather, perhaps, it is a phrase that means different things to different people. For many learning professionals it provokes a sense of fear – should they be doing some of *it*? – and a sense of panic – *how* should they be doing *it*? A good place to begin is with what could be described as the classic or textbook definition of training/learning evaluation provided in the *Glossary of Terms* by the Manpower Services Commission (1981):

> *The assessment of the total value of a training/*learning *system, training course or programme/*learning intervention *in social as well as financial terms. Evaluation differs from validation in that it attempts to measure the overall cost benefit of the course or programme in social as well as financial terms.* [Our additions not in italics.]

Fear and panic setting in? Don't despair – take a deep breath and read on. It is recognised that this is a very ambitious definition. We believe a more useful and practical definition is that provided by Hamblin (1974) in his classic text on this subject:

> *Any attempt to obtain information (feedback) on the effects of a training/*learning *programme, and to assess the value of training/*learning *in the light of that information.* [Our additions not in italics.]

Some might argue that this definition is too loose, too unspecific, and suggests an undisciplined approach. However, we believe that evaluation is often not attempted *because* people think that it involves large, sophisticated (and expensive!) studies. In fact, we will show that there are many ways to evaluate learning – each provides some information or some window into the process – and we would argue that any attempt at evaluation is better than none at all. The purpose of this section is to introduce a structured way of looking at evaluation and then to discuss a range of tools and techniques that can be used in the evaluation process.

The first chapter, Chapter 16, sets the scene by looking at some purposes and principles of evaluation. It also sets out a multi-level model that will form the basis for the structure of Chapters 18 to 21. However, first, Chapter 17 provides the basic building-blocks for the rest of the section in describing how to set about collecting the data. Chapters 18 to 20 address the issues of why and how to tackle evaluation at each of the main evaluation levels. Chapter 21 considers the cost-effectiveness and cost/benefit of learning interventions. Chapter 22 then provides a starting-point for analysing evaluation results. It introduces some simple techniques and refers the reader to other sources of information for more sophisticated approaches. The final chapter, Chapter 23, looks at some of the issues associated with the presentation and use of evaluation results.

So, now we begin our journey round the final section of the Learning Wheel.

READING AND REFERENCE

HAMBLIN A. C. (1974), *Evaluation and Control of Training*, Maidenhead, McGraw-Hill.
MANPOWER SERVICES COMMISSION (1981), *Glossary of Terms*, London, HMSO.

Figure 11 | **The Learning Wheel – evaluating the learning**

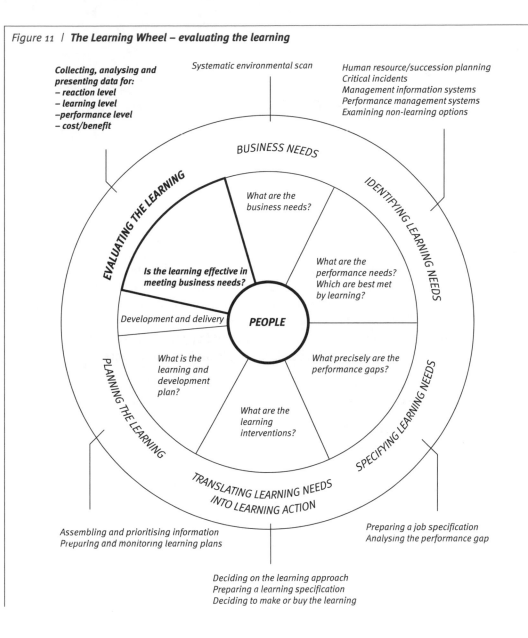

Collecting, analysing and presenting data for:
– reaction level
– learning level
–performance level
– cost/benefit

Systematic environmental scan

Human resource/succession planning
Critical incidents
Management information systems
Performance management systems
Examining non-learning options

BUSINESS NEEDS

EVALUATING THE LEARNING

IDENTIFYING LEARNING NEEDS

What are the business needs?

What are the performance needs? Which are best met by learning?

Is the learning effective in meeting business needs?

PEOPLE

Development and delivery

What is the learning and development plan?

What precisely are the performance gaps?

What are the learning interventions?

PLANNING THE LEARNING

SPECIFYING LEARNING NEEDS

TRANSLATING LEARNING NEEDS INTO LEARNING ACTION

Assembling and prioritising information
Preparing and monitoring learning plans

Preparing a job specification
Analysing the performance gap

Deciding on the learning approach
Preparing a learning specification
Deciding to make or buy the learning

16

Setting the scene

INTRODUCTION

This is a key chapter which, as the title suggests, 'sets the scene' for the rest of this section on evaluation. We start by describing the main purposes of evaluation and what we believe are the key principles that should underpin all evaluation activity. We then examine how evaluation is both dependent on, and mirrors, the learning needs analysis (LNA) process. Next, we describe a multi-level model that provides the basis for a structured approach to evaluation. Finally, we comment on the contribution made by Investors in People and the importance of a learning and development culture.

THE PURPOSES OF EVALUATION

Learning evaluation is carried out for a wide range of purposes, which can be categorised generally under four main headings:

- to improve the quality of the learning, in terms of the delivery – eg facilitator skills, learning methods used, the length of the intervention; and the appropriateness of the learning objectives – eg their content and level
- to assess the effectiveness – of the overall learning intervention, facilitator and learning methods – and the extent to which it has met the learning needs, performance requirements and business needs
- to justify the intervention – to prove that the benefits outweigh the costs
- to justify the role of learning in the organisation – for budget purposes, and especially in cutback situations.

Usually the evaluation has one of these purposes as its primary focus. For example:

- If there has been a number of general complaints about a learning programme, the evaluation will be directed primarily at identifying the causes and improving the quality.
- If there are concerns that the learning intervention is not achieving what was intended, the evaluation will start by looking at the effectiveness issues.

- If there are concerns about the costs of the learning intervention or whether there is a cheaper way of achieving the same results, it will focus first on justification.

- If the organisation has a tough budget-setting process or is looking for cutbacks, the emphasis may then be on providing the proof that learning justifies the investment in it.

These purposes are clearly all interlinked, and to some extent any evaluation will address all four purposes. However, being clear on the primary purpose will help focus the evaluation on the appropriate issues and determine the best approach from the outset.

The results from evaluation studies can also provide invaluable information on how effective the learning has been in meeting *individual learners'* needs. The results can therefore be used to provide each learner with feedback and to identify whether and what further interventions might be required. It can also help the individual learner understand the impact of the learning on his or her own performance and its contribution to team and organisational performance. In the same way, assessments that are set up primarily to assess the individual learner – eg tests used as the basis for licensing an individual to do a job – can also be used to provide evaluation information on the effectiveness of the whole learning intervention.

Given all these purposes, many would be forgiven for wondering how it was possible to get away with *not* evaluating learning. Surely everyone wants to strive continuously for improved quality? Surely everyone wants to assess the effectiveness of its product, staff and methods? And finally, *surely* you must have to demonstrate that learning represents a good investment? Yet the evidence suggests that the evaluation carried out is often very limited. In some ways it seems extraordinary that what can be quite a considerable investment appears to escape the normal quality and financial criteria. One of the results of this has undoubtedly been to make the learning budget a soft target for cuts at times of financial stringency.

We hope that we have convinced you of the need to read on!

EVALUATION THAT MAKES A DIFFERENCE

Michael Patton coined the term 'utilisation-focused evaluation' in the context of evaluating social programmes. However, many of the principles that Patton suggests can be soundly transferred from the world of general evaluation to the specific area of evaluating learning and development interventions. Patton (1997) describes his approach as follows:

> *Utilization-Focused Evaluation begins with the premise that evaluations should be judged by their utility and actual use; therefore, evaluators should facilitate the evaluation process and design any evaluation with careful consideration of how everything that is done, from beginning to end, will affect use.*

The message is that there is no point in carrying out evaluation for its own sake – it must lead to information that will be used to make a difference to the quality of learning and development and its impact on individual, team and organisational performance. So Patton puts the spotlight on the whole *process* of evaluation – who and how you involve people, as well as the 'technical' tools of questionnaires, etc. *Our first key principle for successful evaluation is to take a utilisation-based approach.*

EVALUATION AS PART OF THE LEARNING PROCESS

Our second key principle is that the foundation for successful evaluation lies in good learning needs analysis. In the first part of this book we define the LNA process as:

- starting with the business needs – what is happening, or is forecast to be happening, in the organisation that suggests there is a need to change the performance/behaviour of individual(s)

- identifying the performance gap – what the gap is between the required performance/behaviour and current performance/behaviour

- investigating whether learning is the appropriate solution (perhaps there is a technological solution, job structure solution, etc)

- analysing the learning required in terms of knowledge, skills, attitudes and behaviours to bridge the performance gap and setting out the learning objectives

- specifying how best those learning needs could be met – eg through a traditional classroom-based course, e-learning solution, coaching on-the-job, etc.

The evaluation process mirrors the LNA process in reverse. It seeks to answer the questions:

- Have the learning needs been met?

- Has the performance gap been bridged?

- Have the business needs been met?

If the LNA process is sound, then the evaluation sets off from secure foundations. Many of the 'problems' faced in evaluation are due to a shaky or sometimes non-existent LNA stage. *In an ideal world the evaluation should be planned at the learning needs analysis stage – this is our third key principle.* It is not always possible. For example, we are frequently asked to come in and evaluate a learning intervention after it has taken place. Given that we know our readers live in the real world, we will help you deal with this situation too!

A MULTI-LEVEL MODEL

The traditional and probably the most commonly used model for learning evaluation dates back to the 1960s and the work of Kirkpatrick (1967) and Warr, Bird and Rackham (1970). It is often referred to as the Kirkpatrick model. The model sets out four levels at which learning interventions can be evaluated. These are:

- *reaction level* – which measures what the learners *think* or *feel* about the learning event (covered in detail in Chapter 18)

- *immediate/learning level* – which measures what the learners actually *learned* from the event (covered in detail in Chapter 19)

- *intermediate/job behaviour level* – which measures the effect of the learning on the learner's *job behaviours* (covered in detail in Chapter 20)

- *ultimate/results level* – which measures the effect of the learning on the *results* of the organisation, ie *organisational performance*. Hamblin (1974) divides this fourth level into two, distinguishing the impact of the learning on organisational objectives – such as sales, productivity, customer complaints – and looking at the economic question – ie some form of cost/benefit analysis (Chapter 20 covers the 'results' parts and Chapter 21 the cost/benefit issues).

(We use the terminology of reaction, learning, job behaviour and results to refer to the four levels. Some organisations refer to the above levels as Level 1 to Level 4.)

You will see that this model exactly matches the process and answers the question posed earlier, with the additional level of participants' reactions.

Using the model

The usefulness of the model derives from the way it can be employed as a diagnostic process or audit trail. The ultimate aim of most evaluation activity is either to prove some form of cost-benefit for the learning, or impact on organisational objectives, or at least some demonstrable change of performance/behaviours of those involved – ie the results and job-behaviour levels of the model. It can be tempting to focus only on those levels. However, all the levels are useful because each contributes to building up a complete picture of the process.

For example, if the results are poor at, say, the job-behaviour level – if, in other words, the performance/behaviour of all or some of the learners has not changed in the way anticipated – you may be left not knowing where the problem lies. The obvious spotlight tends to fall on the learning programme itself – perhaps the facilitator lacked the appropriate skills, the learning methods were unsuitable, the programme was too short/too long, etc. However, the problem can, and often does, lie elsewhere.

Before the learning intervention

Problems can occur either during the LNA process or during the process of selecting learners for the programme. This is the situation where some or all of the learning objectives may not be relevant to learners' needs or pitched at an inappropriate level. See the case study below.

CASE STUDY

The double whammy (1)

A salutary example of this occurred with a learning intervention to provide a *whole* department with project management skills. The focus of the intervention was on using an appropriate computer package to manage projects. Some of the learners' jobs did not involve projects at all! For others, the programme included skills in using the software package that they simply did not need. This had the double-whammy effect of causing frustration at learning skills for which they could not see the relevance and leaving insufficient time for the learning of the skills that they did need!

After the learning intervention

Problems can also occur during the transfer of the learning back into the workplace.

- Perhaps there are no opportunities to use or practise the new skills. See the two case studies below.

CASE STUDY

The double whammy (2)

Taking again the example of the project management skills programme described above – a number of problems occurred, but one of the most significant was that many of the participants did not get access to a computer for several months after the learning event. By the time they did, most had forgotten what they had learned.

There is often quite a short window of opportunity to use new skills before they are lost. It may seem surprising that such an obvious issue is overlooked, but it often happens even with major interventions of the kind described above. It is sometimes not even recognised as an issue.

CASE STUDY

Facilitating Facilitating

In a learning programme to provide managers with the ability to facilitate group discussion, it emerged that at least a third would not have the opportunity to use these skills in the general course of their work in the immediate future. In this situation, opportunities had to be devised especially to provide for the practice of these skills. This problem is even more likely to happen if the learning is not part of a major intervention – for example, when a learner seeks to develop his or her presentation skills by going on an open programme.

- Perhaps there is no support from the learners' managers or colleagues in helping to implement the new skills. A commonly quoted example is in the fraught area of customer care training, where learners will often comment that it was difficult to apply the new skills without the 100 per cent support of their organisation/manager/colleagues. This lack of support can take many forms, as for example if:
  - the organisation does not supply the appropriate conditions for using the new skills – eg through poor procedures
  - managers do not take an interest or do not provide feedback on the use of the skills
  - colleagues sabotage the implementation either passively by cynicism or actively by not supporting the new approach through their own methods of working/behaviours.

By using all the stages in the model, you can begin to eliminate some of the variables. For example, carrying out the second stage, the learning level, checks the extent to which the learning objectives have been met. This provides a check on the efficacy of the actual learning event itself. So in our situation of poor job behaviour level evaluation described earlier, if the learning level results are sound, then the problem lies in one of the two areas described above: either the learning objectives are inappropriate or some factor or factors has/have intervened after the learning. The first level of evaluation – the reaction level – can provide invaluable information on problems that have arisen during the learning event itself and often an insight into the causes if the intervention is less than effective.

Focus on outputs and processes

Traditionally, the focus of evaluation studies has tended to be on outcomes – what the learning intervention has *achieved* in terms of the development/improvement of knowledge, skills, attitudes and behaviours. However, evaluation is essentially itself a learning process – finding out what type of learning intervention works, so that it can be repeated. Also, we human beings are incredibly complex and the way we learn is also very complex. Learning facilitators are only too well aware that no two learning interventions are ever the same. You may in theory be delivering the identical programme, but each learner's reaction to the programme will be unique, and the interaction between the facilitator and the learners and the learners with each other will also be unique. This of course raises the vexed question – if you have evaluated a learning intervention with positive results, how can you guarantee that it will be equally effective with another group? Basically, you cannot, unless you have sought to understand the process underlying the learning intervention and why it was effective.

Evaluation that focuses solely on outcomes does not tend to provide helpful information which addresses the 'why?'/'what?'/'how?' questions – for example:

- Why did the programme achieve better results for some objectives/skills/areas of knowledge/competencies?
- What were the reasons for the programme achieving better results with some learners than others who experienced the same programme?
- How did the participants learn from a specific exercise?

Unless you know the answers to these questions it is very hard to make meaningful decisions about revising the learning process. For example, if the performance of the learners has not reached the required standard, unless one has some idea of why, it is very hard to know what to do. Should the learning objectives be tackled or the learning methods examined, and if so, in what way – or should the facilitators be replaced? Or should the specific learning programme be jettisoned altogether? Perhaps it is not the right intervention at all. Maybe the problem lies in the organisation of the work or with the management of the team rather than in the performance of the learners themselves.

As well as focusing on outcomes, it is important to explore these 'why?'/'what?'/'how?' questions during the evaluation process.

INVESTORS IN PEOPLE

The now well-known Investors in People Standard has done an enormous amount to put evaluation on the learning agenda. It sets out a national standard for effective investment in people. Any organisation can work towards this standard, and once it has been assessed as meeting the standard, it can be publicly recognised as an *Investor in People* and use the logo in its advertising, letter-headings and so forth. According to the latest *Company Report*: 'one in four of the working population is now employed by an accredited Investor in People organisation' (Investors in People UK, 2002).

The four over-arching principles of the Standard are:

1. *commitment* – An Investor in People is fully committed to developing its people in order to achieve its aims and objectives.

2. *planning* – An Investor in People is clear about its aims and its objectives and what its people need to do to achieve them.

3. *action* – An Investor in People develops its people effectively in order to improve its performance.

4. *evaluation* – An *Investor in People* understands the impact of its investment in people on its performance.

   (Source: Investors in People, UK 2002)

Essentially, through providing evidence against these principles, an organisation is assessed for the Standard, among other things, on the whole learning and development process – from the commitment to learning as an important contribution to the overall strategy of the organisation, through the planning and implementation stages, to reviewing the effectiveness of the learning.

Underpinning each of these principles is a series of assessment indicators. The indicators for the evaluation principle, with their associated evidence guides, are shown below.

Indicators	Evidence
10 The development of people improves the performance of the organisation, teams and individuals.	The organisation can show that the development of people has improved the performance of the organisation, teams and individuals.
11 People understand the impact of the development of people on the performance of the organisation, teams and individuals.	Top management understands the overall costs and benefits of the development of people and its impact on performance. People can explain the impact of their development on their performance, and the performance of their team and the organisation as a whole.
12 The organisation gets better at developing its people.	People can give examples of relevant and timely improvements that have been made to development activities.

Source: Investors in People, UK 2002

The comprehensive and systematic collection of evidence required to meet the 'evaluation principle' of the Standard is central to the content and philosophy of this book.

A LEARNING AND DEVELOPMENT CULTURE

For learning evaluation to make the fullest contribution to improving the quality of learning and development and its impact on performance, it is important that it is supported by what we call a learning and development culture. An important foundation-stone is usually a learning and development strategy that articulates key values and policies (see Chapter 15). At the heart of such a culture is that learners and their managers take joint ownership for learning – working in partnership to:

- identify the learning needs
- ensure that the most appropriate learning solution is provided
- facilitate the transfer of the learning back into the workplace.

This will usually mean that learners and their managers meet regularly to discuss performance and learning and development issues. It also means that everyone in the organisation understands the contribution that learning and development makes, to their own performance, to their team's performance and to the organisation's ability to meet its objectives.

The learning and development strategy would also include an evaluation strategy and plan that would set out:

- the organisation's support for evaluation and the contribution it can make to the effectiveness of learning and development in the organisation
- the policies and approach to be adopted – eg criteria for selecting learning interventions to be evaluated and at what level, who will be responsible for learning evaluation, how the process will be monitored, how the results will be fed back, etc
- a plan of evaluation activity over the time period of the learning and development plan
- a budget for evaluation.

Having an evaluation strategy has a double advantage – it means that your evaluation activity is planned *and* is taken seriously as part of the overall learning and development work.

CONCLUSION

Evaluation is often viewed as putting an additional burden of cost on the learning and development budget. However, we would argue that money spent on good LNA and useful evaluation will result in less money spent on learning delivery, but that money will be targeted on the learning that makes the most difference to organisational goals and the learning will be provided in the most cost-effective way. In other words, learning needs analysis and evaluation will pay for themselves!

In Chapter 17 we cover the important issue of how to collect the data that is a key part of any evaluation activity. (Those readers that want to focus on the evaluation process specifically might want to skip over this chapter in the first instance and read Chapters 18 to 20, which describe the different levels of evaluation – then return to discover more about this important subject.)

READING AND REFERENCE

HAMBLIN A. C. (1974), *Evaluation and Control of Training*, Maidenhead, McGraw-Hill.

INVESTORS IN PEOPLE UK (2002), *Investors in People UK Company Report 2001–2002*, Investors in People UK. www.iipuk.co.uk

INVESTORS IN PEOPLE UK (2002), *The Standard*, Investors in People UK (2002), www.iipuk.co.uk

KIRKPATRICK D. L. (1967), 'Evaluation of training', in Craig R. L. and Bittel L. R. (eds) *Training and Evaluation Handbook*, New York, McGraw-Hill.

PATTON M. Q. (1997), *Utilization-Focused Evaluation*, 3rd edn, London, Sage Publications.

WARR P., BIRD M. *and* RACKHAM N. (1970), *Evaluation of Management Training*, London, Gower.

17

Collecting the data

INTRODUCTION

How the data is collected is a key issue. The first, vital stage in any data collection exercise is to *plan* it. You must ask the questions:

- Why am I collecting the data? What is the purpose of the survey or data collection exercise? What are my objectives?
- Based on my objectives, what do I *need* to know? It is essential to be crystal clear about what information you need, and in what form. It is also important not to be side-tracked into collecting information that might be useful or seems interesting! The downfall of many data collection exercises is that they get bogged down by attempts to collect too much data. *It is crucial to remain focused on your objectives*.

You then need to decide on:

- the design of the study itself
- methods of data collection
- issues of validity and reliability.

This chapter looks at each of these areas in turn.

DESIGNING THE EVALUATION STUDY

There are three key design issues that must be considered:

- what the population of interest is
- whether to use a census or a sample
- what experimental design to use.

The population of interest

The first key issue you should think about is who you are going to get information from – ie who is the population of interest for the evaluation study. That population could, for example, include any or all of the following groups:

- the learners from some or all of the programmes
- their managers
- their staff
- their colleagues
- internal or external customers
- the facilitators of the learning programmes.

The first group is the obvious one – it would be an unusual evaluation study which did not seek information from the learners! However, if you are seeking information about performance or changes in performance, then the next four groups may provide useful perspectives. Finally, the other key participants in the process are the facilitators, who are likely to have views about how well the programme met its objectives, the types of learning methods used, and so on.

Census or samples

The next design issue involves deciding for each population of interest whether you should be conducting:

- a census – ie collecting data from everyone, or
- a sample – ie collecting data from only a subgroup of that population.

The option of sampling becomes important when evaluating large learning programmes, perhaps involving all or major sections of the organisation, when to carry out a census would prove very costly and time-consuming. If the sample is chosen properly – ie randomly – it is possible to draw conclusions about the whole population from the sample results. The selection of samples – there are several different methods – and using sample results is quite a complex issue and beyond the scope of this book. For further information on this subject we suggest reading *Managing Information and Statistics* (Bee and Bee, 1999).

Experimental design

This is a rather grand name for some quite simple but important concepts. In essence, every learner who undertakes a learning programme is involved in an experiment – will the learning programme achieve what it is supposed to do? This is just like trialing a new drug: you want to try it out and see if it works.

There is a range of experimental design approaches that can be adopted for a particular evaluation study. The two simplest involve only the participants in the learning programme. These are:

- taking measurements *after* the learning programme only, which usually involves comparisons against some target of desired performance
- taking measurements *before and after* the learning programme, and assessing any gains in performance.

The first approach allows for checking that the learning programme has achieved its objectives. However, without a starting-level there is no way of assessing how much the intervention has *contributed* to the achievement of these objectives. Perhaps all the learners could have achieved similar results without going through the programme!

The second approach does allow for the measurement of the gain in performance as a result of the learning programme. But hold on a minute – perhaps if this learning programme was spread over a period of time, the learners would have achieved this gain or a good part of it without the learning programme, just through experience on the job.

This leads us on to the more sophisticated design approaches that involve the use of *control groups*. However, before we go on to these more complex approaches we would like to reassure those of you that are feeling a little nervous that most evaluation studies use the very simple experimental designs described so far.

Control groups are used as a method of trying to eliminate the effects of other factors that might influence the results of the evaluation. A control group is chosen to be as similar as possible to the study group – ie the group receiving the learning. Both groups are assessed at the start. The study group receives the learning intervention, the control group does not, and both groups are assessed at the end. The gain in performance of the study group is then compared with the gain in performance of the control group. The difference in gain should at that point reflect the impact of the learning intervention over and above the other factors.

These different approaches are referred to as *experimental designs*. The designs can become even more complex. For example, there is evidence that merely being the recipient of attention in some form can have an effect on performance. In other words, simply being subject to the learning intervention (attention) may be causing some or all of the performance gain. This is often referred to as 'the Hawthorne effect' (see Chapter 10). It is an effect that can be counter-acted by giving the control group something to act as a sort of 'placebo' – ie to mimic the attention given by receiving the learning. Now using a placebo is a relatively simple concept – for example, in drug experiments where it can be represented by a sugar-pill that looks and tastes just like the drug. In the context of learning evaluation experiments it is not nearly so easy. In some studies the placebo used has been a form of team briefing. However, it is hard to find a placebo that would not have some sort of effect in its own right. One possibility is that the control group could receive a learning intervention in an area totally unrelated to the performance needs being addressed by the learning programme under study. To deal with this issue, some more sophisticated designs introduce a second control group which is given the placebo, while the first control group remains subject to no action.

Yet a further complication is added if it is felt that the results are affected simply by taking the measurements at the start – then a third control group is added which is only assessed at the end. These designs can be illustrated diagramatically as shown in Figure 12.

Figure 12 / ***Experimental designs***

Measuring against a target performance:				
A		*learning* ───────────	B	*measure*
Measuring changes in performance:				
• *no control group*				
A	*measure*	*learning* ───────────	B	*measure*
• *one control group (non-learning effects)*				
A	*measure*	*learning* ───────────	B	*measure*
C	*measure*	*no action* ───────────	D	*measure*
• *two control groups (Hawthorne effect)*				
A	*measure*	*learning* ───────────	B	*measure*
C	*measure*	*no action* ───────────	D	*measure*
E	*measure*	*placebo* ───────────	F	*measure*
• *three control groups (pre-learning measurement effect)*				
A	*measure*	*learning* ───────────	B	*measure*
C	*measure*	*no action* ───────────	D	*measure*
E	*measure*	*placebo* ───────────	F	*measure*
G		*no action* ───────────	H	*measure*

Source: (based on) Whitelaw (1972)

In practice it is difficult to find control groups that are similar to the group receiving the learning, and the difficulty is clearly compounded if more than one control group is required. In practice most evaluation studies either use no control group or at most one, either with or without the introduction of a placebo. However, understanding the purpose of the different designs helps towards understanding also the limitations of whatever design is chosen.

METHODS OF DATA COLLECTION

There are four main methods of collecting data (which are the same methods covered in Chapter 10: *Investigating the performance gap*):

- self-complete questionnaires
- interviews
- observation
- desk research.

Each method has its advantages and disadvantages which have to be taken into account when deciding on the best approach to collecting data for a particular evaluation purpose. We look briefly at each in turn and then cover the process of questionnaire design. Finally, we look at ways of integrating the data collection tools with the learning event itself.

Self-complete questionnaires

This is a very common form of data collection and basically the evaluator trades depth of information either to get breadth of coverage or for reduced costs.

Table 10 | *Advantages and disadvantages of self-complete questionnaires for collecting data*

Advantages	Disadvantages	Tips

• *a low-cost way to gather data*
 • *can be a quick way to gather data*
 • *makes least demands on the time of the participants in the survey*
 • *involves no 'observer/ interviewer' effects*
 • *if carefully designed, provides results that can be readily analysed*
	• *possibility of low response rates, which can lead to biased results – eg only those with a particular axe to grind will respond*
	 • *unsuitable for generating in-depth information*
	 • *not always suited to the target population – eg participants who do not normally complete forms/do office-type work as part of their normal jobs and therefore might find the completion of such forms difficult or off-putting*
	 • *requires very careful design to ensure clarity and lack of ambiguity*
		• *control/encourage the return of questionnaires by:*
		   – *monitoring and following up*
		   – *inducements – eg participating in a draw*
		 • *keep the questionnaire short and easy to complete, which generally means it must be highly structured – ie tick box options, with only a few questions allowing free or open comment*
		 • *consider using e-mail, disk format, etc, for ease of completion and return*

The development of organisational intranets has revolutionised the technology of self-complete questionnaires. Now these can be completed on-line and returned at the press of a button, making it easier both to complete and to return these questionnaires.

Interviews

There are four possible interview approaches available:

- the traditional face-to-face 1:1 interview
- the telephone interview
- group interviews
- video-conferencing interviews.

The traditional *face-to-face 1:1 interview* has the attributes listed in Table 11.

The *telephone interview* can be considerably cheaper, but is a less sensitive tool and the quality of probing and exploration of issues is reduced. Often the telephone interviews are highly structured, asking for tick-box-type responses, and become more similar to the self-complete questionnaires.

Group interviews, often referred to as focus groups, are excellent for raising and discussing issues. Their advantage is that they can provide powerful qualitative information on the learning experience and are particularly good for clarifying problem areas and establishing causes of effective and ineffective learning. Their disadvantage is that the group can be led down particular paths by one or two individuals with strong views.

Video-conferencing interviews make use of the power of the Internet/intranet to enable either

Table 11 | *Advantages and disadvantages of the face-to-face interview for collecting data*

Advantages	Disadvantages	Tips
• ensures a response! • enables responses on specific questions/issues to be clarified and probed • enables complex issues to be explored and generally allows for more in-depth information to be collected • although it is important to plan and structure the interview, this is usually an easier process than designing a self-complete questionnaire	• relatively costly • requires skilled interviewers • the involvement of an 'interviewer' can affect the results – ie interviewer bias as the respondent picks up overt or covert signals of how the interviewer expects the interviewee to respond • can be difficult to analyse because it usually generates qualitative data	• ensure that respondents are clear on the purpose of the interview • develop the interviewers' skills in research interview techniques and in the purpose of the data-collection exercise • include some structured questions – with range of responses listed on a card • include some semi-structured questions – ie interviewer categorises the response

1:1 interviews or group interviews to be carried out without the participants having to be together in the same place. This can reduce the costs of the interview approach considerably.

The *design* of interviews ranges from unstructured to highly structured. At one end of the spectrum, at its most simplistic, an unstructured approach would perhaps involve the interviewer asking the respondent to 'Tell me about the learning experience.' Any structuring would be simply to guide and focus the discussion along the way, and would not be predesigned but responsive to the information that was forthcoming.

In the middle of the spectrum lie interview designs that have pre-decided areas for questioning, with perhaps even specific questions identified and with varying degrees of freedom to probe and follow-up responses.

At the highly structured end are two types of interview designs:

- The first are similar to self-complete questionnaires, with specific questions, often with coded/structured responses – eg choosing a number on a scale, a particular option – and with the more open questions precisely worded.

- The second involve very specific and precise approaches to the interviewing process – eg critical incident interviews and repertory grid interviews; these are most commonly used for learning needs analysis (see Chapter 10), but can also be used in evaluation.

Observation

Observation is an important method of data collection in learning evaluation because learning is very often directed at skills/behaviour development.

Table 12 | *Advantages and disadvantages of observation for collecting data*

Advantages	Disadvantages	Tips
• *the skill/behaviour is being assessed directly* • *with many practical skills, it is the best method of assessment*	• *can be costly as there is usually a minimum observer-to-learner ratio of 1:1, and with some types of skill 2:1* • *can be a time-consuming approach* • *the results can be influenced by the Hawthorne effect – basically where people's behaviour is affected simply by the fact that they are being watched* • *if taking place in the workplace, can be disruptive*	• *use carefully designed observation sheets* • *develop the observers' skills in how to observe and in the detail of the specific observation study*

Desk research

This involves making use of data that has already been collected for other purposes and is therefore sometimes referred to as secondary research. It is an important method of data collection for results level evaluation where data on organisational performance will be required, and for monitoring performance data on individuals and/or work groups such as productivity and sales. Other examples are using the results of performance review interviews to monitor performance, project plans to monitor effectiveness of project planning programmes, etc. Desk research is also used for other purposes – eg to make comparisons with other organisations, to take into account non-learning effects on results such as economic conditions, etc. In addition, it covers activities such as reading up on evaluation studies carried out previously within the organisation and by other organisations.

See Table 13.

Table 13 | Advantages and disadvantages of desk research for collecting data

Advantages	Disadvantages	Tips
• *usually a low-cost method – the data has been collected (or will be collected) for another primary purpose* • *data can often be collected quickly*	• *the data is not always in exactly the form that it is required and it is important to be aware of its limitations – eg does it cover all employees or only particular groups, how accurate and reliable is it?* • *the data may be out of date* • *the data may be difficult to access owing to its confidentiality, or just the way the information may be held on the computer, etc*	• *As with any method of data collection it is vital to plan how the data is to be collected. However, with this method, since it does not usually involve the design of some sort of formal survey instrument such as a questionnaire, it is all too easy to leap straight in without a plan. This can lead to a considerable waste of time and, even worse, the wrong data being collected – so the message is: plan and design your desk research in just the same way as you would any more formal survey*

Design of data collection tools

Questionnaires in one guise or another feature in all the data collection methods:

- The self-complete questionnaire method requires a questionnaire that will stand on its own without the benefit of the further explanation that could be given by an interviewer or observer. It is usually highly structured.

- The interview method requires an interview form, which can range in format from a form that it is almost as highly structured as a self-complete questionnaire to one which just sets out the main areas or subject headings that are to be covered.

- The observation method requires an observation sheet to record the observed behaviour. These sheets can include questions ranging from simple yes/no statements to whether the particular behaviour or skill has been observed, noting the frequency of the behaviour occurring, through to rating the level of skill observed and making comments.

- The desk research method requires a recording plan which can vary from subject headings through to a detailed layout for the recording of the relevant data.

It is vital that the questionnaires are well designed. Questionnaires that are going to be used as formal survey instruments should go through the following stages:

- initial design
- pre-test – an informal trial, trying out the self-complete questionnaire or interview form, etc, on a small group as similar to the target population as possible
- redesign as necessary
- pilot survey – a small-scale test survey of the target population
- redesign as necessary
- full survey.

Appendix 17.1 provides a short introduction to questionnaire design covering the types of questions that can be asked and some useful tips particularly directed at the design of self-complete questionnaires. It also provides references for some useful further reading on the subject.

(NB It is important always to consider the inclusion of classification questions so that it is possible to monitor whether the effects of the learning have varied between different groups. Examples of classification questions have been included in appendix 17.1, but for the sake of brevity such questions have not been included in the sample questionnaires shown in the Appendices to Chapters 18 to 20.)

INTEGRATING EVALUATION WITH THE LEARNING

Some managers may see evaluation as an unnecessary cost, arguing that the money would be better spent on the learning intervention itself. There are, therefore, considerable advantages when choosing the methodology in looking for creative ways to use existing opportunities presented by the learning intervention itself as a means of data collection. Three examples of this approach are action plans/projects, reflection sheets/journals and e-learning tests.

Action plans/projects

Action plans are an example of the data collection opportunities that occur naturally within a learning intervention. Many learning programmes use action plans as an important way of helping the transfer of the learning back into the workplace. However, they also offer an excellent source of evaluation information. To what extent have the action plans been achieved? How relevant/useful were they on return to the workplace? If not, why were they not? See the next case study.

CASE STUDY

Timely actions

In the case of a time management programme, action plans provided a very fertile source of information on outcomes because they set out how the learners proposed to change the way they did their jobs. These outcomes were then used as the starting-point for a follow-up survey. It revealed that factors in the workplace intervened to make some of the proposed changes – eg the use of voice mail facilities and agreeing times with colleagues when they could work without interruptions – difficult to implement. This resulted in the following actions:

- an organisation-wide guide on the appropriate use of voice mail was drawn up
- in future programmes, more focus was to be given to negotiating and implementing 'quiet time' agreements.

Sometimes projects can be used as a very powerful way of measuring the benefits of a learning intervention in money terms. For example, consider an action learning programme where the focus of the learning was round a project for improving, in some way, the profitability of the organisation. It might be through improving productivity, reducing costs, increasing sales, or tackling waste. In these situations there will be a real quantifiable benefit at the end, and an added benefit is that the evaluation process simply has to assemble the information rather than directly collect it because the projects are set up to measure and record the benefits. See the case study below.

Profitable projects

A senior management programme for an international company, which was rather like a mini-MBA programme in content, included an individual practical project as the last module of the programme. It resulted in both a written project report and a real outcome for the organisation. An evaluation study looked at the outcomes of these projects and was able to arrive at a financial benefit. In addition, the written report on the way the learners tackled the project provided very useful information on how well the learning from the different modules had been applied.

Reflection sheets/journals

Another very useful source of evaluation information can be the use of reflection sheets/journals, etc. These are often used in programmes to encourage learners to reflect for themselves on key issues that have come up, learning points, areas to be followed up, etc. In their own right they can give a fascinating and often quite detailed insight into the learning that is going on during the programme. With planning they can also give even better evaluation information on the process of the learning event – for example, by including specific questions asking the learners to reflect on the process, such as on the learning methods or the facilitator's style, perhaps – as they experience the learning event.

Again this approach has a double-edged effect. The data is collected free for the evaluation (since it is part of the learning intervention) and the method of collecting the data encourages the learner to reflect on the learning process, which can have a very beneficial effect on the learning intervention itself. A good example of this was a programme for learning facilitators in carrying out learning needs analysis. One of the reflection sessions built into this programme raised concerns about the relevance of an LNA case study that was being used and allowed for change to be introduced there and then during the programme.

e-learning tests

Most e-learning/technology-based learning programmes incorporate some form of self-assessment as part of the package. These often take the form of tests to check the participant's initial knowledge and skills and then the participant's knowledge and skills after completion of the programme. Such information can clearly be very useful in evaluating the effectiveness of the learning programme (see Chapter 19).

VALIDITY AND RELIABILITY

There are three key aspects that must be considered in any evaluation study:

- internal validity
- external validity
- reliability.

(Please note that we are not talking about 'validation', which is a term that is sometimes used as an alternative to 'evaluation' when talking about whether learning objectives have been met.)

The *internal validity* of an evaluation study is concerned with how well the study measures what we want or are aiming to find out. This usually involves the adequacy and appropriateness of the measuring tool, the instrument, used for the data collection. For example, if we are using a questionnaire, are the questions appropriately worded to elicit the information that is required? Does the knowledge test effectively measure the knowledge that has been learned? Does the skills test include all the critical steps, and are the measurement scales used appropriate? If we are measuring work performance, have we established the appropriate indicators? Approaches such as testing the instruments widely, using alternative approaches to measure the same attribute, all help towards establishing the internal validity of the study.

The *external validity* of an evaluation study is concerned with the extent that the findings can be applied beyond the group involved in the study. If a study has measured the effectiveness of a specific learning programme using 50 learners from perhaps 200 learners that had been on the programme, can the results be applied to the whole 200? Here we are entering the realms of sampling that go beyond the remit of this book. However, the answer is a tentative yes, subject to the sample of 50 learners having been chosen appropriately (ie so that they represent the whole group) and acknowledging that any results are only estimates for the whole population and therefore that the actual result for the whole population lies somewhere in a range around the estimate. As we explained earlier in this chapter, sampling is quite a complex subject: some suggested further reading material is given at the end of this chapter.

On a wider scale, if a learning programme has been assessed as effective in one area of the organisation, can you generalise the conclusions to the whole organisation? Well again, we are afraid it all depends... How similar are the learners in their starting levels of knowledge and skills, their experience of the organisation, etc? If you demonstrate that one, two, three... learning programmes are effective, does this mean that they all are? It depends! It is often very tempting to use the results of evaluation studies beyond their original purpose. The message from this section is that you need to take care when you do so, and be very clear what assumptions you are making when you do.

The last issue that must be considered is that of reliability. The *reliability* of an evaluation study is the extent to which the results can be replicated – ie if the study was repeated, the results would be the same. The obvious approach to dealing with this issue is to repeat tests and observations. Also, techniques such as including the same question but in different forms, using multiple observers, etc, can be helpful.

This list of issues that must be considered can sometimes sound rather daunting – how can you possibly design an evaluation study that passes all these *tests*? The answer is that in practice you cannot – what is important is that you are *aware* of the issues and that as far as is practicable you have designed and then used your study in as professional a way as is possible.

Often the issue of reliability and reducing errors tends to dominate. Patton (1997) uses the lovely parable:

A man found his neighbour down on his knees under a street lamp looking for something. 'What have you lost, friend?'

'My key,' replied the man on his knees.

After a few minutes of helping him to search the neighbour asked, 'Where did you drop it?'

'In that dark pasture,' answered his friend.

'Then why, for heaven's sake, are you looking for it here?'

'Because there is more light here.'

Often we are tempted to use measures because they are available, easy to use, reliable, etc, and we lose sight of whether they will actually help us answer our evaluation question. There is no point in having very accurate data that does not provide useful information. The message is to keep the focus on the evaluation question and then do your best to optimise the quality and integrity of your data.

CONCLUSION

In this chapter we have introduced the issues concerned with the design of an evaluation study and examined the different methods of collecting data. Because some form of questionnaire is at the heart of all the data collection methods, the basic principles of questionnaire design are also set out. In addition, we suggest looking at ways in which the evaluation can be integrated with the learning process – which has the double benefit of providing low-cost information and reinforcing the learning process. Finally, we have looked at the key issues of how valid and reliable our evaluation results are. We move on now to tackling learning evaluation at the first level – reaction level evaluation.

READING AND REFERENCE

BEE R. *and* BEE F. (1999), *Managing Information and Statistics*, London, CIPD.

PATTON M. Q. (1997), *Utilization-Focused Evaluation*, 3rd edn, London, Sage Publications.

WHITELAM M. (1972), *The Evaluation of Management Training* – a preview, London IPM.

INTRODUCTION TO QUESTIONNAIRE DESIGN

In this Appendix we provide a brief introduction to questionnaire design and cover:

- the types of questions that can be used
- some useful do's and don'ts for the design of questionnaires, particularly the self-complete variety.

Types of questions

There are five main types of question:

- classification questions
- coded/structured questions
- open questions
- semantic-differential-type questions
- Lickert-type questions.

We will look at each of these types of question in turn.

Classification questions

DESCRIPTION

Questions to enable respondents to be 'classified' into particular groups

PURPOSE

- for analysis of the data, to identify the effect of the learning intervention on different groups of learners
- to check how representative the sample is of the whole population against criteria such as age, gender, ethnic origin, occupation, grade, department.

EXAMPLES

GENDER (tick one box)

Male ☐   Female ☐

ETHNIC GROUP

Choose ONE section from A to E, then tick the appropriate box to indicate your cultural background.

A White

☐ British
☐ Irish
☐ Any other White background, please write in . . . .

B Mixed Black

☐ White and Black Caribbean
☐ White and Black African
☐ White and Asian
☐ White and other Mixed background, please write in . . . .

C Asian or Asian British

☐ Indian
☐ Pakistani
☐ Bangladeshi
☐ Any other Asian background, please write in . . . .

D Black or Black British

☐ Caribbean
☐ African
☐ Any other Black background, please write in . . . .

E Chinese

☐ Chinese
☐ Any other background, please write In . . . .

Source of ethnic origin categories: www.cre.gov.uk.

ISSUES

- When to ask the questions – at the beginning or the end of a questionnaire? On balance, we would advise at the end, because this type of question can inhibit people from responding
- If the questionnaire is being completed anonymously, it is important that the combination of classification questions do not identify an individual.
- Ensure that a full range of options is included.

Coded/structured questions

DESCRIPTION

The respondent is given a limited choice of answers

PURPOSE

- to test knowledge
- to establish facts
- to measure attitudes.

EXAMPLES

- How long must an employee have been employed before s/he can bring a claim for unfair dismissal on the grounds of race or sex? Please tick the appropriate box:

One year	☐
Two years	☐
No time limit	☐
Don't know	☐

- Please indicate the five most important purposes of team briefings.
  Put a 1 against the most important, a 2 against the next most important, and so on.

Give information on objectives/targets	☐
Receive information/feedback	☐
Discuss company issues	☐
Discuss job issues	☐
....	
....	
Other, please describe: _____	

ADVANTAGES

- quick and easy to complete
- easy to analyse.

DISADVANTAGES

- hard to design because it is important to offer a comprehensive/complete set of options
- forces choice, may cause bias.

Open questions

DESCRIPTION

The respondent is free to give any answer

PURPOSE

- to test knowledge, usually of more complex areas/issues
- to measure attitudes.

EXAMPLES

What information should be included in the record of . . .?
Describe what you would do if . . .
What do you think about the new proposals for . . .?

ADVANTAGES

- gives no hints to the answers
- allows free expression of views
- no bias
- easy to design.

DISADVANTAGES

- difficult to analyse
- requires a strong marking frame – ie a framework for assessing the answers in the case of knowledge tests and for coding and categorising attitude and opinion information.

Semantic – differential type questions

DESCRIPTION

The respondent is asked to assess something on a 7-point scale. Other number scales can be used.

PURPOSE

- to assess skills
- to measure attitudes.

EXAMPLE

Please assess the chairing skills of the learner, by circling the appropriate rating.

Strong control	1	2	3	4	5	6	7	Weak control
Listened well	1	2	3	4	5	6	7	Did not listen

....

....

What are your views on bullying in the workplace?

Very serious issue	1	2	3	4	5	6	7	Not a serious issue
Occurs frequently	1	2	3	4	5	6	7	Occurs not at all

ADVANTAGES

- allows for a structured range of responses
- easy to analyse.

DISADVANTAGES

- subjective judgements made on rating scale – ie what is a 3 to one individual might be a 4 to another.

ISSUES

- whether or not to be consistent with which is the favourable extreme – ie left or right
- what range of scale to use – common ranges are 4 to 10
- whether to have a middle option – ie to use an even-number scale to force a choice between the top half and the bottom half of the scale and avoid respondents' tendency to go for the middle option.

Lickert-type questions

DESCRIPTION

The respondent is asked to indicate his or her views against a rating that is specified

PURPOSE

- to assess skills
- to measure attitudes/opinions.

EXAMPLES

Please indicate your views on the new disciplinary procedures, by ticking the appropriate box.

	Strongly agree	Agree	Not sure	Disagree	Strongly disagree
Easy to understand	☐	☐	☐	☐	☐
Will improve discipline	☐	☐	☐	☐	☐
....					
....					

Please assess the chairing skills of the learner, by ticking the appropriate box.

	Poor	Fair	Good	Very Good
Control of meeting	☐	☐	☐	☐
Listening skills	☐	☐	☐	☐
....				
....				

ADVANTAGES

- allows for a structured range of responses
- specifies the meaning of the scale.

DISADVANTAGES

- constrains response
- can cause bias.

ISSUES

- important to have a balanced set of response options – ie of favourable/unfavourable responses
- whether to have a middle option (for the same reasons as listed for the semantic-differential-type question).

The do's and don'ts of questionnaire design (self-complete questionnaires)

- Keep the questionnaire as short as possible.

- Keep questions as short and simple as possible.

- Use simple language – avoid technical/jargon words/acronyms.

  eg How many Special Incidents have you been involved in?
      How many DP forms are there?
      Give examples of when and how you have used DCF techniques.

- Avoid questions that rely heavily on memory – use the appropriate timespan.

  eg How many learning programmes have you been on in the last five years? [*Can
      you remember how many learning programmes you have been on in the last five
      years? A year may be the more appropriate timespan.*]
      How many times have you used a particular computer package – eg a
      spreadsheet package – in the last six months?
      [*One month might be more appropriate.*]

- Avoid ambiguous questions.

  eg How many employees are you responsible for?
      [*What does 'responsible for' mean? The employees that directly work for you, all
      the employees in the department that you head, those that you are professionally
      responsible for?*]
      Do you have a computer?
      [*What does 'have' mean? At home or at work, for your sole use, or access to?*]

- Avoid leading questions and using emotive words.

  eg Do you feel that your manager should be *more* supportive?
      Do you think the company should *forbid* the use of telephones for personal
      calls?

- Avoid multiple questions.

  eg Do you think the department needs more and better team briefings?

- Avoid double negatives.

  eg Please indicate whether you agree or disagree with the following statement:
      Managers should not be required to record their time on duty.
      Agree   ☐
      Disagree   ☐

- Try to avoid hypothetical questions – you will get a hypothetical answer!

  eg What would you do if a customer was shouting and being abusive on the shop
      floor?
      [*It is more productive to probe experience – eg What did you do when . . . ?*]

- If you are providing a structured list of choices, always give a Don't Know, Not Applicable, Other, Please Specify option.
- PAY ATTENTION TO DETAIL

    eg. Instructions for completing the questionnaire or individual questions, eg
    - tick one box only
    - routing or skip-to instructions – if Yes, go to Q6 . . .
    - contiguous, not overlapping categories – age 21–25, 26–30, 31–35
      not 21–25, 25–30, 30–35.

Reading and Reference

For a good all-round introduction to questionnaire design, try Oppenheim (2000). For an easy-to-read lively guide to primarily the structuring and wording of questions and some pitfalls to avoid, try Converse and Presser (1986).

CONVERSE J. M. *and* PRESSER S. (1986), *Survey Questions: Handcrafting the standardised questionnaire*, London, Sage Publications.

OPPENHEIM A. N. (2000), *Questionnaire Design, Interviewing and Attitude Measurement*, Continuum International Publishing.

18
Reaction level evaluation (level 1)

INTRODUCTION

This is the first stage of the multi-level model introduced in Chapter 16. It explores the participants' reactions to the learning programme and basically answers the questions:

- how satisfied were they with the learning experience?
- how effective did they *feel* it had been in meeting their learning needs?

This is the most common form of evaluation carried out – largely because it is a relatively quick and low-cost approach. Most organisations carry out some form of reaction level evaluation.

WHAT DOES REACTION LEVEL EVALUATION TELL US?

There is some scepticism about the value of this type of evaluation, which is essentially subjective and is often referred to rather derogatively as 'happy-sheets'! However, in our view, it has four useful purposes:

- As part of a diagnostic process or audit trail it can help detect possible causes when a learning programme is identified as not being effective at one of the higher levels of evaluation – eg when monitoring behaviour in the job.

- Using a properly designed instrument, it can be argued that the learners themselves have the best insight into whether the intervention has met their own learning needs.

- Intuitively, one feels that if participants have found a learning intervention enjoyable, satisfying, stimulating, etc, it is more likely that they will be willing to put the new learning into action.

- On a very practical level, the participants will have the most relevant views on the quality of the venue, catering, accommodation, etc.

However, equally, it is important to note that learners' 'happiness' with a programme does not necessarily mean that the learning intervention will be effective in changing their job behaviour or in meeting business needs. The approach has the following main limitations:

- As we note in later chapters, the participants may have a good learning experience but the learning may not be appropriate for their work, or other factors in the workplace can intervene to affect the transfer of the learning back to the job.

- Participants may not always be honest in their feedback – they may temper any negative feedback for fear of upsetting/offending the facilitators, or alternatively, exaggerate their negative feedback, perhaps, if they feel that they have not participated or performed appropriately during the learning event.

- Participants may have found the learning personally challenging at the time and signalled 'unhappiness' through the reaction-level evaluation – but then go on to make changes in the way they work.

The other 'reactions' that can usefully be explored are those of the facilitators and, where relevant, any observers (sometimes involved in pilots or as part of quality-control systems).

HOW DO WE DO IT?

This form of evaluation is normally undertaken using a self-complete questionnaire. The questionnaire is usually highly structured – ie the learner has to choose between a range of options – with one or two general open questions at the end. These questionnaires are not hard to design and usually cover the areas of:

- the existence/adequacy of pre-course briefing
- the extent to which learners *feel* that the learning objectives of the course have been met
- relevance to the learning need
- the competence of the facilitator(s)
- the effectiveness of the learning methods used
- the quality/usefulness of learning materials – eg hand-outs, videos
- facilities – eg the venue, catering, accommodation
- the adequacy of support for any special needs of the participants
- administration – both before and during the event.

The length and detail of the questionnaire depends on the nature of the programme and the type of participants involved. Some examples of reaction-level questionnaires are provided in appendices at the end of this chapter. Appendix 18.1 is a detailed questionnaire and might be most useful for management programmes. Appendix 18.2 might be used for short courses or for technical and basic vocational learning programmes where a simpler questionnaire might be appropriate.

The evaluation is usually carried out at the end of a programme, although it can be carried out at the end of various stages – eg at the end of each day, or at the end of specific sections of the programme. If a programme is longer than a week, it is sensible to seek the participants' reactions at the end of discrete parts, such as modules. If a programme is being piloted, it may be useful (subject to participant fatigue!) to complete questionnaires at the end of each session.

SOME KEY ISSUES

Two key issues are whether the questionnaires should be:

- completed during the programme, rather than being taken out and completed by participants away from the programme environment
- completed anonymously.

The first is a much-debated issue. There is little doubt that the traditional approach of completing these questionnaires in the last half-hour of a learning event causes a number of problems. The learners may:

- not have had time to reflect on the issues being raised by the questionnaire
- be tired (and keen to get off home!)
- be influenced by the group view
- be too aware of the presence of the facilitator, which may inhibit honest responses.

An alternative approach is to ask the learners to complete the questionnaires after the programme and return them. This overcomes most of the above problems. However, many organisations try this approach and then find that it founders on the difficulty of getting the questionnaires returned. The result is either a low response rate or considerable administrative effort to ensure a decent level of return. The situation can be improved by using on-line questionnaires and workflow systems that enable returns to be chased electronically and automatically.

In practice, the best approach is probably to have the questionnaires completed during the programme, but to follow some simple guidelines:

- Introduce and hand out the questionnaires at the *beginning* of the programme, so that participants can reflect on the questions during the event.
- Emphasise that the purpose of the questionnaires is to ensure that the learning is meeting their needs and to continuously monitor and improve quality.
- Schedule time for completion of the questionnaires in the programme.
- Brief the facilitators on how to introduce and administer the questionnaires.

The second issue is anonymity. Again there are pros and cons. Clearly, participants may feel more able to give honest feedback if they cannot be identified. This may particularly be the case in small organisations who use internal facilitators perceived as colleagues. The major drawback is that responses cannot be followed up. So, for example, if some learners rate some aspect of the programme, or the whole of it, as poor, it is not possible to go back and find out more details. Also, from a customer-care perspective there are considerable benefits to be gained from following up on your dissatisfied customers.

SOME USEFUL APPROACHES

Although self-complete questionnaires are by far the most common approach, there are a number of other methods that can be used:

- Telephone interviews provide the opportunity to explore reactions in more depth and probe any problem areas. This is clearly a more costly approach.

- Focus groups of learners can again provide more in-depth information. Using a neutral facilitator (ie not the one that facilitated the learning event itself) is preferable. This approach can be very helpful in getting to the root of any problem areas and coming up with solutions. It is a particularly useful technique when piloting new programmes. The disadvantage of this approach is that it may prove difficult to distinguish issues affecting individuals from wider issues affecting the group.

- Self-complete flipcharts are a more informal way of recording reactions. A flipchart is put up and learners invited to write their comments, either directly or using Post-It notes, on the chart. These can be used during the learning event as a means of generating feedback and enabling the facilitator to respond during the event or at the end to record reaction-level information in a more dynamic and informal way. Structuring the chart – eg into quadrants and using symbols (see Appendix 18.3 in Appendix 18.3) – will make it more effective.

The other important 'reactions' it might be helpful to monitor at this stage are those of the other key players in the process – the facilitators. They will probably provide the best insight into why certain learning objectives might not have been met – perhaps because of the starting-levels of knowledge and skills of that particular group or because it became apparent that these were not relevant or less relevant than some other areas of the learning programme. Their comments on the general content, level, length of the programme and learning methods used may be particularly useful in the early stages of a learning programme's life. As with the learners, the facilitators' views on the practical aspects of the programme – eg quality of learning facilities – are particularly relevant. An example of a facilitator feedback form is provided in Appendix 18.4. Some organisations use these, but their use is not as widespread as might be expected given what a simple and cheap form of information they provide.

Remember, it is also important to evaluate external learning events. This sometimes gets overlooked because these types of interventions are often used for individual learning needs rather than for groups. However, it is equally important to monitor the quality and effectiveness of this type of learning intervention.

USING THE RESULTS

It is important to analyse the results and then demonstrate that these results are used, with clear actions flowing from them, to improve learning interventions in your organisation. See the two case studies overleaf.

> ### CASE STUDY
>
> **Tight timing**
>
> In a major corporation, a one-day learning programme had been set up to help middle managers develop their strategic planning skills. The reaction level questionnaires after the first tranche of programmes were showing disappointing results on the extent to which the learners felt the learning objectives had been met. A clue to the problem lay in a question which asked about the pace and intensity of the course – a high proportion of learners were signalling that there was just not enough time to do justice to the exercises and to reflect and discuss the issues. The programme was redesigned to span two days, and worked well thereafter.

> ### CASE STUDY
>
> **Charity begins in-house**
>
> A charity sent a number of its staff on an open programme on customer care. The organisation asked the staff to complete the same reaction level questionnaire as was used for internal programmes. The results were generally poor. Because the questionnaire used was a very simple one with tick-box answers, it was decided to telephone the learners and get some more in-depth responses. The common theme was that the facilitators of the programme had little understanding of the customer-care issues of charities. Also, there were concerns that the facilitators reacted badly to feedback offered early in the programme, and comments such as 'abrupt, unhelpful, dismissive' were made. The learning manager contacted the company running the open programmes with this feedback and secured a substantial discount of the fees for the programme. She also decided to research other open programmes on customer care, with some very specific questions about their suitability for charity staff, and investigate the costs of running a tailored in-house programme.

The great advantage of reaction level evaluation is that the feedback comes quickly. So if you are running a number of programmes, it is possible to make an early intervention which will benefit later cohorts. Often it is only a 'light hand on the tiller' required – such as updating learning materials.

CONCLUSION

As noted earlier, this level of evaluation can provide a lot of information at a relatively low cost. Once they have been designed (and organisations mostly use a couple of standard questionnaires which are then only customised in a minor way – perhaps to make changes to the learning objectives), the data collection is free in that the forms are usually administered and collected by the learning facilitators. The approach of generic questionnaires has a double advantage: it cuts down the design costs, and more importantly allows comparisons to be made easily between different learning programmes. However, reaction level evaluation can generate an enormous amount of data. Many organisations now design their questionnaires so that they can be scanned directly into a computer and analysed using specifically developed computer programs.

We shall go on now to look at the next level of evaluation – the learning level.

APPENDIX 18.1

REACTION LEVEL QUESTIONNAIRES FOR LEARNERS (DETAILED FORMAT)

LEARNER ASSESSMENT OF THE LEARNING PROGRAMME

Programme title: _____   Programme date: _____

Name: _____   Manager's name: _____

Job title: _____   Job title: _____

Department: _____

We want to ensure that the learning you undertake is of high quality and of relevance to your job. We would be grateful if you would complete this questionnaire as honestly and as fully as possible.

1 PRE-PROGRAMME BRIEFING

Did you receive a pre-programme briefing from your manager?   Yes ☐   No ☐

If Yes, please indicate the extent to which the briefing helped you prepare for the programme by circling the appropriate rating (1 indicating of little or no help ... 6 indicating of great help).

Knowing what the learning objectives of the programme were   1   2   3   4   5   6

Understanding why you were on the programme   1   2   3   4   5   6

Understanding how the programme related to your job   1   2   3   4   5   6

2 LEARNING OBJECTIVES

Please indicate the extent to which you feel the learning objectives were met by circling the appropriate rating (1 indicating not met at all ... 6 indicating fully met).

1 _____   1   2   3   4   5   6

2 _____   1   2   3   4   5   6

3 _____   1   2   3   4   5   6

4 _____   1   2   3   4   5   6

5 _____   1   2   3   4   5   6

6 _____   1   2   3   4   5   6

3 PRACTICAL RELEVANCE

Please indicate the practical relevance of the programme to your job by circling the appropriate rating.

Not relevant   1   2   3   4   5   6   Very relevant

4 LEARNING METHODS

In the development of your understanding and skills, please comment on the usefulness of the following learning methods. Please circle the appropriate rating (1 indicating of no use … 6 of great use) or the Not Used category.

Input sessions	1	2	3	4	5	6	Not Used
Group discussions	1	2	3	4	5	6	Not Used
Case studies	1	2	3	4	5	6	Not Used
Role-plays	1	2	3	4	5	6	Not Used
Practical exercises	1	2	3	4	5	6	Not Used
Videos	1	2	3	4	5	6	Not Used
Hand-outs	1	2	3	4	5	6	Not Used
Other _____	1	2	3	4	5	6	

5 FACILITATOR(S)

In the development of your understanding and skills, please comment on the quality of your facilitator(s) by circling the appropriate rating (1 indicating low quality … 6 high quality).

Lead facilitator

Appropriate pace	1	2	3	4	5	6
Knowledgeable	1	2	3	4	5	6
Creating interest	1	2	3	4	5	6
Involving the group	1	2	3	4	5	6

Second facilitator

Appropriate pace	1	2	3	4	5	6
Knowledgeable	1	2	3	4	5	6
Creating interest	1	2	3	4	5	6
Involving the group	1	2	3	4	5	6

Other speakers/facilitators

_____	1	2	3	4	5	6
_____	1	2	3	4	5	6

6 FACILITIES AND ADMINISTRATION

Please indicate your satisfaction with the quality of the facilities and administration by circling the appropriate rating (1 indicating low quality . . . 6 indicating high quality) or the Not Used category.

Facilities

Learning room(s)	1	2	3	4	5	6	Not Used
Catering	1	2	3	4	5	6	Not Used
Accommodation	1	2	3	4	5	6	Not Used
Convenience of location	1	2	3	4	5	6	Not Used
Other _____	1	2	3	4	5	6	

Administration

Joining instructions

− timeliness	1	2	3	4	5	6	Not Used
− adequacy	1	2	3	4	5	6	Not Used
Handling of any enquiries	1	2	3	4	5	6	Not Used
Other _____	1	2	3	4	5	6	

Special Needs

If you had any special needs, please set out what these were and comment on how well they were met.

7 GENERAL COMMENTS

Please add any comments that may help us improve the quality of the learning experience − ie in terms of meeting your expectations and needs, making the programme more relevant to your job, providing a high quality of learning and facilities.

APPENDIX 18.2

REACTION LEVEL QUESTIONNAIRE FOR LEARNERS (SIMPLE FORMAT)

LEARNER ASSESSMENT OF THE LEARNING PROGRAMME

Programme title: _____   Programme date: _____

Name: _____   Manager's name: _____

Job title/grade: _____   Job title/grade: _____

Department: _____

We want to ensure that the learning you receive is of high quality and of relevance to your job. We would be grateful if you would complete this questionnaire as honestly and as fully as possible.

---

1 BEFORE THE PROGRAMME

Did you receive a pre-programme briefing from your manager?   Yes ☐   No ☐

Did you receive joining instructions for the programme?   Yes ☐   No ☐

If Yes, please indicate your views on the quality of the briefing and instructions by ticking the appropriate box.

	Poor quality	Fair quality	Good quality	Very good quality
Briefing prepared me well for the programme (about what I was supposed to learn, why I was on the course, relevance to my job)	☐	☐	☐	☐
Instructions received in good time	☐	☐	☐	☐
Instructions were clear	☐	☐	☐	☐

2 ON THE PROGRAMME

Please indicate your views on the quality of the programme by ticking the appropriate box.

	Poor quality	Fair quality	Good quality	Very good quality
Meeting your learning objectives	☐	☐	☐	☐
Relevance to your job	☐	☐	☐	☐
The facilitator(s) helping you to learn	☐	☐	☐	☐
The hand-outs clear and useful	☐	☐	☐	☐
The adequacy of the learning room(s)	☐	☐	☐	☐
The quality of the catering	☐	☐	☐	☐

3 GENERAL COMMENTS

Please add any comments that may help us improve the quality of your learning experience.

APPENDIX 18.3

REACTION LEVEL FLIPCHART FOR LEARNERS

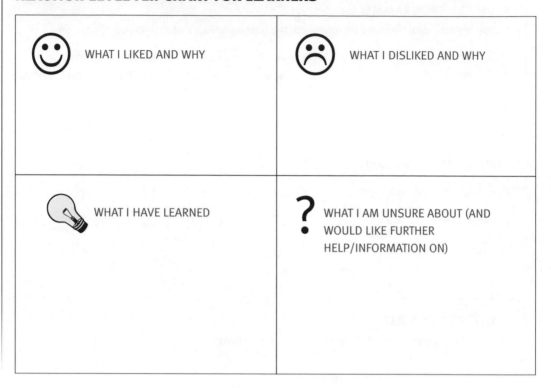

:) WHAT I LIKED AND WHY	:(WHAT I DISLIKED AND WHY
💡 WHAT I HAVE LEARNED	? WHAT I AM UNSURE ABOUT (AND WOULD LIKE FURTHER HELP/INFORMATION ON)

REACTION LEVEL QUESTIONNAIRE FOR FACILITATORS

FACILITATOR FEEDBACK ON THE LEARNING PROGRAMME

Programme title: _____   Programme date: _____

Name: _____   Organisation: _____
(if applicable)

Did you develop the programme?   Yes   ☐
No   ☐

How many times have you delivered this programme?   Only this once   ☐
2–5 times   ☐
6+ times   ☐

We want to ensure that the learning taking place is as effective as possible. We would be grateful if you would complete this questionnaire.

---

1 LEARNING OBJECTIVES

Please comment on the extent to which you felt the learning objectives of the programme were met, and on any factors that might have affected their achievement.

---

2 CONTENT, LEVEL AND LENGTH

Please comment on whether you felt the content, level and length of the programme were about right. If not, please put forward some ideas for how the programme can be improved.

---

3 LEARNING METHODS

Please comment on the effectiveness of the learning methods used in meeting the learning objectives.

4 FACILITIES AND ADMINISTRATION

a) Please comment on the adequacy and quality of the facilities.

b) Please comment on the adequacy and quality of the general accommodation, catering and service.

c) Please comment on the quality of the administration both before and during the programme.

5 GENERAL COMMENTS

a) Please comment on whether you changed the content, learning methods, etc for this particular learning group, and if so, the reasons for doing so.

b) Please add any comments which may help us improve the quality of the learning experience – ie in terms of meeting the learners' expectations and needs, making the programme more relevant to their jobs, providing a high quality of learning and facilities.

19

Learning level evaluation (level 2)

INTRODUCTION

We have dealt with reaction level evaluation, a stage probably familiar to most readers, and now move on to the possibly more uncharted waters of learning level evaluation. However, this level of evaluation will provide some key information in our 'detective' work in assessing the effectiveness of our learning interventions. It is the second stage of the multi-level model introduced in Chapter 16. This stage is sometimes referred to as 'immediate level' or 'level 2' evaluation. It seeks to assess what learning has taken place, and takes as its starting-point or foundation the learning objectives for the intervention.

WHAT DOES LEARNING LEVEL EVALUATION TELL US?

There are two types of assessment involved:

- The first measures whether the learning objectives have been achieved – ie whether the learners have met the required level of knowledge, skills, attitudes or behaviour.

- The second measures the gain in learning, for which reason assessment is required before and after the intervention.

A key point is that the assessment takes place in the learning environment rather than during normal work performance. It is *not* assessing whether the learning has been transferred into the workplace, but simply what has been learned from the programme. Most commonly it takes place at the end, or at the end of stages, of the learning event and takes the form of a 'test'. Occasionally, it may take place in the work environment but under learning/test conditions – as, for example, a learner train driver might be tested on a train with an accompanying instructor.

For individual assessment

Learning level evaluation is most commonly carried out in situations where it is important that the learner reaches a certain standard before being able to operate in the 'real' world. Obvious examples are train drivers, doctors, electricians, police officers, etc, for whom it is clearly essential to have a certain level of knowledge and skills before they start to carry out their jobs. The primary purpose of this activity is assessment of the participants rather than evaluation of the event, and individual results are often not combined nor any lessons learned from the process.

As a diagnostic tool – exploring the audit trail

However, learning level evaluation also provides important information for the *audit trail* we discussed in Chapter 16 because it gives direct feedback on the learning delivery process itself and can help identify issues/problems with the learning needs analysis. Poor results will indicate that the intervention has been ineffective in meeting the learning objectives.

There are basically two types of poor result:

- The results are poor for only a small number of learners.
- The results are generally poor for all learners.

If the results are poor for only for one or two learners, this might suggest that:

- the intervention was inappropriate for those particular learners – ie there was a poor fit between their learning needs and the learning offered
- those learners had not approached the learning in a positive way, for whatever reason
- the relationship between the facilitator and these learners had not proved productive.

Clearly, it is important to identify the cause of the problem so that appropriate action can be taken to remedy the situation for those specific learners. The evaluator must also keep a weather eye out for patterns – is it always learners from an ethnic minority group or a particular department who achieve poor results? If such a pattern emerges, then a more major investigation might be required because it might suggest that the learning is culturally biased, that the facilitator had difficulty relating to particular groups, that the learning style or methods are less appropriate to participants from particular backgrounds, or that something else of the sort was wrong.

However, the more critical situation arises when the results are generally poor. Identifying the causes requires some nifty detective work. Among the possible causes might be:

- the performance of the facilitator(s)
- the learning methods used
- the content/level of the event
- any combination of these.

The first two are concerned with the development and delivery part of the learning process, and the third would suggest that the LNA was inadequate in that it had not correctly specified the learning need. This is when the reaction level evaluation can be very useful because it is likely that the learners themselves will have identified the problem area. The other obvious source of readily available information is the facilitator – which is when facilitator reaction level questionnaires (which are used on all CIPD learning events) come into their own. If the case is still unsolved, interviewing the facilitator and a sample of the learners may provide the answers.

Doing more learning level assessment/evaluation

Finally, it can be argued that we are perhaps a little cavalier in our attitudes to establishing whether people have adequate levels of knowledge, skills and behaviours to do their jobs. What is the potential harm done to the business by someone handling a customer complaint badly, carrying out a performance review interview poorly, writing incomprehensible reports? Commonly, learners on customer care programmes, performance review interviewing programmes, report writing programmes are not formally assessed as to whether they meet required standards. It may be done informally by the facilitator through observing the learner during the various exercises. There can be a strong case for introducing learning level assessment with these types of programmes, which would have the double benefit of ensuring minimum standards of performance on return to work as well as providing evaluation information.

HOW DO WE DO IT?

Obviously, the target population for learning level evaluation is always the learners. How we tackle learning level evaluation usually depends on the nature of the learning that is taking place. Chapter 9 describes the main types of competencies and hence learning:

- knowledge
- skills
- attitudes and behaviours.

We look at each in turn.

Knowledge

Knowledge learning is most often assessed using some form of self-complete questionnaire – we are familiar with the concept of a written test or exam. There are three basic types:

- a simple questionnaire that requires the learner to answer either yes/no/don't know or true/false/don't know to a list of statements
- a multiple-choice questionnaire which may offer the learner a number of choices of answer
- an open-ended questionnaire which requires free-form essay-type answers.

The first two types of questionnaire are most useful for testing knowledge of rules and regulations and simple procedures. The third type of questionnaire is most useful for testing learners' understanding of more complex subjects or how they may react to more complex situations. The first two types of questionnaire require very careful design, but then are quick and straightforward to assess. Care needs to be taken over how the questions are phrased and, in the case of the multi-choice questionnaire, the range of choices and the positioning of the correct choice has to be thought through. The open-ended questionnaire is usually easier to design, but the answers are more difficult to assess. It is important to draw up a clear and comprehensive marking scheme for this type of questionnaire. With all the questionnaires it is important that the questions are clear and unambiguous.

Examples of the three types of knowledge-assessment questionnaires are shown as appendices 19.1 to 19.3. These are all based on a learning programme on how to handle disciplinary situations in a particular organisation. It can be seen that the first two deal with the fairly simple concepts of the knowledge of relevant employment law and organisational procedures. The third questionnaire is trying to assess learners' knowledge and *understanding* of the procedures, and how they would handle particular situations.

E-learning/TBT packages will normally have some form of knowledge assessment built into them. These are often used in a *formative* way – ie for the learner to use the results as part of the learning process. The learner will know which questions he or she has got wrong and be invited to revisit that part of the programme. They can also be built in as *summative* tools – ie as final assessments. Often these packages enable the assessments to be carried out in an imaginative way – for example, to set up simulated situations and use graphics and video clips.

Occasionally, interviews are also used to explore complex areas of knowledge, where probing and follow-up questions may be needed. It is important that such interviews are structured as much as possible in order to ensure consistency of assessment, and similarly that there is a well-designed marking structure.

'Now, hang on a moment,' you might be saying. 'Surely there is more to this than just simple knowledge? Surely the learners will need to develop some skills in handling the people involved in disciplinary situations?' Yes, most certainly – see the next section on skills assessment. Most learning interventions involve both knowledge and skills learning, and a range of assessment methods may therefore be required.

Assessing knowledge can be carried out for two purposes:

- to ensure that a required standard or level of competence has been reached – this will often be expressed in terms of achieving a minimum mark of, say, 80 per cent

- to assess the gain in learning – which is often expressed in terms of a gain ratio (see Chapter 23).

The first approach is essential if a required standard must be reached before the learners can take on a new job or some new duties – eg knowledge of safety procedures for driving a train or cash-handling knowledge for operating a checkout. Often, in these cases, establishing a learning gain is not relevant because the starting knowledge is assumed to be zero or close to zero. The second approach – assessing the gain in learning – is more useful where there is no absolute requirement for a certain level of knowledge to be achieved before the participant leaves the programme, and where participants may come to the learning programme with different starting-levels of knowledge. It is most often used for management programmes, and usually its primary purpose is the assessment of the programme rather than of the participants, although the after-learning results can also provide useful feedback on whether further help or support is required by individuals.

Skills

Skills-based learning is assessed by observation. Successful skill assessment is based on two key factors:

- the design of the assessment/observation process and form
- the use of skilled observers.

First, a skill must be broken down into its main elements. For a relatively simple practical skill – eg changing an electrical plug – there may be only four or five elements. For a more complex skill – eg wiring a fire-alarm board – there may be considerably more. The assessment form will list all the different elements and each of these will be assessed. Since many technical skills require some form of qualification or licence, the methods and approaches for assessing technical skills are usually well established. The assessment may call for the use of sophisticated simulation equipment – eg as exists for testing train-driving skills. Practical skills can also sometimes be assessed by observation of a finished product or work sample – for example, a properly laid-out table (for a catering programme), a completed Gantt chart (for a project management programme).

The assessment of personal/interpersonal skills is generally less well-developed, largely because it is rare to find a qualification of any sort as a prerequisite for the job in the same way as there often is for jobs that demand technical and professional skills. Also, the assessment of personal/interpersonal skills is sometimes perceived as difficult to do, with the result that often attempts are limited to knowledge assessments. However, the skill assessment is based on exactly the same principle of breaking down the skill into its key elements. The equivalent to the simulation set-up is to use some form of role-play – eg assessing a mock selection interview or a mock presentation.

However, with skills such as interviewing, dealing with grievances, giving feedback, etc, the standards to be achieved – and hence the assessment – are less clear-cut than with, say, a technical skill, where generally there is only one correct way and the standard of the finished product can be very precisely defined. There is a much greater potential for subjectivity so that the need for a well-designed observation process and form, and for skilled observers, becomes even more important. Also, because of the element of subjectivity and the complexity of what is being observed, it is often helpful to have more than one observer.

Assessing skills is far more resource-intensive than assessing knowledge because the ratio of observers to participants is probably one-to-one at the assessment stage. It can in addition extend the length of the programme for the participants. This is another reason why, if there is not an absolute requirement for participants to have reached a specific standard, this type of assessment is often not done. The skills will be practised, using role-plays, etc, and observed with feedback given as part of the *development* of the skill, but then not *assessed* that a required level has been reached. Instead, some learning programmes build in an assessment in the workplace – ie a job behaviour level assessment – for example, observing someone facilitating a learning programme for real, or a manager chairing an actual meeting. We discuss this form of assessment in the next chapter. However, as soon as you move outside the learning environment, other factors can start to intervene. How much opportunity for practice has there been? How much coaching/support has been received from the learner's manager? How do you standardise the situation being assessed – eg the degree of difficulty or complexity of a meeting? The direct assessment of learning from the programme is lost.

Appendix 19.4 provides an example of an observation sheet for assessing personal/ interpersonal skills, those used in selection interviewing, and Appendix 19.5 provides a more complex assessment form for assessing the skills involved in carrying out a disciplinary hearing. This latter form comprised part of a package of assessment tools, together with the knowledge forms in Appendices 19.1–19.3, for assessing all aspects of a learning programme for handling disciplinary situations in a particular organisation.

Forms such as these can also be used for the next level of evaluation – assessment of performance back in the job, where observing a *real* interview or disciplinary hearing would be the basis for the assessment.

As with the assessment of knowledge learning, skill assessment can be carried out for the two purposes of:

- ensuring that a required standard of competence is achieved – eg passing the driving test, gaining a certificate/licence in welding
- assessing the gain in skills.

In practice, it is usually the first question that is addressed. This is often either because the skill is new and therefore the starting-point is *no skill*, or because establishing a starting-point is impractical in view of the difficulties (in cost and time) of assessment.

Attitudes and behaviours

Often, people talk about a third type of learning – that aimed at addressing attitudes. Assessing this third type of learning is particularly difficult. That is because participants are all too frequently aware of the *right* answers to give. Also, it can be argued that it is very difficult to change attitudes, and what you are aiming to change is the way people actually behave. This can be both a long process and one in which the results are best measured where the behaviours will operate – ie in the workplace – as is discussed further in the next chapter on job beheviour level evaluation.

SOME KEY ISSUES

We look at three key issues:

- the importance of good learning objectives
- developing effective evaluation tools and maintaining standards
- explaining the purpose of assessments to learners.

Learning objectives

One of the keys to successful learning level evaluation lies in the quality of the learning objectives. Learning level evaluation is straightforward if the learning objectives of the intervention:

- embody the full extent of the learning that is required
- are expressed in such a way that their achievement can be measured.

We described the concept of well-formed learning objectives in Chapter 12. Well-formed learning objectives set out:

- performance – what the learners will be able to do
- conditions – the conditions (if any) under which performance will occur
- criteria – the standards for acceptable performance.

In fact, all you need to carry out your learning level evaluation! So the message is that it is vital to get your learning objectives right.

Developing your evaluation tools

Developing evaluation tools usually requires specialist knowledge and necessitates liaison between the facilitator, evaluator and the specialist manager in the area. We recommend that these tools are designed at the same time as the learning programme is being developed. This is because developing them puts the learning objectives under great scrutiny and can be a very useful way of ensuring that the learning objectives *do* reflect the learning required from the programme.

Equally, it is vital that the assessment tools truly assess learners on what the learning objectives actually state the participants will be able to do, and neither more nor less. For example, if one learning objective is that the participant will be able to complete a specific form – eg an accident report form – then the assessment should involve the completion of that form based, say, on the description of an accident. In assessing whether this objective has been achieved, it would not be much use to ask the learner only to state the sections that must be filled in, or, on the other hand, to require the learner to write a management report on all the action to be taken as result of the accident!

It is important, also, to keep assessment tools up-to-date. For example, procedures and standards can change. Sometimes, because learning level assessment tools demand a considerable effort to develop, they can get set in tablets of stone and continue to be used when they have ceased to be an appropriate method of assessment.

Another potential issue to be aware of is a creeping reduction in standards through sloppy administration of assessments. For example, assessment questions can get to be well known, and facilitators can develop bad habits of giving heavy hints about what the questions are going to be. Marking standards can also drift if they are not monitored.

It is very important, too, to keep in mind the two purposes that assessment tools are used for, namely:

- to *license* individual learners as competent in a particular knowledge area or skill
- to measure the effectiveness of the programme in meeting the learning objectives.

The first purpose can usually be addressed in a relatively straightforward way – eg by setting a standard that the learner must achieve an 80 per cent result in a knowledge test or a particular rating in a skills test. The second purpose involves taking the results as a whole and perhaps looking at the proportion of delegates that *passed* the test, the average mark or score gained, or where appropriate the average learning gain.

Explaining the purpose

Finally, be aware that some learners may see assessment as daunting and worrying. It is important to make it very clear what the assessment is for:

- If it is to assess whether the learner has reached a particular standard, this should be explained at least at the outset of the programme and preferably before the learner goes on the programme. It should be made crystal clear how the assessment is going to be made – eg through written tests, skill simulation – and the standard that is required. It is also important that the learner knows what will happen if he or she does *not* reach the required standard. Can the learner resit the test, and if so, how many times, over what period? If not, or if the learner fails the resits, what happens then?

- If it is primarily to measure the effectiveness of the learning, make this clear. However, you will need to think about confidentiality. Who will have access to the results, particularly individual results?

Care must be taken when introducing assessment for the first time on to a programme, and even more so where it involves participants who are not used to being assessed – for example, on management courses. Otherwise, the prospect of the 'testing' can dominate the programme at the expense of the learning experience.

USING THE RESULTS

As with all the levels of evaluation it is important to demonstrate that the results have been used to make a difference to the learning process in the organisation. As with reaction-level evaluation, information is available directly after the learning intervention has been completed, and there is therefore opportunity to take action early. See the case studies below.

CASE STUDY

Death by overhead

A large transport organisation was introducing a new set of health and safety procedures. It was essential that staff received a totally consistent and accurate statement of the procedures, and also that the learning was delivered very quickly. A half-day learning programme was therefore designed that consisted of over 100 slides delivered in lecture format, with set notes, with the opportunity for questions at pre-defined stages. The learners' knowledge of the procedures was assessed at the end using a multi-choice questionnaire. The results from this knowledge test were analysed for the first three programmes – and more than 55 per cent of the learners failed to achieve the pass mark.

A group of the learners that had failed the test were asked to attend a focus group session. From that session it became clear that they had found the programme boring and had difficulty seeing the relevance of many of the procedures to their particular work. The learning intervention was redesigned. The new procedures were set out in a clear and lively way in a booklet. The learning programme was then structured around a series of group exercises that required the learners to relate the procedures to their own jobs. The same multi-choice questionnaire was used. This time more than 90 per cent of the learners achieved the pass mark.

The original course had become known as 'death by overhead' by the facilitators delivering it! The wider learning was that this learning method for operational staff was unlikely to be effective.

Basic beginnings

A financial institution was keen to improve the quality of its recruitment processes and was introducing competency-based interviewing. A two-day programme was developed on the basis that the target population for the learning comprised already experienced interviewers so that the learning need was around understanding and applying the competency-based approach. On the last afternoon the learners conducted a competency-based interview which was videoed. The learners were assessed against a checklist of behaviours. The results of this assessment showed that 65 per cent of the learners had inadequate basic interviewing skills – eg building rapport, questioning and active listening. The programme was redesigned to include the development of these basic interviewing skills.

The wider learning for the organisation was to investigate the starting knowledge and skills of the target learning population in more detail.

CONCLUSION

Learning level evaluation is an important stage in the evaluation process. It directly measures the extent to which the learning objectives have been achieved. Successful learning level evaluation depends critically on the learning objectives being well-formed, and a useful by-product of this level of evaluation is that it puts the spotlight on the learning objectives. We now move on to the next two evaluation levels – measuring the effects of learning on job behaviour and results.

SIMPLE KNOWLEDGE ASSESSMENT QUESTIONNAIRE (SIMPLE)
(Handling disciplinary issues programme)

The purpose of the questionnaire is to get feedback on how successful the programme has been. Individual results will be regarded as confidential. Please answer the following questions. Do not dwell too long over your answers but rely on your initial reaction. Circle the answer you have selected – T for a true statement, F for false, and DK for don't know. Please do not guess – if you do not know the answer, circle DK.

---

1   The sole purpose of discipline is punishment.   T   F   DK

---

2   After hearing all the evidence you should always adjourn a disciplinary   T   F   DK
    hearing to consider your decision.

---

3   Circumstances should always be taken into account when deciding on   T   F   DK
    a case of discipline.

---

4   It can be fair for people to be given different punishments   T   F   DK
    even though they have committed the same 'crime'.

---

5   The disciplinary process should be used to teach employees the 'rules'.   T   F   DK

---

6   Under the disciplinary procedure an employee is entitled to have union   T   F   DK
    representation when a witness statement is being taken down.

---

7   Gross misconduct is generally seen as misconduct serious enough to   T   F   DK
    destroy the contract and make any further working relationship and trust
    impossible.

---

8   The rules of natural justice provide that a person subject to the disciplinary T   F   DK
    process may call witnesses in his or her defence.

---

9   The circumstances of the case against a shop steward should be discussed
    with a full-time official before any disciplinary action is taken.   T   F   DK

---

10 An appeal should be made within five working days of receipt of notice of the   T   F   DK
     punishment.

_____

11 Breaches of disciplinary rules should be disregarded after a specified   T   F   DK
     period of time.

_____

12 An employee can appeal against an informal oral warning.   T   F   DK

_____

13 An employee may be dismissed for a 'first offence'.   T   F   DK

_____

14 A 'final written caution' will warn that dismissal will result if there is no   T   F   DK
     satisfactory improvement.

_____

15 An employee has to have been employed by the company for one year   T   F   DK
     before he or she can bring a claim for race or sex discrimination.

_____

16 A written warning will always set out the right of appeal.   T   F   DK

_____

17 An employment tribunal will take into account the details of a case and the   T   F   DK
     way it has been handled.

_____

18 Except in cases of race or sex discrimination, an employee has to have   T   F   DK
     been employed by the company for one year before he or she can bring
     a claim for unfair dismissal.

_____

19 Shop stewards are subject to the same disciplinary standards as any other   T   F   DK
     employee.

_____

20 Sexual and racial harassment will always be considered by the company a   T   F   DK
     reason for disciplinary action.

_____

KNOWLEDGE ASSESSMENT QUESTIONNAIRE (MULTIPLE CHOICE)
(Handling disciplinary issues programme)

The purpose of this questionnaire is to assess the effectiveness of the programme. Individual results will be treated as confidential. Please tick the appropriate box. Please do not guess – if you don't know the answer, tick the 'don't know' option.

1 The main purpose of discipline is:	Punishment ☐ Teaching a lesson ☐ Improved performance ☐ Don't know ☐
2 When you have heard the evidence at a disciplinary hearing you should adjourn to consider your decision:	Always ☐ Sometimes ☐ Never ☐ Don't know ☐
3 When deciding on what punishment is appropriate for a breach of discipline, circumstances should be taken into account:	Always ☐ Sometimes ☐ Never ☐ Don't know ☐
4 It can be fair for people to be given different punishments even though they have committed the same 'crime':	Always ☐ Sometimes ☐ Never ☐ Don't know ☐

5 The witness statements for a disciplinary hearing are given to the accused person:	Never ☐
	At the disciplinary hearing ☐
	Before the disciplinary hearing ☐
	Don't know ☐
6 An employee is entitled to have a union representative or workplace colleague present when a witness statement is being taken:	Always ☐
	At the manager's discretion ☐
	Never ☐
	Don't know ☐
7 'Gross misconduct' is the term given to describe behaviour which:	Is very serious and requires disciplinary action to be taken ☐
	Is serious enough to make any further working relationship and trust impossible ☐
	Requires a very heavy sentence ☐
	Don't know ☐
8 Among other things, the rules of natural justice provide that persons subject to the disciplinary process:	Can remain silent if they wish ☐
	May call witnesses in their defence ☐
	Can choose who will take their disciplinary hearing ☐
	Don't know ☐

9 taken against a shop steward, the case against him or her should always be discussed with:	Before disciplinary action is A workplace colleague not in a position of authority over the accused ☐ A senior personnel officer ☐ A full-time union official ☐ Don't know ☐
10 An appeal against a disciplinary penalty should be made within:	Eleven working days of notification ☐ Three working days of notification ☐ Five working days of notification ☐ Don't know ☐
11 A first written warning should be disregarded if a similar offence has not been committed within:	It is never disregarded ☐ One year ☐ Two years ☐ Don't know ☐
12 An employee may not appeal against:	A written warning ☐ A verbal warning ☐ An informal oral warning ☐ Don't know ☐
13 An employee may be dismissed for a first offence:	When gross misconduct or negligence is proven ☐ At the discretion of the manager ☐ Never ☐ Don't know ☐

14 A final written warning will state that:	Dismissal will take place the next time he or she is accused of negligence ☐
	Dismissal will ensue if he or she fails to meet the required standards ☐
	Neither of the above ☐
	Don't know ☐
15 Except in cases of race or sex discrimination, an employee bringing a claim for unfair dismissal must have been employed by the company for at least:	Six months ☐
	One year ☐
	Two years ☐
	Don't know ☐
16 A written warning will always set out:	The time limit after which it may be disregarded for further disciplinary action ☐
	The right of appeal ☐
	The penalty for offending again ☐
	Don't know ☐
17 An employment tribunal will always take into account the details of the case and:	Who is involved at the hearing ☐
	The race and sex of the person making the appeal ☐
	The way the case has been handled ☐
	Don't know ☐

18 Before an employee can bring a claim for race or sex discrimination he or she has to have been employed by the company for at least:	One year ☐
	Two years ☐
	No time limit ☐
	Don't know ☐
19 Shop stewards are subject to:	Softer disciplinary standards than any other employee ☐
	Harsher disciplinary standards than any other employee ☐
	The same disciplinary standards as any other employee ☐
	Don't know ☐
20 harassment will be considered by the company a reason for disciplinary action:	Sexual and/or racial Always ☐
	Sometimes ☐
	Never ☐
	Don't know ☐

KNOWLEDGE ASSESSMENT QUESTIONNAIRE (OPEN QUESTIONS)
(Handling disciplinary issues programme)

The purpose of this questionnaire is to assess the effectiveness of the programme. Individual results will be treated as confidential. Listed below are six questions about handling a disciplinary hearing. Please answer all the questions on the answer sheets provided.

Time allowed: 30 minutes

1. When should a defendant get copies of the witness statements, and why at this time?

2. If you are chairing a disciplinary hearing and the defendant will not answer questions, what should you do?

3. If you are chairing a disciplinary hearing and a defendant walks out in the middle of the proceedings, what should you do?

4. If you are chairing a disciplinary hearing and the defendant or his/her representative become abusive, what are your options?

5. After having heard the evidence and deciding that the defendant is guilty of the offence, what factors should you take into account in deciding on the penalty?

6. What information should be included in the record of the disciplinary hearing?

APPENDIX 19.4

SKILLS ASSESSMENT OBSERVATION SHEET
(Recruitment interviewing programme)

For use:

1. at the end of a selection/recruitment learning programme for observing a role-play

or

2. three to six months after a selection/recruitment learning programme for observing an actual interview.

The observer(s) – ideally for the role-play assessment there would be two observers – should be positioned so that they are unobtrusive, but have a clear view of both interviewer and interviewee.

The form is intended to assess current levels of skill and provide a structured means of giving feedback. As well as providing for a grading, there is space for comments to record reasons for the grading – examples of good practice and of where there is room for improvement. All observers should read the notes 'How to give feedback' before carrying out the assessment observer role.

Grading – the interview technique was of: 1 poor quality

2 fair quality

3 good quality

4 very good quality

INTRODUCTORY STAGE					COMMENTS
Warm welcome – made the candidate feel at ease	1	2	3	4	
Clear, useful introduction of himself/herself (name, title, role)	1	2	3	4	
Clear statement of the purpose and structure of the interview	1	2	3	4	
Positive statement about note-taking	1	2	3	4	

ACQUIRING INFORMATION					COMMENTS
Good use of open questions to open up topic areas	1	2	3	4	
Good use of probing questions to follow up areas of interest	1	2	3	4	
Avoidance of leading questions	1	2	3	4	
Good listening skills – indicated by following up leads, showing active listening	1	2	3	4	

GIVING INFORMATION   **COMMENTS**

Clear and relevant details   1   2   3   4
of the job

Clear and appropriate details   1   2   3   4
of the organisation

Clear and appropriate details   1   2   3   4
of conditions and pay

ENDING STAGE   **COMMENTS**

Sufficient and supportive   1   2   3   4
opportunities for questions
from the interviewee

Clear indication of what will   1   2   3   4
happen after the interview

Sincere and warm 'Thank you'   1   2   3   4

OVERALL   **COMMENTS**

Good balance of time   1   2   3   4
spent talking by interviewer
[1 > 60%, 2 40–60%, 3 25–40% , 4 < 25%]

Good listening skills –   1   2   3   4
indicated by following
up leads, showing active
listening

Good rapport (relationship)   1   2   3   4
between interviewer/
interviewee

No indications of gender   1   2   3   4
or race bias

GENERAL COMMENTS

APPENDIX 19.5

SKILLS ASSESSMENT OBSERVATION SHEET
(Handling disciplinary issues programme)

For use:

1 at the end of a learning programme on handling disciplinary issues for observing a role-play
    or

2 three to six months after a learning programme on handling disciplinary issues for observing an actual disciplinary hearing.

The observer(s) – ideally for the role-play assessment there would be two observers – should be positioned in such a way that they are unobtrusive but have a clear view of the proceedings.

The form is intended to assess current levels of skill and provide a structured means of giving feedback. As well as providing for a grading, there is space for comments to record reasons for the grading – examples of good practice and of where there is room for improvement. All observers should read the notes 'How to give feedback' before carrying out the assessment observer role.

Grading – the technique was of: 1 poor quality
                                    2 fair quality
                                    3 good quality
                                    4 very good quality

CONDUCT OF THE DISCIPLINARY HEARING

OPENING					COMMENTS
Clear introduction of himself/herself	1	2	3	4	
Clear introduction of other panel members	1	2	3	4	
Details of defendant checked	1	2	3	4	
Clear statement that the hearing is part of the disciplinary procedure	1	2	3	4	
Clear statement of charge	1	2	3	4	
Right to representation covered appropriately	1	2	3	4	

MAIN PART					**COMMENTS**
Good use of open questions to open up issues of concern	1	2	3	4	
Good use of probing questions to follow up issues of concern	1	2	3	4	
Avoidance of leading questions	1	2	3	4	
Good listening skills demonstrated	1	2	3	4	
Calm approach	1	2	3	4	
Effective control of hearing	1	2	3	4	
Impartiality displayed	1	2	3	4	
All evidence covered	1	2	3	4	
Adequate opportunity for defence provided	1	2	3	4	
Circumstances fully covered	1	2	3	4	

Was an adjournment granted?   Yes ☐   No ☐ (please tick)

Comments:

GIVING THE DECISION					COMMENTS
Clear statement of decision	1	2	3	4	
Clear statement of penalty, taking account of previous disciplinary record	1	2	3	4	
Clear statement of penalty with any circumstances affecting it	1	2	3	4	
Clear statement of improvement sought (standard/target and time-scale)	1	2	3	4	
Competent handling of any questions	1	2	3	4	
Full explanation of appeals process	1	2	3	4	

QUALITY OF THE PROCESS

PREPARATION					COMMENTS
Notification to defendant timely and appropriate	1	2	3	4	
Location/layout/arrangements appropriate	1	2	3	4	
Evidence assembled competently	1	2	3	4	

DECISION-MAKING					COMMENTS
Appropriate decision made	1	2	3	4	
Circumstances properly taken into account	1	2	3	4	
Precedents taken into account	1	2	3	4	
Appropriate penalty given	1	2	3	4	
Appropriate documentation completed	1	2	3	4	

20

Performance level evaluation (levels 3 and 4)

INTRODUCTION

In Chapter 19 we looked at how we evaluate what learning has taken place. This chapter takes the evaluation one stage further on – it focuses on whether this learning has been successfully transferred back into the workplace. It assesses whether job performance has improved, and in particular whether the identified performance gap has been bridged. There is little point in developing skills, etc, if they are not transferred back into the workplace. For most learning interventions this is probably the most crucial level of evaluation. It is perhaps surprising, therefore, that this level of evaluation is so infrequently carried out in any systematic way – particularly as it provides the learning professional with both a really interesting and exciting challenge and a fascinating insight into the learning process, the people, the jobs and the organisational culture.

In terms of the multi-level model introduced in Chapter 16, this chapter covers:

- the third level – the job behaviour level (sometimes referred to as the intermediate level)

and

- the fourth level – the results level (sometimes referred to as the 'ultimate' level).

We are combining these two levels because very often evaluation of them is carried out together and because both provide information on the impact of the learning intervention on how learners perform back in the workplace. We describe this level of evaluation as the *performance* level. There are therefore essentially two elements to this stage of evaluation, looking at:

- the job behaviours – ie the way people do their jobs
- the results of those behaviours – ie the contribution to organisational objectives.

WHAT DOES PERFORMANCE LEVEL EVALUATION TELL US?

Behaviours v results

There is a school of thought which argues that *how* people do their jobs is not important, only the results achieved. However, we take the view that both have a part to play. Let us take a simple example of a learning intervention aimed at improving the performance of sales people to sell their products or services. At this evaluation stage, you might look at the way they make a sale – ie you might observe a sales transaction with a customer, to assess whether they were using the appropriate behaviours (eg building rapport, asking relevant questions), how they handled the close of the sale, etc. Or you might look at the results of those behaviours – ie the level of sales. Many people might argue that it is surely the results that matter. However, there are two advantages to also looking at the behaviours:

- From the audit trail perspective, if the results evaluation is poor, you will want to know why – and looking at the behaviours will be one part of that investigation.

- You may be interested from a long-term customer-relations perspective that your sales people are behaving appropriately with your customers. They may be generating extra sales in the short term but selling products that the customer does not really want and which may result in the return of the product rather than the customer!

Also, with some learning intervention it is very difficult to measure specific results, such as in many areas of management learning or soft skills learning. For example, with learning interventions aimed at improving time management skills or leadership skills, it is sometimes better to look at the behaviours rather than take time trying to make a direct link with results. Or sometimes, perhaps where there are some relevant performance indicators, a combined approach is helpful.

Intervening factors

Another important issue to consider with this level of evaluation is the other factors that can affect job behaviour and the results achieved. As soon as the learners return to the workplace they are subject to a wide range of influences, which we will call *intervening factors*, that could affect the way they do their jobs. These can have both positive and negative effects – for example:

- They may receive extra coaching or learning on the job, or alternatively receive little support from their manager.

- New equipment or procedures might be introduced which could be helpful, or unhelpful.

- There may not be the opportunities to practise the new skills and behaviours – a very important factor. There is considerable evidence to show that if a new skill or behaviour is not used within a relatively short time, the learning degrades very rapidly. A particularly good (or bad!) example of this is with computer skills, such as learning to use a new software package.

- There may be a lack of peer support. For example, if a learner comes back from a learning programme motivated and able to deliver a different standard of customer care, and his or her colleagues think it is a waste of time or do not support, through their own work, the same standard of customer care, then it is easy for the learner simply not to implement the new learning.

These are all internal factors and will impact directly on the behaviours and through them the results achieved.

There is also the possibility that external factors may intervene – for example:

- A change in general economic activity, perhaps as a result of interest rate or exchange rate movements, could make it harder or easier to generate sales.

- The emergence of a new competitor could also influence sales or labour turnover.

- Competitor activity, in the form of new service standards, could influence customer satisfaction levels.

Such external factors tend to affect the results rather than the behaviours.

There are essentially two ways to tackle these intervening factors:

- through using control groups – This is where you compare the behaviours and results (in fact, usually results) of your learning group with those of another group of staff who are doing the same work but who have not received the same learning intervention. It is important that this control group is as similar as possible to the learning group in terms of experience, gender mix, etc. You may use more than one control group. In Chapter 17 we described the various design approaches that can be adopted

- by exploring the existence of the intervening factors and seeking to estimate the extent of their influence – For example, you ask learners and/or their managers to identify any intervening factors and ask them then to estimate how much such factors may have impacted on the performance/results.

There can be difficulties with using the control group approach. It may be hard to find a control group, for example, if the whole workforce doing a particular job attends the learning intervention at the same time. The time and resources required to identify and monitor a control group adds to the costs of the evaluation. In many cases it is the second approach – of estimating the influence of the intervening factors – that offers the more practical way forward. It will not be as statistically correct as the control group approach, but can often provide sufficient evidence to answer any questions raised.

As a diagnostic tool – exploring the audit trail

So what happens if there are poor performance level evaluation results? Consider, again, the two situations:

- the results are poor only for a few learners

- the results are generally poor.

If the outcomes are poor for only a few learners, the starting-point is to look at the learning level evaluation results for those learners:

- If the learning level evaluation results were fine, it would suggest that there were specific factors in the workplace or personal to the individuals that hampered the transfer of the learning back to the job. These could be the sort of factors discussed earlier. It could also simply be that the learning was not relevant to their jobs, and that those particular learners should not have been sent on the learning intervention at all.

- If the learning level evaluation results were poor, these cases need to be investigated – and again, as for the other levels of evaluation, it is important to be on the lookout for patterns and trends. Is it always particular departments, particular types of learner, etc?

If the outcomes are generally poor, you should start once more with the learning level results:

- If these were poor then the poor job level outcomes would not be surprising! However, it would beg the question of why no action was taken in response to the poor learning level results. It highlights the extremely important point that it is *vital* to act on evaluation results. Only one thing is worse than ineffective learning interventions, and that is knowing the learning is ineffective and doing nothing about it!

- However, if the learning level results were fine (and if, of course, the learning level evaluation was valid and reliable), then it will have been established that the learning objectives of the intervention had been achieved. This would suggest that either:

  - the intervention had not tackled the right learning issues – ie that the learning objectives were inappropriate – and that the LNA on which they had been based was therefore flawed in some way
  or

  - it is possible that there are some general factors/obstacles in the workplace that have hindered the transfer of learning back into the job. It may be that these could have been anticipated during the LNA process and addressed by the intervention, or they may have occurred subsequently – a change of management, perhaps, leading to different priorities. The evaluator must again don his or her deerstalker, take up the magnifying glass, and do some more detective work!

If there are no learning level results, the detective work becomes harder. You do not know whether it is the delivery of the learning that is the problem or whether the learning intervention was ill-conceived, or whether there are factors in the workplace that are affecting the results. The reaction level evaluation will prove a useful starting-point again, and follow-up interviews with learners and their managers could be helpful. Some organisations very successfully use focus group discussions involving learners and their managers to investigate these sorts of issues – see the case study overleaf.

Reviews revisited

An organisation had been concerned about the way managers were handling performance review interviews and their associated paperwork. Performance reviews were often conducted very late and the relevant forms completed poorly – sections were missed or inadequately completed. It had been decided that all managers should undergo a quick refresher learning programme on how to conduct performance reviews. A performance level evaluation was carried out a year after, which identified that there had been little improvement in either the delays in completing the reviews or the quality of the review forms. A focus group of participants in the programme was carried out. Two clear messages came through:

- The programme had focused on the mechanics of the process – how to complete the forms, conduct an interview. There had been little time spent on the objectives and importance of performance reviews. There was considerable cynicism about the usefulness of the whole process, and these issues had not been addressed by the learning intervention.
- There was considerable criticism of the process itself. The managers felt that the forms were poorly designed, there was no system of reminders to carry out the reviews, etc.

This was a good example of where a quick response to a perceived need without any real LNA being carried out had proved to be an almost complete waste of time and money!

HOW DO WE DO IT?

The approach will vary depending on whether you are looking at job behaviours or measuring results.

Job behaviours

There is a range of approaches which involves decisions about:

- who does the assessment
- what method of assessment is used.

Who does the assessment?

There are usually three main choices of who does the assessment:

- the learner – ie self-assessment
- the learner's manager
- an external/independent assessor.

The most common approach is for self-assessment and manager assessment, or, quite often, a combination of the two. The advantages are that such assessments can usually form part of the normal working situation and are therefore low-cost. They can also reinforce the coaching/mentoring role of the manager. The advantages of external assessors are that they are usually skilled in the task, arguably make more objective assessments, and can ensure consistency of standards.

For some sorts of learning interventions other assessors may come into play – for example:

- learners' staff – for learning programmes on, say, leadership, performance reviews, etc. Clearly, this can present sensitivity issues since in many organisations upward assessment is not well developed. In one organisation this problem was addressed by using the regular anonymous employee satisfaction survey as the vehicle for the assessment. It was a credible approach because the learning programme was being addressed at all managers in specific business units.

- learners' colleagues – for learning programmes on, say, teamworking, time management, etc. Again, this sort of approach may need careful handling because peer assessment is similarly not well established in many organisations.

- learners' customers, who could be internal or external customers – for learning programmes on customer care, call centre telephone skills, etc. Often customer surveys are used to provide information from this key group.

Methods of assessment

The methods of assessment are the familiar choice (see Chapters 10 and 17) of:

- observation
- self-complete questionnaires
- interviews.

Observation

It is, perhaps, obvious that the most direct way to assess *how* something is done is usually to observe it. What one would really like to do is be the proverbial 'fly on the wall'. In practice, observing behaviour in the workplace has a number of problems. If it is specially organised for assessment purposes – ie *formal* observation – it can be a time-consuming and costly approach. It probably requires an observer:learner ratio of at least one-to-one. If what is to be observed is a particular skill – for example, a technical skill such as welding a joint – then the observation can be very focused and of relatively short duration. Similarly, if it is a management skill, such as giving a presentation, the observation can be based on the specific occasion on which the presentation is given. However, if it is a management skill, such as handling poor performance situations which are not pre-planned, then it may require a considerable period of observation to witness the situations that give rise to the behaviour being assessed.

Also, where any formal observation is involved, and in particular if formal observers (ie observers who would not normally form part of the workplace environment) are used, then the very presence of the observer(s) can have an effect on the result (see Chapter 10, the Hawthorne effect). If formal observation is used, the same types of assessment form as those used for the learning evaluation of skills are appropriate (see Appendix 19.4 and 19.5). The only difference here is that the learner is performing the skill in the real environment of the workplace rather than under the simulated conditions of the learning environment.

If organisations have well-developed competency frameworks, these can often form the basis of the assessment tools. National Vocational Qualifications (NVQs) and Scottish Vocational Qualifications (SVQs) can additionally provide a competency structure and process for assessing many jobs. Many organisations are now designing their learning programmes so that the measure of success of the effectiveness of the programme is the award of an NVQ/SVQ.

The alternative to the formal observation is the *informal* observation available through the normal manager–staff relationship as part of the performance management process. The manager observes the learner over a period of time performing the job areas addressed by the learning intervention, and forms a view of the level of competency achieved. This can then be used as a basis to ensure that the learner has reached the appropriate standard and/or compared with a starting competency level to assess the gain in competency.

Appendix 20.1 sets out one approach to performance level evaluation. It takes the learner and his or her manager through from nomination for a particular learning intervention to assessing the effectiveness three months (or whatever period is chosen) after the learning event. It incorporates a set of forms to be completed jointly by the learner and his or her manager that takes them through the process. It includes:

- a nomination form, setting out the business need, performance gap, why the particular learning solution was chosen, details of timing, etc

- a pre-programme briefing form, covering the learning objectives, how the learning relates to the learner's job, identifying pre-programme preparation work, any problems which may affect the learner's ability to make the most effective use of the learning

- an evaluation form (reaction level), completed immediately after the learning has been completed, to note the learner's reaction to the programme, identify any particular learning needs not met and any action that is required to aid the transference of the learning to the job

- an evaluation form (performance level), completed three months after the learning (or any period considered appropriate) to assess the effect of the programme on job performance and in meeting the business need.

The exact format and content of each of these forms can be varied to reflect the needs of the organisation. The balance of descriptive information and quantitative information (rating scales, etc) will depend on the culture of the organisation, the reporting system used, etc.

The main output from this system is generally qualitative information (for example, describing the change in performance, the way the business need has been met) with the addition of some quantitative information from the rating scales/tick-box questions included. One approach to dealing with the qualitative information is to do so on an exception-reporting basis. Where the results from the rating scales suggest there are problems, the qualitative information can provide the detail and depth to indicate where the problems may lie and where any investigation might start.

With a new recruit or on promotion or transfer into a new job, where the learning intervention is directed at providing the learner with the full range of knowledge and skills required for the job, it is likely that the assessment will take place shortly after the learning intervention and the full range of competencies for the job will need to be measured. Where the learning intervention is to improve or extend performance in an existing job, when practice and experience is part of the learning process, the full assessment may not be appropriate until some months after the event (see later under *Some key issues*). Assessment will probably only be against a partial set of competencies. The assessments can be based on either the formal or informal observation methods described earlier.

This approach to performance level evaluation can have the additional and very important benefit of supporting the transference of the learning back into the job. It requires both the manager and the learner to focus on the learning process from start to finish – ie from the identification of need and nomination through to the assessment of whether the learning intervention has achieved the objectives in terms of job performance. It provides a structured means of ensuring that support is given at all stages and action taken when problems occur. *It could be argued that this additional benefit is of equal and possibly even greater value than the original evaluation objective.*

Where a performance review system is in place, this approach can be linked in with it. This is particularly appropriate if the system is based on more frequent meetings than the traditional annual review.

The disadvantages with this approach are that:

- It requires a considerable investment of time by both learners and their managers. However, it could be argued that the types of meetings/discussions which underpin these approaches should be taking place anyway. All that is additional is the completion of the forms.

- Such systems can require considerable administrative effort to work effectively – both in ensuring that the various questionnaires/forms are completed at the appropriate times and in reporting the results. However, the use of on-line questionnaires and workflow systems which can be set up to trigger the various stages can make a big difference to the success of this approach.

The approach can be perceived as overly bureaucratic and there can therefore be an unwillingness to participate fully, resulting in patchy/poor-quality information which can undermine the usefulness of the approach. *It is essential that the results are seen as useful both to the individual learner and his or her manager, and that they are used to make a difference to the quality of the learning interventions.* (More about this in Chapter 23.)

Self-complete questionnaires

The alternatives to observation are interviews and self-complete questionnaires.

Self-complete questionnaires have the advantage that they are a relatively low-cost method of collecting information. Again, they can be directed at the learners, their managers, or both (or any other groups involved – eg colleagues). However, in order to extract the quite complex information that is required, self-complete questionnaires have to be carefully designed to keep them as short and structured as possible. The types of question that it is useful to ask are:

- How often has the skill/knowledge been used?
- How successful was the use of the skill/knowledge? – either using a rating scale of some sort, or asking for examples of outcomes
- How competent was the learner rated both before and after the learning intervention?
- What barriers are there to, or problems with, using the skill/knowledge acquired?

An example of a self-complete questionnaire designed to assess the effects of a time management programme on job performance is provided as Appendix 20.2.

Clearly, there are advantages and disadvantages to relying only on self-assessment. It could well be argued that the learner is the best source of information on his or her own behaviour. Hamblin (1974) argues in his classic text that the problems associated with *objective* observation are such that:

> ... *we shall regard the trainee himself* [sic] *as the main source of information* ...

... On the other hand, there is the question of whether the learner either will be willing to self-assess honestly or be able to self-assess accurately. On the first point, a key question is anonymity. It is likely that the learner will be more willing to assess his or her own performance honestly if there is no danger of the information being used for other purposes – eg the annual pay round! However, with this approach there is no opportunity to respond to the answers and take action where there are problems. To complete Hamblin's quote above:

> ... *and we shall regard the evaluator as being primarily a catalyst whose aim is to achieve rapport with the trainee and so help the trainee to understand his [sic] own behaviour and plan how to change it.*

Hamblin strongly took the view that the evaluation must be for the benefit of the learner. In the case of self-complete questionnaires there is the possibility of conflict between the objective of the evaluation for assessing the effectiveness of the learning intervention, when anonymity may be advantageous, and meeting the needs of the learner by providing further help and support if the learning intervention has been ineffective in some way.

Interviews

The last method for consideration is that of interviews. There are the four potential approaches noted earlier (Chapter 17):

- one-to-one face-to-face interviews
- telephone interviews

- group interviews
- video-conferencing interviews.

The first approach is quite a common method in use although it falls between the two stools of low cost (self-complete questionnaires) and the most direct method (observation). Face-to-face interviews are costly – but with skilled interviewers a much greater degree of probing can take place than with a self-complete questionnaire. Also, the use of more sophisticated approaches, such as using repertory grid methods (see Chapter 10), can provide more rigorous and objective information. The compromise is building the evaluation into the normal review system, as suggested earlier, and simply adding questions specifically aimed at the job performance which is the subject of the evaluation on to the normal review interview.

An alternative approach can be to use group interviews or discussions, normally either with learners and/or their managers. As well as a direct method of assessment, this approach can be a particularly useful way at identifying problem areas. For example, if the evaluation using self-complete questionnaire surveys or manager-assessment is coming up with poor results, group discussion can be a very effective way of distilling out the causes (see the case study *Reviews revisited* earlier in this chapter).

Results

The second aspect of performance level evaluation is measuring performance in terms of the results achieved – ie the contribution to organisational objectives. The most common method is some form of 'desk research'. This can best be viewed as a five-stage process:

1 Identify the *key indicator(s)/measures(s)* of organisational performance that will be used for the assessment. These should be identified at the LNA stage and fall directly out of the statement of business need that gives rise to the learning intervention. Examples of the sorts of performance indicators that could be used are shown in Table 14. These are generally of two types:
   - measures that are already used for monitoring performance – eg sales, productivity
   - measures that may have to be set up specially for the evaluation – eg a customer satisfaction survey, statistics on projects that overrun or overspend.

2 Ensure that results are available and in the right form for the *before-learning* period – ie you have a 'before-learning' benchmark. There is nothing more frustrating than realising after the event that there is no previous data available on the measure (eg statistics on project performance), or that data is perhaps not available at the required level of detail (eg error rates broken down by production lines), etc.

3 Decide *how long* the learning will take *to affect the indicator*. This encompasses the need for practice and skill development, and also the time it will take before the changed performance will show up in the particular indicator. For example, improved selling skills may take several months to impact on orders taken and finally sales generated. This decision will also depend on how regularly the performance indicator is measured. For example, customer satisfaction surveys may be undertaken only every six months.

4 Identify *the other factors* that might intervene and consider methods for minimising or measuring the effects of those other factors – for example, by comparing results with other parts of the business where learning has not taken place (ie using a form of control group). If the measure was sales performance, then both groups (the learning group and non-learning group) would have experienced the same economic and competitive conditions. (Clearly, it is important to ensure that this is the case – ie that the control group is similar to the learning group in all relevant respects – see Chapter 17.)

5 Set up appropriate *systems to monitor the results*. This is particularly important if the results are not usually monitored either at all or in the form required for evaluation purposes, and also if the results are being monitored over a long period.

You might argue that this is the key area of evaluation – surely the primary and *ultimate* purpose of learning is to improve organisational performance? People can change the way they do their jobs until the cows come home, but if this does not impact on the organisational performance, then surely the learning intervention has failed? The answer to this question must be 'yes' – particularly since we take as the starting-point for this book that learning must be directed to business needs. The starting-point of any LNA is *what is the business need?* and the closing point of any evaluation must be whether the need has been met. Or maybe not quite the closing point, for a further question may be whether the need has been met at an acceptable cost or in the most cost effective way – see Chapter 21.

Table 14 | Examples of measures/indicators of organisational performance

Type of learning	Results that could be measured
Customer care	*Number of customer complaints (analysed by type of complaint)*
	Customer satisfaction using surveys
	Number of customers
	Level of orders or sales
	Number of referrals from existing customers
	Number of lost customers
	Amount of repeat business
	Employee satisfaction using surveys (for internal customer care)
Performance management	*Productivity measures*
	Levels of output/sales
	Wastage rates
	Error rates
	Absenteeism
	Customer satisfaction
	Employee satisfaction
	Number of disciplinary hearings

Table 14 | *Examples of measures/indicators of organisational performance*

Type of learning	Results that could be measured
Selection interview	Percentage of offers accepted Percentage of recruits deemed fully competent at the end of probation period Average length of time recruits stay
Safety	Number of accidents (analysed by type and degree of seriousness) Results of safety audits Lost time due to injuries
Project management	Number of projects that overrun/come in on time Number of projects that are over budget/come in on budget Project team satisfaction using surveys
Team-building/ supervisory/ management skills	Output/sales of team Productivity of team Absenteeism Staff turnover Employee satisfaction using surveys Number of formal grievances

SOME KEY ISSUES

Perhaps the most important issue to take into account is that this level of evaluation involves assessment *in the workplace*. It will be vital to:

- secure the co-operation of all concerned, and this means communicating clearly and in good time the purpose and benefits of the evaluation. It can mean sharing at the outset who is going to get the evaluation results and how they will be used

- ensure wherever possible that it is of benefit to the individual learners, so that it reinforces the learning messages and deals with unmet needs

- minimise the impact on the workplace – this usually means in terms of the time of those involved, usually the learner and his or her manager.

Another important issue is that of timing – *when* the assessment should take place. This will depend on:

- whether the learning is required to carry out a new job or take on new skills, in which case the assessment is likely to be relatively soon after the learning intervention

- whether the learning requires a period of practising the skills in the workplace, in which case it will depend on the period of time required. For example, if the skills are used on an everyday basis (such as receptionist skills, computing skills, etc), then the period of time may be quite short – perhaps a month or two. However, if the skill is practised less frequently (eg selection interviewing by a line manager, presentation skills, dealing with an emergency situation) or requires a longer period to develop the skills (eg leadership, time management skills), then a considerably longer period of time may have to elapse – three months or more

- whether the evaluation requires observation and whether informal observation is being used (eg by the learner's manager), in which case there will have to be sufficient opportunity for such observation to take place.

Ideally, with performance level evaluation that involves the improvement of existing skills it is important to have an assessment of the skills before the learning begins. If that option is not available, an alternative approach is to establish the starting-point – ie the before-learning level – at the time of the post-learning assessment. This clearly has the disadvantage that it may be hard to focus on behaviours of the past. However, it does have the advantage (and arguably this is a significant advantage when self-assessment is involved) that participants at the later stage (ie after the learning intervention) will have a much clearer picture of the behaviours and standards of behaviours being assessed than before the event. In terms of the learning model analogy (that people progress from unconscious incompetence through conscious incompetence to conscious competence and finally unconscious competence) it could be argued that before the learning started people were in a state of unconscious incompetence as to the quality of their skills!

USING THE RESULTS

This is a key level of evaluation because many problems with the learning intervention will only show up when a learner's ability to perform his or her job is assessed. See the two case studies below.

CASE STUDY

Prioritising problems

A classic example occurred in a major utility. A learning need for team leaders was identified as being able 'to prioritise their own and their team's work'. A series of one-day learning interventions took place. The reaction level evaluation produced glowing results. It showed that the learners felt they had really mastered the skill of prioritising. The facilitator had used the device of putting up the learning objectives on flipcharts on the wall and inviting learners to put up a gold star when they felt they had achieved that learning objective. These flipcharts were covered in gold stars. No formal learning level evaluation was carried out. After three months a survey was carried out asking the learners and their managers to what extent they had put the learning into action. The results showed there had been little change in the way the learners organised their work, and few could identify times when they had used their prioritising skills. Both learners and their managers commented that the problem was that the pressure was so great that they simply reacted to crises as they came along. The real learning needs were for better time management skills generally and the key learning need was for their managers and those above them!

The wider learning for the organisation was to carry out better LNA!

After-sales assumptions

A mail order company received a lot of complaints about the quality of the after-sales service being offered. The company immediately launched into a customer care initiative which involved a series of learning interventions addressing the importance of retaining customer loyalty, knowledge of systems and procedures, telephone skills, handling queries and complaints. These were universally enjoyed, with excellent reaction level evaluation. Some testing of knowledge took place and a sample of learners were tested on their telephone skills and ability to handle queries and complaints. The results were encouraging. However, six months later the level of complaints remained the same. A follow-up survey of the learners was carried out. The simple message came back that their performance and bonuses depended on the level of *new* sales generated. There was no incentive to spend time on after-sales service. The company revised its incentive scheme.

The wider learning for the company was that it was vital not to jump to the conclusion that a learning intervention was the solution to all problems!

CONCLUSION

Performance level evaluation is potentially the most valuable source of information for assessing the effectiveness of learning interventions. However, it is also the level of assessment that requires the most careful and thoughtful planning and implementation to ensure that the information gathered is relevant and of good quality and at the same time causes least disruption in the workplace. Clear objectives, consultation with the all key players and careful testing of the assessment instruments used are all the essential ingredients of a successful evaluation study. We will continue this theme in the next chapter, which looks at the issues of cost-effectiveness and cost-benefit.

READING AND REFERENCE

HAMBLIN A. C. (1974), *Evaluation and Control of Training*, Maidenhead, McGraw-Hill.

APPENDIX 20.1

LEARNING EVALUATION PACKAGE

PURPOSE

Learning is designed to achieve improved workplace performance. To ensure that the learning is as effective as possible requires a partnership between:

- the learner – in preparing for the learning programme, actively and conscientiously participating in the learning, and then applying the learning back into the job

- his or her manager – in providing support before and after the learning

- the learning manager – in ensuring that the right learning intervention is chosen and evaluating the effectiveness of the learning programme

- the learning facilitator – in ensuring that the quality of the learning delivery is as high as possible.

The first stage is to identify clearly the business need and the gap between current standards and the required standards of performance. It is important to consider non-learning solutions and informal learning approaches before opting for a formal learning intervention. The learning need must then be closely matched to an appropriate learning programme.

This package is designed to ensure that the learning delivered is as effective as possible. It involves a number of stages:

- the nomination of the learner for the programme

- the preparation of the learner for the programme

- the professional delivery of the learning

- the support and monitoring of the learner after the event to maximise and measure the transference of the learning to the job.

STAGES IN THE PACKAGE

1   The nomination of the learner for the programme (Forms A and B). This should be a joint approach to ensure that:

- the business need is clearly identified

- the current and required levels of performance are assessed

- all other approaches to bridging the gap are investigated

- a method and time-scale for assessing performance after learning is established

- any other details – eg any preferences for timing, deliverer, learning methods, any special needs – are specified.

2   Pre-learning briefing for the learner from his or her manager (Forms C and D) to ensure that:

- the learning objectives of the course are understood

- the learner clearly understands why he or she is on the programme

- the learner understands how the course relates to his or her job

- any pre-course preparation work required is identified

- any problems are identified which may affect the learner's ability to make the most effective use of the learning.

3   Post-learning briefing and appraisal meetings (Forms E and F):

- immediately following the learning, a meeting between the manager and learner to:

   a) discuss the learner's reaction to the programme

   b) dentify any particular learning needs not met and any action that is required to aid the transference of the learning to the job

- three months after the learning or any period considered appropriate to assess the effect of the programme on job performance and in meeting the business need
- at later stages if required.

FORM A DETAILS

Learner's name: _____

Manager's name: _____

Job title/grade: _____

Job title/grade: _____

Department: _____

Learning manager: _____

FORM B NOMINATION

Describe the business need.

Describe the current level and the required level of performance.

Describe the knowledge and skills learning needed.

Why have you chosen a learning solution? (If appropriate, include what other solutions have been considered.)

What support will be given to ensure that the benefits of the learning will be transferred to the job?

Explain how and when the effectiveness of the learning will be measured.

Details of the proposed learning intervention:

Date the learning is required by:

Any dates when learner is not available:

Any comments on type of learning approach preferred:

FORM C DETAILS OF LEARNING

Title: _____   Ref No. (if applicable): _____

Delivery dates: _____

Facilitator(s): _____

Learning objectives: A

B

C

D

E

F

FORM D PRE-LEARNING BRIEFING

The pre-learning briefing should take place ideally one to two weeks before the learning programme.

The purpose is to ensure that the learner is as well prepared as possible for the learning programme.

The areas to be covered are:

1   the competencies in the job that the learning is addressing
2   the learning objectives of the programme
3   any preparation work required before the programme
4   any problems or concerns that the learner might have that might affect his or her ability to make the best use of the programme.

Date of briefing:

Comments:

Signed: Signed:

Learner   Manager

Date   Date

FORM E POST-LEARNING BRIEFING – COMPLETED IMMEDIATELY AFTER THE LEARNING PROGRAMME

This form should be completed within two weeks of the learner's return from the learning programme. Its purpose is to gauge the learner's overall reaction to the programme and identify any immediate areas of unmet needs and any further action that may be required at this stage.

Details of how the full competency appraisal is to be carried out should also be discussed.

Date of briefing:

To what extent were the learning objectives achieved? Please circle the appropriate rating (1 not achieved at all . . . 6 fully achieved).

Learning objectives							
	A	1	2	3	4	5	6
	B	1	2	3	4	5	6
	C	1	2	3	4	5	6
	D	1	2	3	4	5	6
	E	1	2	3	4	5	6
	F	1	2	3	4	5	6

How does the learner rate the programme overall in preparing him or her for carrying out the job? Please tick:

poor quality ☐
fair quality ☐
good quality ☐
very good quality ☐

Comment on why the programme was fair or poor quality.

Are there any areas where further action is required at this stage? Please tick: Yes ☐   No ☐

If Yes, please complete the section below.

AREAS WHERE FURTHER ACTION IS REQUIRED

This could take the form of manager support/coaching, self-learning, further learning, a work/project assignment, any other appropriate activity.

AREA	PROPOSAL FOR ACTION	REVIEW DATE

Signed: Signed:
Learner   Manager
Date   Date

FORM F EVALUATION

This form is to be completed three months (or whatever period is considered appropriate) after the learning. The purpose is to assess how effectively the learning has met the learning needs and business needs identified in the Nomination Form B.

Date of evaluation form completion:

Describe the current level of job performance in the areas addressed by the learning. Is the job performance up to the required standard? Please indicate how performance has been assessed.

Please rate the programme's effectiveness in meeting the job performance needs. Circle the appropriate rating.

Not effective at all   1   2   3   4   5   6   Completely effective

Describe if and how the business need has been met. Please include any quantitative/financial assessments of the benefits to the organisation.

Please rate the programme's effectiveness in meeting the business needs. Circle the appropriate rating.

Not effective at all   1   2   3   4   5   6   Completely effective

If the job performance is not up to the required standard and/or the business need has not been met, identify the reasons for this.

Proposals for further action, if required.

Signed: Signed:

Learner   Manager

Date   Date

APPENDIX 20.2

SELF COMPLETE QUESTIONNAIRE FOR LEARNERS
(Time management programme)

The purpose of this survey is to evaluate how effective the time management programme that you attended has been in improving your performance in your job. It is emphasised that individual information collected will be treated confidentially – only the overall results will be reported. It is important that you answer the questions as honestly and fully as possible.

1   To what extent has the programme helped you to prioritise and plan your workload? Please circle the appropriate rating.

Not at all   1   2   3   4   5   6   Very much

2   Please tick if you were using any of the following techniques:

	Before the programme	Now
Time log	☐	☐
A diary planner	☐	☐
Sorting in-tray	☐	☐
Other planning tools, please specify:		
_____	☐	☐
_____	☐	☐

3   To what extent has the programme helped you to control interruptions more effectively? Please circle the appropriate rating.

Not at all   1   2   3   4   5   6   Very much

4   Please tick if you were using any of the following techniques:

	Before the programme	Now	N/A
Keeping an interruptions log	☐	☐	
Secretary screening calls/visitors	☐	☐	☐
Colleague screening calls/visitors	☐	☐	☐
Use of surgery times	☐	☐	
Working in quiet place	☐	☐	
Booking meetings with yourself	☐	☐	
Others, please specify:			
_____	☐	☐	
_____	☐	☐	

5 How many meetings have you chaired since the programme? Please tick the appropriate box.

No meetings ☐
1–3 meetings ☐
4–6 meetings ☐
7 or more meetings ☐

If your answer was *No meetings*, please go to Q8.

6 To what extent has the programme helped you to chair meetings more effectively? Please circle the appropriate rating.

Not at all   1   2   3   4   5   6   Very much

7 Please tick if you were/are using any of the following techniques:

	Before the programme	Now
Having clear meeting objectives	☐	☐
Using an agenda	☐	☐
Sending an agenda out in advance	☐	☐
Allocating times to agenda items	☐	☐
Specifying type of outcome for items –eg for information/decision	☐	☐
Others, please specify:		
_____	☐	☐
_____	☐	☐

8 How many meetings have you participated in since the programme (other than as the chair)? Please tick the appropriate box.

No meetings ☐
1–3 meetings ☐
4–6 meetings ☐
7 or more meetings ☐

If your answer was *No meetings*, please go to Q11.

9 To what extent has the programme helped you to participate in meetings more effectively? Please circle the appropriate rating.

Not at all   1   2   3   4   5   6   Very much

10. Please tick if you were using any of the following techniques:

	Before the programme	Now
Requesting an agenda	☐	☐
Setting aside time to prepare for meeting	☐	☐
Attending for specific items only	☐	☐
Sending written contributions when only involved in minor items	☐	☐

Others, please specify:

_____ ☐ ☐

_____ ☐ ☐

11. To what extent has the programme helped you to delegate more effectively? Please circle the appropriate rating.

Not at all   1   2   3   4   5   6   N/A Very much

If your answer is *N/A*, please go to Q13.

12. Please tick if you were using any of the following delegation techniques:

	Before the programme	Now
Prepare written brief	☐	☐
Clarify use of resources	☐	☐
Set clear time-scales	☐	☐
Set up review meetings	☐	☐
Give feedback on results	☐	☐

13. Were there any other ways in which the programme helped you improve your time management skills? If so, please describe them.

14. Are there any problems or barriers to your implementing the time management skills that you learned on the programme?

15. Overall, how would you rate your time management skill before the programme and now? Please circle the appropriate rating (1 indicates poor time management skills ... 6 indicates very good time management skills).

Before the programme   1   2   3   4   5   6

Now   1   2   3   4   5   6

16. Looking back on the programme, what comments or changes would you like to make for improving its effectiveness?

21
Cost effectiveness and the cost/benefit of learning

INTRODUCTION

The evaluation process outlined so far has looked at answering the following questions:

- How have the learners reacted to the learning – to what extent has the learning met the their satisfaction objectives?

- What have they learned – to what extent has the learning intervention met the learning objectives set out for it?

- How has their job behaviour and the results achieved changed – to what extent has the learning intervention met the job objectives and organisational objectives?

Another vital element in the equation, however, is the cost of the learning. It is a rare organisation in which cost is of no concern! There are two other important questions that must therefore be considered:

- Has the learning been delivered in the most cost-effective way – ie at the least cost for achieving the objectives?

- Do the benefits of the learning outweigh the costs, or, expressed a little differently, does the learning provide an adequate return on the investment made in it?

HOW COST-EFFECTIVE IS THE LEARNING?

To a large extent the first of these questions will or should have been addressed through the process of systematic LNA outlined in the earlier sections of this book. This process will have ensured that:

- the learning is to meet a clearly defined business need

- a learning intervention is the most appropriate way of meeting that business need

- the learning intervention has been specified very precisely – in terms of target audience, measurable learning objectives, etc

- the issue of 'make or buy' has been investigated – ranging from developing and delivering the intervention in-house to sending learners on open programmes.

One of the most difficult decisions to make is how the learning is delivered. There is a wide variety of approaches, from the traditional classroom-based approach, e-learning interventions, distance learning packages, etc, through to coaching on-the-job and/or a mixture of these! The type of approach adopted may have a significant impact on the cost of the intervention.

Usually the decision is based on a mixture of such factors as:

- the learning styles of the target population
- job constraints – eg those which might make it difficult for learners to be released as a group
- the type of learning – eg knowledge-based learning lends itself well to e-learning/TBT solutions and distance learning approaches
- the learning culture/strategy of the organisation, which might be encouraging the use of approaches such as action learning or self-managed learning
- the experience of the learning professionals involved, which might favour more traditional approaches, such as classroom-based learning.
- the size of the target population – eg tailored IT-based solutions are costly to develop and cheap to deliver so they usually require a large target audience to make them a cost-effective solution.

There has been quite a lot of research done on comparing e-learning/TBT approaches and distance learning approaches with more traditional learning interventions, but very little on comparing other approaches. The assessment is usually carried out *prior* to the intervention, as part of the LNA process, to decide on the most cost-effective approach – ie how to achieve the learning objectives at the minimum cost.

Cost-effectiveness evaluation is where two or more different learning interventions designed to meet the same learning objectives and ultimately the same business need are evaluated and compared. This type of evaluation is done very infrequently, and is of most benefit for major ongoing learning programmes where there is a significant financial investment in the learning, such as induction programmes or programmes for new job entrants – eg police officers, train drivers, etc (see the case study overleaf).

Cost-effectiveness study – innovative induction

Happy Hotels is a chain of 72 hotels. All new staff currently receive an induction programme based on a two-day classroom-type learning intervention delivered by internal facilitators which had development costs of £4,000. Around 2,000 new staff are taken on each year. It has been decided to investigate whether a TBT solution would provide a more cost-effective way of meeting the learning needs of the new staff. An interactive multimedia package was developed at a cost of £75,000 and launched at six hotels. The delivery costs are assessed at £80 per head for the classroom programme and £30 per head for the TBT solution. The results were benchmarked against a control group of six hotels similar in terms of size, turnover and customer satisfaction level which continued to use the existing induction training package.

The performance indicators chosen were:

- overall customer satisfaction levels
- staff turnover during first year.

The results were as follows:

Indicator	IT-based learning	Traditional learning – control group	Difference
Customer satisfaction	Increased from 70% to 86%	Increased from 70% to 75%	Additional 11% satisfaction ratings
Staff turnover	7% reduction, saving £14,000 in first year	2% reduction, saving £4,000 in first year	Saving of £10,000 in first year

If you compared the two approaches on a purely cost basis, then across the whole chain, with 2,000 new staff/year in the first year:

IT-based learning		Traditional learning	
Development costs	£75,000	Development costs	£4,000
Delivery costs	£30 × 2000 = £60,000	Delivery costs	£80 × 2000 = £160,000
Total costs	£135,000	Total costs	£164,000

The IT-based solution pays for itself in less than a year.

The results show that it also provides a more effective solution.

DO THE BENEFITS OF THE LEARNING INTERVENTION JUSTIFY THE EXPENDITURE ON IT?

This second question is perhaps the most fundamental as well as the most difficult question to address in the whole of the evaluation arena. Learning is often described as an investment – usually because the term 'investment' is perceived as more positive than describing it as a cost! However, because it is an investment in just the same way as building a new factory, buying a new item of equipment, buying stocks and shares – requiring an expenditure of money and resources by the organisation – a return will be expected. Most major investments by organisations have to be justified in advance of the agreement to proceed. This is often done using some form of investment appraisal process that involves:

- assessing the expenditure required and the timing of the expenditure
- estimating the benefits that will result from the expenditure in monetary terms and when these benefits will accrue
- taking into account the time value of money (discounting the value) – ie that the benefits are worth more the sooner they are achieved.

The investment appraisal of general projects usually results in one of three measures:

- the payback period – ie the period of time it takes to recoup the expenditure from the flow of benefits
- the net present value for the project, expressed as a sum of money which represents the present value (the value in today's terms) of a future flow of benefits over and above the original investment
- the internal rate of return for the project – eg 6 per cent, which is similar in concept to the interest rate that would be received if the money had been invested in a bank or building society.

With many types of investment – such as a new warehouse, a refurbished department store, a new computer system – the benefits will continue over a number of years: the lifetime of the asset. Hence the focus on looking at the flow of benefits over a period of years and taking into account the time value of money. Exactly the same process can be used for learning interventions. However, the focus tends to be only on one year's benefits, and perhaps occasionally two years. This is because of the following factors:

- the problem of intervening events – the longer the period following the intervention, the greater the possible effect of these (see Chapter 20)
- the extent to which some of the learning might have taken place through simply doing the job
- the needs of the job change
- the inevitable moving of individuals on to new jobs, etc.

The measures that tend to be used for the appraisal of learning projects are:

- payback period

- net value = benefits − costs

- percentage return on investment $= \dfrac{\text{benefits}}{\text{costs}} \times 100$.

Although we have described the process as an appraisal before the investment takes place to justify proceeding with it, the process is exactly the same for testing whether an investment that has taken place is worthwhile – ie for learning evaluation.

Learning projects often escape the rigorous financial discipline of this form of investment appraisal before the decision to proceed and indeed frequently avoid any financial assessment after the event. The downside of this more financially relaxed approach has been that in times of cutback the learning budget often appears a soft option. It can be difficult to show any tangible financial rewards from learning interventions, whereas usually the production manager can *prove* what the effects would be of closing down a production line, or what would be the rewards from investment in new equipment, and the distribution director can *prove* what the effects would be of cutting back the warehouse staff or the rewards would be from a new computerised stock control system.

So assessing the costs and benefits or working out the rate of return from learning would seem to have considerable merits. Why, then, is it not done more frequently? The assessment of the cost side of the equation is tedious but generally not hard. Chapter 13 sets out the costs of developing and delivering learning programmes. However, the other side of the equation, quantifying the benefits or returns from the learning in *monetary* terms, can be very challenging.

Let's look at three ways of assessing the benefits:

- using performance indicators
- using a value added approach
- from learning projects.

Assessing benefits using performance indicators

Sometimes it can be straightforward to quantify the benefits – as for example when the learning can be shown to produce a quantifiable:

- increase in sales
- increase in productivity/output
- reduction in wastage and hence in production costs
- reduction in accidents/equipment downtime, etc, and hence in costs
- reduction in absence rates, labour turnover and hence in labour costs.

To demonstrate the principles let's take some simple case studies. In the two case studies below, the first uses the payback period measure and also illustrates that there will be other unquantifiable benefits as well. It is always worthwhile identifying these as part of the evaluation study. The second case study uses a simple return-on-investment approach. However, it also includes a way of dealing with an intervening factor – in this case the impact of external market conditions on sales performance.

Cost/benefit study – wasteful warehouse

A large retail organisation in East Anglia was experiencing problems with wastage and damage of stock during the storage, picking and delivery of goods, and also problems with back injuries. It was decided to run a learning programme in the proper handling of stock, including good lifting techniques. All the warehouse and the transport staff who were involved in handling the goods – 64 staff in total – participated in a series of one-day learning events. The programme was developed and run by a specialist consultant, in liaison with the in-house learning manager, and run partly in a seminar room in a local hotel (half a day) and partly in the warehouse (half a day). Eight programmes were run.

Costs	
Cost of developing the programme (Consultant's fee)	£2,000
Cost of delivering the programme (8 × £1,000 per day)	£8,000
Cost of seminar room (including lunch etc) (8 × £90)	£720
Cost of learners' time = 64 × £90 (Cost per day for each learner = £90, based on salary + on-cost)	£5,760
Total costs	£16,480

Benefits	
Wastage and damage Wastage and damage was measured before and after the learning intervention. In three months before, average loss was 1.5% of stock value In three months after, average loss was 0.8% of stock value Savings in wastage of stock thus 0.7% of stock Over a year average value of stock 5 £1,500,000 Annual savings in wastage is forecast 5 £10,500	£10,500
Reduction in days lost through back injuries In three months before, 13 days lost In three months after, 3 days lost Savings in days thus 10 Over a year, forecast saving: 40 days Cost per day for each learner: £90 (based on salary + on-cost)	£3,600
Total benefits	£14,100

CASE STUDY continued

Additional benefits
It was felt that morale and motivation had improved as staff now took more interest in their work (based on a focus group session with the supervisors).
There was an improvement in absenteeism and time-keeping – these were not quantified because the learning intervention had coincided with a tightening of the disciplinary procedures in this area – however, the supervisors felt that the programme had also contributed to this.
There were savings in the administration costs at the store in dealing with damaged and mis-picked goods and associated customer complaints – these were not quantified.
Relationships between the store staff and warehouse staff had improved as a result of the reduction in damaged and mis-picked goods that reached the store (based on anecdotal evidence from managers at the store and supervisors at the warehouse).
There was a reduction in pain and suffering for warehouse staff due to back injuries.

In financial terms, the programme paid for itself in just over a year.

The actual payback period

$$= \frac{16,480}{14,100}$$

$$= 1.17 \text{ years}$$

$$= 1 \text{ year } 62 \text{ days}$$

Cost/benefit study – soaring sales

A medium-sized manufacturing company has been concerned that it is sales are lagging behind the industry average. A one-week learning programme for sales representatives has been set up at a total cost per programme (including opportunity costs of lost sales while learners are on the programme) of £50,000. A group of sales representatives are chosen at random to go on the programme and their sales performance is monitored for a year afterwards. Their performance is compared with a comparable group of sales representatives who did not participate in the learning programme. The use of the control group is to take into account other factors such as the economic and competitive situation and any natural trend in sales performance. If a control group had not been used, it would be important to take into account these other factors some other way – perhaps, for example, by adjusting for the industry-wide increases in sales or simply by estimating what the expected sales might have been without the benefit of the learning intervention.

The increase in sales of the learning group over the control group was £75,000.

$$\text{Return on investment} = \frac{\text{benefits}}{\text{costs}} \times 100\%$$

$$= \frac{75,000}{50,000} \%$$

$$= 150\%$$

Not a bad return!

Cost/benefit evaluations are not often attempted on learning programmes in which it is difficult to identify monetary performance indicators. However, British Telecom (Coaley, 1993) carried out a very interesting study to determine the 'financial' worth of some of their management learning programmes. They set out first to identify *failure costs* due to poor performance by junior managers in the business. This was achieved by carrying out critical incident interviews (see Chapter 10) with the line managers. Performance ratings of the junior managers were made before and after the learning. Achievement of a certain rating post learning indicated that performance was 'normal, effective, acceptable' and therefore the failure costs due to poor performance would no longer occur. It was reported in *Personnel Management Plus* (January 1994) that the £7 million investment in the learning programme was estimated to have brought a £280 million return to the company (the net present value or worth to the company today of a flow of benefits over six years). Most finance directors would consider this an excellent return from their investment!

Assessing benefits using a value added approach

So, on now to the more tricky assessment of, say, a general management programme. In theory it may be possible to identify and measure performance indicators such as productivity increases, reduction in wastage, failure costs as British Telecom did, etc. However, in practice this can be very difficult and it is worth considering an alternative approach. It is based on the concept developed by Cascio and Ramos (Cascio, 1991) that salary is the starting-point for putting a value on performance:

Assuming an organisation's compensation program reflects current market rates for jobs, then the economic value of each employee's labour is reflected best in his or her annual wage or salary.

Using salary as the starting-point for putting a value on performance is the fundamental concept. There are the further issues of whether labour on-costs such as pension, National Insurance, cost of accommodation, etc, or an individual's contribution to profit should also be included.

The approach at its simplest is based on assessing the performance of the learner before the learning event, either on the whole job or on the part that is being addressed by the learning, and then again after learning event. See the case study below.

CASE STUDY

Cost/benefit study – super supervisor

Taking a very simple example, suppose that a supervisor whose salary is £20,000pa is being developed in leadership skills at a cost of £1,500. A job analysis identifies that the competencies being learned form 25 per cent of the full job. The learner is assessed at being 50 per cent competent in this area before the event and 80 per cent three months after the event.

$$\text{Added value from learning per year} = \text{value of salary paid for leadership competencies} \times \text{percentage gain in competence}$$

$$= £ (0.25 \times 20{,}000) \times \frac{(80 - 50)}{100}$$

$$= £ 5{,}000 \times 0.3$$

$$= £1{,}500$$

Let us assume that the benefits of the learning are £1,500 for the first year, but that it is estimated that without the learning the supervisor would have increased in competence to 70 per cent through experience and coaching on the job after one year. The benefit for the second year would then be £500. After two years it is assumed that the supervisor would have reached full competency without the programme.

The appraisal would be based on:

end of year	cash flow
0	− £1,500
1	+ £1,500
2	+ £500

$$\text{The return on investment over two years} = \frac{2{,}000}{1{,}500} \times 100\%$$

$$= 133\%$$

'Hang on a minute,' I hear you say. 'This looks nice and easy!' Well, yes, in a way it is – the concept is a very simple one. The hard part is the bit that is skipped over – assessing the competence level before and after the programme, and also taking a view about the way the benefits fall away over the period of time. Clearly, this is a subjective assessment for someone – probably the learner's manager can assist. There are various approaches to analysing the job and assessing competence level or performance level, including the use of performance grids and what is referred to as DIF (difficulty, importance, frequency) analysis. Cascio (1991), although rather complex, and Jackson (1989) provide useful further reading on these approaches.

Assessing benefits through learning-related projects

Another way of generating financial information on benefits is through costing the results of learning-related projects. For example, on a middle management learning intervention all the learners had to complete a project that made direct use of the knowledge and skills they were learning. These projects were then assessed on whether the objectives of the project had been achieved, on the approach and methodology used, and *on the financial benefits resulting*. The return on investment based on these projects alone was over 300 per cent! However, an issue here was the extent to which the projects might have been carried out and delivered some or all of the results without the learning intervention. In this case the organisation was not bothered about this caveat: it was delighted with the results.

For a more in-depth look at this fascinating area, readers might consult Phillips (1997). The book takes a very simple and straightforward approach and includes a wide variety of different case studies

CONCLUSION

Carrying out some form of cost/benefit analysis or investment appraisal requires thought and effort. For major learning interventions this should be an essential activity, and there are considerable benefits from using the discipline of this approach for most reasonable-sized learning projects. It is very difficult, if not impossible, to carry out the *perfect* appraisal. What is required is a reasonable best attempt! All cost/benefit analyses and investment appraisals are littered with assumptions of one sort or another. So take heart and give it a try. The more you do them and experiment with different approaches, the better you will become. As ever, always be clear and open about what has been done and what assumptions have been made. At least you will now be able to proffer some hard evidence to support the belief that learning is worthwhile!

READING AND REFERENCE

Cascio W. F. (1991), *Costing Human Resources,* 3rd edn, Massachusetts, Plus-Kent.

Coaley K. (1993), *Financial Value and Management Training,* Management Development Review, vol 6, no 2.

Jackson T. (1989), *Evaluation: Relating training to business performance*, London, Kogan Page.

Phillips J. (1997), *Return on Investment in Training and Performance Improvement Programs*, Houston Gulf Publishing Company.

22

Analysing evaluation results

INTRODUCTION

Evaluation studies can generate a large quantity of what can be called 'raw data', the basic numbers that cascade out of our questionnaires, interviews, monitoring of performance indicators, etc. However, these numbers as they stand do not tell us very much. In our book on managing information and statistics (Bee and Bee, 1999) we state:

> *Data on its own is meaningless. It must be converted into information before it can be used in the decision-making process.*

This chapter will look at some of the most useful techniques for converting data into useful information. The purpose is to introduce you to the techniques and how they can be used. It is not the intention to bury you in statistical theory and formulae but, if you want to find out more about a technique, to refer you on to a couple of books in the field.

The advent of simple but sophisticated computer software has opened up the field of statistics to a much wider audience. Standard spreadsheet packages such as MS Excel™ enable complex statistical functions to be calculated at the press of a button, and statistical charts and diagrams to be produced in seconds. This is both good news and bad news for the learning professional embarking on an analysis of evaluation results. The good news is that you can undertake quite sophisticated statistical analysis quite easily. The bad news is that you can be tempted down a sophisticated statistical path without really understanding what you are doing and therefore what the information produced is really telling you, and perhaps more importantly what it is not telling you. There are two basic messages to come out of this homily:

- Keep your analysis as simple as possible.
- If you do use a more sophisticated technique, make sure you understand it either by undertaking further reading or by seeking help from a friendly statistician (they do exist!).

The starting-point for any evaluation study must be the purpose or objective(s) of that study. This will guide the methodology and approach to the data collection. The analysis, too, should be undertaken with the objectives clearly in mind.

THE PURPOSE OF ANALYSIS

There are generally four main purposes for analysing evaluation results:

- to summarise data – often a great mass of data is produced and it is necessary reduce it down to a manageable form

- to compare data – results from different programmes, between the different types of learners, etc

- to examine relationships between data – between the results from learning-level evaluation and performance-level evaluation, between the effectiveness of the learning and the size of the learning group, etc

- to highlight specific/problem areas – with meeting a particular learning objective, with a particular facilitator, etc.

TYPES OF DATA

This chapter looks at how to analyse the two types of data, quantitative data and qualitative data. By 'quantitative data' we mean the type of data that has usually been generated by:

- responses to questions with rating scales, tick-boxes

- performance data, such as productivity, output, sales, absentee rates, wastage, costs, etc.

By 'qualitative data' we mean the types of responses generated from open questions – ie questions where the respondent is not limited to a tick-box or circling a score but is usually encouraged to provide his or her own thoughts and views and in-depth information on a particular topic. For example, a learner might be asked about the barriers to implementing learning in the workplace, how a programme might be improved, etc.

ANALYSING QUANTITATIVE DATA

We will look at two main approaches, diagrammatic and numerical. Diagrammatic approaches, as the name suggests, uses diagrams or pictorial representation to describe or present the information. Numerical methods rely on describing or presenting the information using a number or set of numbers. Both approaches are all about *conveying the message* – the message being sent by the evaluation results – in as clear and understandable a way as possible.

Diagrammatic approaches

Presenting data in a diagrammatic form can be a very powerful way of increasing the understanding and impact of that data. The most useful diagrammatic methods are:

- bar charts
- pictograms
- histograms
- pie charts
- graphs
- scatter diagrams.

Bar chart

As the name suggests, this chart presents information in the form of bars, which can be horizontal or vertical (Figure 13). Each bar represents an item of information and the height or length of the bar represents the quantity of that item. This is a simple but very useful way for presenting information, particularly reaction-level results (see Figure 13).

Pictogram

A form of bar chart in which the bars are replaced by pictures representing the item of information (Figure 14). This can be a very eye-catching way of presenting the information and is particularly useful in making presentations and for reports that are aimed at audiences who are less familiar with statistical charts – eg if the evaluation results are being reported back to a group of non-management participants (see Figure 14).

Histogram

A special form of bar chart that is used to present frequency information. It is hard to describe, so take a look at Figure 15 alongside. This shows the ratings (marks out of 100) given to a learning programme by learners over a specific year. It shows the percentage of occasions that the programme received ratings of, for example, 51–60 per cent and 61–70 per cent.

The main difference between bar charts and histograms is that with a bar chart there is no relationship between the bars – ie they can appear in any order – whereas in the histogram there is. For ease of analysis and presentation make sure that your groups are the same size. For instance, in the diagram the data has been divided into 10 per cent ranges.

Pie chart

This is a powerful way to compare sections of the data relative to the whole. As the name suggests, it presents the information in the shape of a pie or a segmented circle. Each segment of the pie represents a part of the data. Figure 16 alongside shows how learners rated a facilitator, split between four categories of ratings – very good, good, fair and poor. A segment can be highlighted by showing it as a cut slice of the pie slightly withdrawn from the whole.

Graph

Graphs can be used to show trends in data over time – see Figure 17 alongside, which shows learning expenditure per employee over a six-year period. Also, these can be used to show relationships between sets of data: see the later section on correlation and regression.

Scatter diagrams

Scatter diagrams are used to show relationships between sets of data – see Figure 18 alongside and the later section on correlation and regression.

Figure 13 | Simple bar chart
Learner ratings of safety programmes

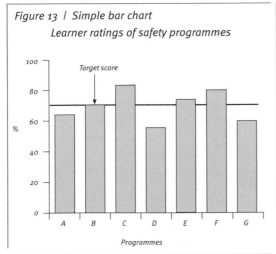

Figure 14 | Pictogram
Success rates on safety programmes

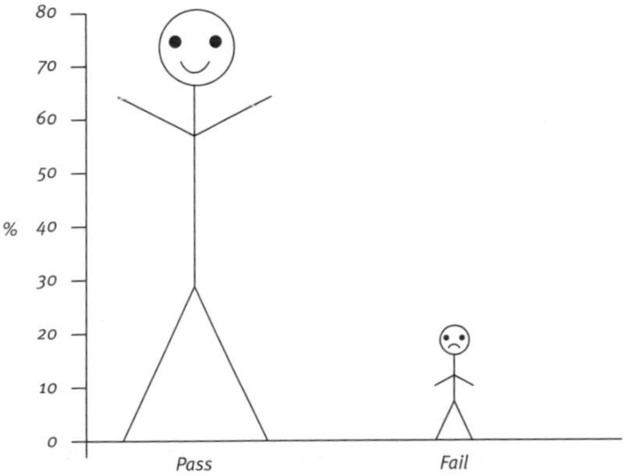

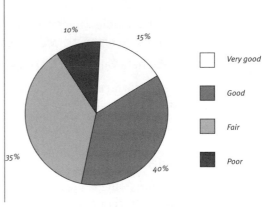

Figure 15 | Histogram
Distribution of scores of programmes in 2002

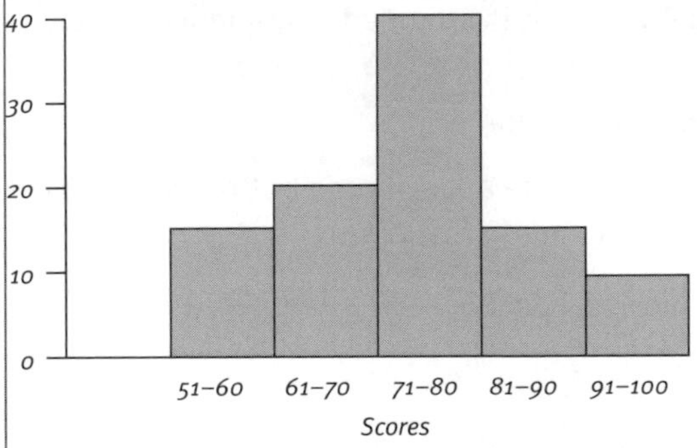

Figure 16 | Pie chart
Paricipant views on facilitator

Very good
Good
Fair
Poor

Figure 17 | Line graph
Learning expenditure/employee 1997–2002

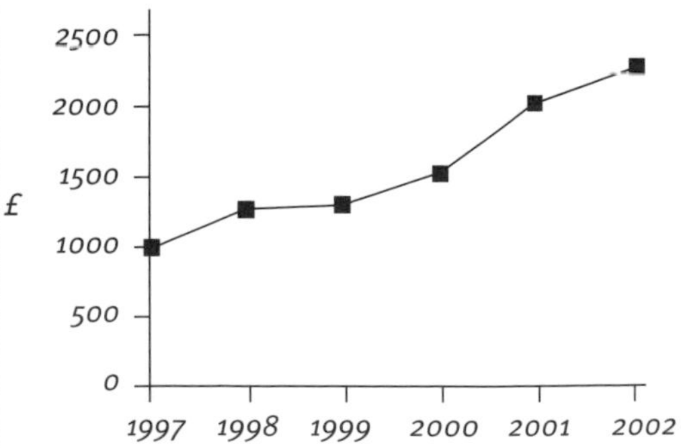

Figure 18 | Scatter diagram and regression line
Relationship between on-the-job scores and
learning scores

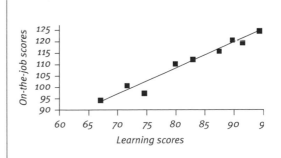

Numerical approaches

The most commonly used numerical methods for analysing evaluation data are:

- measures of location
- measures of dispersion
- scoring methods
- correlation and regression
- sampling, statistical inference and significance-testing.

All of these methods are well covered in the references at the end of the chapter except *scoring*, so we will devote more space to that method than the others.

Measures of location

Measures of location are designed to give information about a certain part or location of the data. The most commonly used ones are measures of the central or middle location. These are:

- the *mean* or *average* calculated by summing all the data items and dividing by the number of data items
- the *median* – the middle value of a set of data when it is arranged in numerical order, either from lowest to highest or vice versa
- the *mode* – the data value which occurs most frequently.

There are two other useful measures of location which provide a feel for the bottom half and the top half of the data respectively. These are related to the median and are:

- the *lower quartile* – the data value *below* which 25 per cent of the data items fall and *above* which 75 per cent of the data items occur (when the data is arranged in numerical order)
- the *upper quartile* – the value *above* which 25 per cent of the data items occur and *below* which 75 per cent of the data items fall (when the data is arranged in numerical order).

Measures of dispersion

Measures of dispersion indicate how variable the data is. There are three measures of dispersion commonly used:

- the *range* – the difference between the lowest and highest value in the data set
- the *inter-quartile* range – the difference between the lower and upper quartile – ie the span of the middle 50 per cent of the data
- the *standard deviation* – a measure of the dispersion or spread of the data around the mean: the higher the standard deviation the more dispersed or variable the data.

Generally with evaluation results you are hoping for as little dispersion as possible. The less variable the data is, the more focused is the message.

Scoring methods

There is a range of scoring methods available. The two most commonly used in evaluation are:

- semantic and Likert-type scales on questionnaires or observation forms – see the first and second examples below
- before and after knowledge-based tests – see the third example below.

EXAMPLE

A SEMANTIC DIFFERENTIAL SCALE

The question asked learners to rate the facilitator on a 6-point scale.

facilitator has poor knowledge of area	1	2	3	4	5	6	facilitator has excellent knowledge of the area
Results: (no of learners)	2	3	3	4	2	1	15 learners

The most commonly used method is to calculate an *average*. In respect of the question above:

$$\text{Average} \quad \frac{(2 \times 1) + (3 \times 2) + (3 \times 3) + (4 \times 4) + (2 \times 5) + (1 \times 6)}{15}$$

$$= \frac{49}{15}$$

$$= 3.3$$

An alternative method is to calculate the *score*.

$$\text{Score} = \frac{(2 \times 1) + (3 \times 2) + (3 \times 3) + (4 \times 4) + (2 \times 5) + (1 \times 6)}{6 \times 15} \times 100$$

$$= \frac{49}{90} \times 100$$

$$= 54\%$$

NB If the bottom end of the scale indicated a zero score – ie no knowledge – then it would be better to use a 0 to 5 scale.

Both the above approaches *assume* that the intervals on the scale are perceived by the respondents as the same size.

Another popular approach is to express the results as a proportion or percentage of the total learners.

The percentage of learners who rated the facilitator as 4, 5 or 6 $= \frac{7}{15} \times 100$

$$= 47\%$$

EXAMPLE

A LIKERT-TYPE SCALE

The question asked learners to tick the box that reflected their views on the quality of the catering on the learning programme.

	Low quality	Fair quality	Good quality	Very good quality	Total
No of learners	2	7	5	1	15

The most obvious approach here is to use the percentage of learners which fall into each category.

The percentage of learners who rated the catering as of good or very good quality

$$= \frac{(5 + 1)}{15} \times 100$$

$$= 40\,\%$$

EXAMPLE

SCORING BEFORE AND AFTER KNOWLEDGE BASED TESTS

Suppose a knowledge test consists of 20 questions and a learner scores 12 before the learning event and 16 after the learning event. Calculate a gain ratio to indicate the gain in learning.

Gain ratio $= \dfrac{\text{post-test score} - \text{pre-test score}}{\text{possible score} - \text{pre-test score}} \times 100$

Gain ratio $= \dfrac{(16 - 12)}{8} \times 100$

$\qquad\quad = \dfrac{4}{8} \times 100$

$\qquad\quad = 50\%$

The gain ratio for the whole course would be the average gain ratio for all learners. Alternatively, the distribution of gain ratios could be presented – eg 60% of learners achieved a gain ratio of 50% or more, 20% achieved a gain ratio of between 30% and up to 50%, and 20% achieved a gain ratio of less than 30%.

Correlation and regression

Correlation measures the relationship between two sets of data, often referred to as variables. Two sets of data are said to be correlated if changes in one are accompanied by changes in the other. The variables are positively correlated if they both move in the same direction – ie as one increases so does the other. The variables are negatively correlated if they move in opposite directions – ie as one increases the other decreases. The strength of the relationship is measured by the *correlation coefficient*. The correlation coefficient takes on values from −1 to +1. The nearer it is to either −1 (negative correlation) or +1 (positive correlation), the stronger is the relationship.

It is shown diagrammatically using a scatter diagram – see Figure 18. This plots the results of the scores gained by learners on a skills test held at the end of a learning programme – ie as part of the learning-level evaluation of the programme – with the results of a skills test conducted back on the job – ie as part of the performance-level evaluation of the programme. Each point on the scatter diagram represents a learner.

Using *regression analysis*, it is possible to fit a straight line to the data points which can then be used to make predictions (see Figure 18). In the example given it would be possible to predict what the on-the-job score would be, based on the learning score.

Sampling, statistical inference and significance testing

Often it is preferable to carry out an evaluation survey on a sample – eg of learners or of programmes – rather than survey the whole population. Sampling has the advantage that it is usually a quicker and cheaper way of obtaining the required information. When the sample is chosen in a statistically correct way, valid conclusions can be drawn about the whole population from the sample results. This process is called *statistical inference*. The sample will provide estimates of what the results would be if the whole population was surveyed. The important concern is how good the estimate is – ie how close it is to the true value for the population. The important decisions are about:

- the size of the sample
- how the sample is selected: there is a range of sampling methods – eg simple random sampling, stratified sampling, cluster sampling, quota sampling, etc.

Significance tests are used to test whether the results from one group are significantly different from those of another group – ie whether the differences are substantial enough that they could not be caused by chance variation. There is a range of significance tests available that are used in different circumstances. These tests can be useful for:

- comparing before and after learning for a particular outcome
- comparing the results of a group that has gone through the learning programme with those of a group that has not (operating as a control group)
- comparing results between different facilitators, different gender groups, etc.

Using computers

As noted in the introduction to this chapter, the advent of simple but sophisticated computer software has greatly increased the accessibility of analysis techniques to the learning professional. Three types of software are potentially of most use:

- spreadsheet packages (such as MS Excel™) – These are most frequently used to produce a wide range of statistical diagrams – eg bar charts, histograms, graphs, pie charts – quickly and easily. They can also be used for both simple and quite sophisticated statistical analyses – eg calculating averages, standard deviations, correlation coefficients, carrying out regression analysis, and significance tests.

- survey packages specifically designed for the preparation of questionnaires, their analysis and the presentation of results

- evaluation packages that have been specifically designed for the evaluation of learning events – These often form part of general training/learning packages which include training/learning needs analysis and training/learning administration. Such packages generally provide basic questionnaires which can be modified, and analysed simply by calculating percentages and averages and presenting the information in the form of bar charts, pie charts and graphs. Most versions currently are directed at reaction-level evaluation or simple recording of before and after competencies.

ANALYSING QUALITATIVE DATA

With qualitative data, the analyst is faced with a large amount of written information. The key to dealing with this information is to seek patterns in the different responses, label these patterns, and then group the responses under the labels – see the example below. Although there are computer programs (eg NUD.IST™) which carry out this work, they are not generally used at present unless there are very large quantities of data involved. For most learning-evaluation studies the analysis is undertaken by hand. Although rather time-consuming and painstaking work, carrying out this type of analysis gives enormous insight into the data.

EXAMPLE

ANALYSING OPEN QUESTIONS

Suppose that 100 learners have been asked to come up with ways that a learning programme could be improved. The first stage is to take a sample of about 20 questionnaires chosen at random. Record all the responses – on a flipchart is often helpful. Then look for patterns/similarities in the types of response – eg those relating to the length of the programme, the quality of hand-outs, the types of case studies, the balance between inputs and exercises, etc. Decide on a set of headings or groupings, then categorise all the responses under these heading as follows:

Programme too long	50
Programme too short	7
Improved hand-outs	20
More case studies	40
etc	

You can now analyse the data using the same techniques as for quantitative data – perhaps commenting that 50 per cent of learners felt the programme was too long, and 40 per cent thought that there should be more case studies, etc.

CONCLUSION

In this chapter we have covered briefly a range of analysis techniques. In summary, remember to:

- focus on the objectives of the evaluation study
- keep your analysis as simple as possible
- identify the messages you are getting from your analysis and then choose the best methods for conveying those messages.

Finally, don't be afraid to seek help – either from those friendly statisticians or by doing some further reading on areas of interest. In the next chapter we will look at the key issues of what to do with all this information once you have got it!

READING AND REFERENCE

This chapter has aimed to provide an introduction and an overview of the various statistical techniques that can be employed to help analyse and present evaluation results. It is beyond the remit of this book to go into detail on the more complex approaches. There are a large number of books on the use and application of statistical techniques. For a gentle introduction to all the techniques try Bee and Bee (1999). For a more in-depth read try Anderson, Sweeney and Williams (2001).

ANDERSON D. R., SWEENEY D. J. *and* WILLIAMS T. A. (2001), *Statistics for Business and Economics*, South Western College Publishing.
BEE R. *and* BEE F. (1999), *Managing Information and Statistics*, London, CIPD.

23
Presenting and using evaluation results

INTRODUCTION

We have planned and designed our study, collected the data and analysed the results. We are now at the final and crucial stage of presenting and using the evaluation information. It is often the stage that is neglected in terms of thinking through the issues and planning the approach. Yet it is without doubt the most important stage if you want to ensure that evaluation really does make a difference to the quality of learning and development in the organisation and its impact on individual, team and organisational performance. You will recall that this was one of our key principles.

The important issues are:

- *who* should have the results?
- *what* and *how* information should be presented.

There are also a number of what may be described as 'political' issues that must be taken into account at this stage.

WHO SHOULD HAVE THE RESULTS

In our *Complete Learning Evaluation Toolkit* (2000) we identify a long list of what we describe as stakeholders in the evaluation process – ranging from the learners themselves and the facilitators through to the customers (both internal and external) of the learners' services, the administrators of the programme, etc. However, we also identify (Bee and Bee, 2000)

the key stakeholders as those who will:

- *use the information produced by the evaluation study and*
- *make decisions resulting from the study which will affect the future quality of learning and development in the organisation.*

It is the key stakeholders who are clearly the primary audience for the results.

However, in addition it is very important to ensure that everyone who has participated in the evaluation study sees the results. They will have usually contributed time, energy and emotion to the process, and it is only fair and a matter of courtesy for them to see the results of their efforts.

Also, nothing undermines the willingness to complete questionnaires, be interviewed, etc, more than when there are no apparent outcomes from all this activity. Participants, too, can sometimes play a very useful role in validating the results. In some of our studies we have either carried out formal presentations or circulated the report to participants and then used focus groups to elicit and discuss their reactions and comments on the findings, judgements and recommendations.

WHAT AND HOW INFORMATION SHOULD BE PRESENTED

It can be a difficult issue to balance how much information is presented to ensure that the recipients have enough information to feel comfortable and confident in the results but at the same time do not suffer serious information overload! It is important that they fully understand the results and their implications, and also how the results have been reached, and therefore their limitations. Often the findings will be based on a mass of data and perhaps quite complex research methods and analysis techniques. It can be very tempting to go for telling them everything – to ensure that the audience is aware of the quality of the evaluation study and therefore the strength of the case for any recommendations. But beware of this approach. There is a great danger that the report will simply end up on the proverbial shelf and no actions will result, merely because the key stakeholders do not have the time and/or interest to plough their way through it. At the other end of the same spectrum, the key stakeholders may blindly accept all the findings without properly understanding them, which can then result in the implementation being flawed.

There are no easy answers to these issues – the important point is to be aware of them. In presenting the evaluation results:

- focus on the objectives – what the evaluation was trying to assess
- think hard about who is the audience – what information do they need, what will be the impact of the results
- be clear about the strengths and weaknesses of the study in terms of methodology and the practicalities of the data collection and analysis
- be constructive – eg highlighting areas for improvement rather than areas of weakness
- present the results in a professional way – writing a clear and succinct report, making good use of diagrammatic methods, etc
- be timely – agree an appropriate time-scale for reporting at the outset of the study and then stick to it, unless there are strong reasons for a change.

SOME KEY ISSUES

The previous chapters have addressed the issues of evaluation in what could almost be described as an artificial environment – where evaluation is seen as *scientific* research into whether learning is effective, where everyone takes an objective and unbiased view of the results of the process. In practice, as we all are well aware, the evaluation will be taking place in the real world of organisations where a number of factors may intervene to 'sully the scientific purity' of the results or how the results are used. Evaluation, almost by definition, implies reviewing somebody's (or rather, usually a number of people's) performance – eg the learning needs analyser, the learning sponsor/initiator, the facilitators, the learners, the learners' managers. Therefore evaluation can be often be perceived as something of a threat to those involved. They may feel they are being judged.

Also, the focus often appears to be on the facilitator, probably because a lot of the evaluation that goes on focuses on the delivery part of the process. We would argue vigorously that the facilitator is only one player, albeit an important one, in the learning experience. Equally key ingredients to the success of the learning process are:

- the quality of the original learning needs analysis – the vital foundation to any learning intervention
- the development and design of the learning intervention
- learners' motivation to take on board and apply the learning in their jobs
- support from learners' managers, peers, etc, to encourage the transfer of learning back into the workplace.

Another issue is that although the articulated objective of the evaluation may be expressed as assessing whether the learning intervention has met the business need, people may have their own agendas about what they want the evaluation process to achieve. Both these issues may affect the way in which people will participate in the evaluation process, either in terms of their willingness to be involved, or in terms of whether they will consciously or subconsciously try to subvert the process and how the results might be used.

Right at the start of this section we set out the importance of being very clear about the purpose of the evaluation at the outset of the whole process. Since this whole book advocates the principle that the clearer the objectives, the more likely you will be to achieve them, it would be surprising if this did not apply to the evaluation process itself! The message here is that if you are initiating and carrying out the evaluation study, be very clear about what all your own objectives are. If you are the initiator, bear in mind that the more you share your objectives with the executor of the study, the more likely the evaluation study will be to meet them. If you are the executor, an important first task may be to tease out all those objectives. Establishing who are the clients, the key stakeholders, is not always straightforward either – eg is it the learning manager or the sponsor of the learning intervention, or both? If there is more than one client, the issue of establishing the purpose of the study becomes more complex.

It is also important at the outset to consider, as far as is possible, how the results will be used and who will have access to those results. An ethical issue can occur when participants in an evaluation study have been told that their individual results will be regarded as confidential. It is vital at the planning stage to think through the implications of confidentiality, and whether in fact it can be achieved. Sometimes it can prove difficult in practice, and if this is the case, it is far better not to suggest that it can be achieved at all.

It would also be naive to suggest that the way evaluation studies are presented and then used will not be affected by organisational and political factors. It is rare that the evaluators themselves can be entirely objective because they will bring to the evaluation:

- some form of baggage by way of preconceptions and assumptions. Sometimes this baggage will be useful and sometimes detrimental. The extent of the baggage will depend probably on the closeness of the relationship between the evaluator and those being evaluated

- some level of concern about what the effects of an apparently critical evaluation will have on themselves, their part of the organisation, etc.

The *outside* evaluator – eg an external consultant – has the advantage and disadvantage that preconceptions and assumptions are more limited. This may mean on the positive side that they go into the evaluation with few preconceived ideas about what the results of the study will show. On the downside they may be operating without an awareness of the values and concerns of those involved or of the organisation as a whole. When presenting the results it is a brave or foolhardy evaluator who will not think about what impact the findings will have on those who are involved, and particularly on the clients and the recipients of the report. At a very obvious level, if one of the clients is the learning manager, to what extent may poor results from the study be seen as criticism of the learning function? Or if the client is the line manager who sponsored or initiated the learning, might poor results seem a reflection on the way he or she reached the decision to undertake the learning in the first place? Or even worse, suppose the learning intervention is a board initiative that turns out to be less than effective! An *inside* evaluator may feel inhibited by these pressures. An outside evaluator *may* be less affected but will also be aware that if the evaluation appears to be critical it may jeopardise the continuing relationship with the client!

USING EVALUATION RESULTS

So, in using evaluation results:

- be aware of the impact of the results on those involved and decide on the appropriate strategy for addressing these issues and sensitivities

- decide who needs to see the results and in what form – eg a presentation and detailed report to the sponsor, a summary to the board, a newsletter to all the participants

- decide what consultation is required, with whom, on what, before deciding on what action is to be taken

- decide on appropriate action as quickly as possible and then take that action as quickly as feasible – set up an action plan with clear targets and time-scales and a process for monitoring progress

- give feedback to those that have participated in the study – eg the learners, their managers, the facilitators: this will help sell the relevance of evaluation, and motivate and encourage further participation.

Evaluation information is just like any other information: decisions made based on it will be affected by a whole range of factors, and rightly so! However, this should not mean that which results and how they are acted upon, relies on chance, how busy the learning professional is at the time or how willing or unwilling key players are to face up to some unpalatable issues. What is important is that whatever decisions are taken – and these may be not to follow up some of the proposals – it is clear why those decisions have been taken.

CONCLUSION

In this whole section we have sought to set out a structured approach to the evaluation of learning interventions based on the multi-level model of Kirkpatrick *et al*. This is an essentially goal-based approach and provides the basis for the strong link with the learning needs analysis approach we have adopted. There are other approaches – eg *goal-free evaluation* which, as the name suggests, is where the evaluator does not set off to measure success against particular objectives but to identify any changes achieved; *responsive evaluation*, which looks at the effects of a learning programme in relation to the different stakeholders; and others. We believe that the traditional model of different levels provides both a structured and a conceptually straightforward approach. This is important because the learning professional will have to *sell* the need for and the benefits of evaluation to the learners, his or her line colleagues, senior managers, etc.

There can be concern that evaluation will result in a plethora of forms, interviews, group discussions, which will swamp the unsuspecting learners, their managers and just about anyone else who has been involved or shown an interest! There will be concern that evaluation will be time-consuming and expensive. The answer lies in keeping a sense of perspective. The most sophisticated evaluation studies should be reserved for the high-expenditure/high-profile programmes. Perhaps decide to evaluate a sample of programmes each year, and involve line colleagues in the choice of which programmes. In Chapter 16 we advocate establishing an evaluation strategy as part of the overall learning and development strategy which will set out the organisation's approach to evaluation. However, the most important contribution to 'selling' evaluation is that it is *seen* to be making a difference to the overall quality of the learning process and having an impact on individual, team and organisational performance. Ensuring that recommendations are followed up is a vital part of the process. Your job does not stop with producing the report – in fact the real work is just beginning: that of implementing the results.

However, we hope that we have convinced you that undertaking learning evaluation is a vital and integral part of the Learning Wheel. Also, that it is not such a daunting challenge as it first appeared! Do not be afraid to tackle it in easy stages, and seek advice and support from your line manager colleagues, friendly statisticians and the finance professionals. Evaluation should be a joint endeavour – the more people that are involved with the design and approach, the more ownership of the results there will be, and most important of all, the greater the likelihood that appropriate action will ensue.

For those of you who are now filled with enthusiasm and energy to carry out learning evaluation, you may like to try our *Toolkit* (Bee & Bee, 2000) for a more in-depth look at this fascinating and crucial area of a learning professional' s work.

READING AND REFERENCE

BEE F. *and* BEE R. (2000), *The Complete Learning Evaluation Toolkit*, London, CIPD.

Section 7
Reflections

Reflections

REFLECTIONS

In our introduction to this book we nailed our colours firmly to the mast in stating our view that the starting-point for *any* learning initiative must be the business needs of the organisation. We have gone on to say that the best way to meet those needs is to be *systematic* in researching who needs the learning, in what areas, with what degree of priority, over what time-scale and by what methods. It is worth reflecting on what the benefits of systematic LNA are. These are that:

- learning interventions are targeted on the needs of the organisation
- learning needs are identified in sufficient time to ensure that they can be met in the most appropriate way
- it allows for prioritising of learning activities to take place in a rational way
- it allows for learning budgets to be prepared on a rational basis
- it enables the learning intervention to be properly planned
- it enables learning resources to be used efficiently and effectively
- it sets the foundation for evaluation that will really make a difference to the quality and effectiveness of learning in the organisation
- it encourages ownership of the learning by all the stakeholders.

We have demonstrated the need to be rigorous in examining all solutions to the business needs analysis, not just the learning option and, once a learning intervention is identified as the preferred option the need to be very precise in defining what is required. We have stressed that when specifying the learning that is required, the outcomes should be stated in measurable, behavioural terms in order to provide the foundation for sound and useful LE.

Finally, we have set out what we believe to be good practice in LE, at the reaction, learning, performance and cost/benefit levels, at all times linking back through the original LNA to the business needs. The benefits of LE extend far beyond the direct and obvious ones of improving the quality of the learning experience and ensuring the effectiveness of the learning intervention. LE provides the basis for the learning function and the learning professional to be considered serious members of the *management team*. By demonstrating that learning delivers results, meets the business needs and represents a good investment of resources, the learning professional will now be operating on the same level playing-field as their line manager and other professional colleagues.

In suggesting a systematic approach to meeting the business/learning needs we introduced the concept of the Learning Wheel. However, we are aware that such a process is not always sequential in that it is not always easy to categorise a particular activity as always preceding, or following, another given activity. In the real world certain activities, which for convenience of explanation we have kept separate, will be rolled up together.

We have also stressed in the book the necessity for the learning professional to be concerned with the wider environment, to be familiar with the language of the manager, the accountant, the economist and the statistician, to be strategic in identifying the needs and in meeting those needs. We recognise that we are not alone in making the case for the learning professional to be proactive, rather than reactive, to what is going on in the organisation. There is a continuing move towards a different role for learning professionals – away from the role of provider of courses to being the focal point of the learning organisation by acting as change agents, and with the learning function at the core of the organisation's business strategy.

We have talked about how LE can make a difference to the quality of learning in our organisations. There are enormous opportunities to explore how we can improve the process of learning, by building on the concepts of blended learning (Schramm, 2002):

> *... to mean the combination of different modes of delivery (that take into account the learner's environment, motivation and learning styles) with different theoretical approaches. This creates a multi-layered and richer palette of learning methods.*

We believe that many organisations have only scratched the surface of the full potential of learning to take them forward into the future. This future, if nothing else, will be one where organisations will need to be more competitive, and where survival and growth will depend on operating at optimum efficiency and effectiveness. It will be a future where a key ingredient to success will be ensuring that all the organisation's human resources, be they full-time or part-time staff, contractors or temporary workers have the most up-to-date knowledge and skills to maximise their contribution. In other words, it will be a future where (Bontis *et al*, 1999):

> *The wealth-creating capacity of the enterprise will be based on the knowledge and capabilities of its people.*

What a challenge for the learning professional!

READING AND REFERENCE

BONTIS N., DRAGONETTI N. C., JACOBSEN K. *and* ROOS G. (1999), 'The knowledge toolbox: A review of the tools available to measure and manage intangible resources', *European Management Journal*, Vol 17 No.4, August.

SCHRAMM J. (2002), *Change Agenda*, London, CIPD.

Index

The Coach's Coach

Personal development for personal developers

Alison Hardingham
with Mike Brearley, Adrian Moorhouse and Brendan Venter

Being a coach is a tricky job, so whether you are an experienced coach or just starting out; a specialist consultant or a coaching manager, this book will help you become better and enjoy coaching more. It will help you to help the people you are coaching improve their performance – which, after all, is why you became a coach in the first place.

Alison Hardingham is a successful business coach and offers advice, techniques and examples drawn from experience of coaching people in all kinds of organisations and with the contributions of three phenomenally successful sports people: Mike Brearley, Adrian Moorhouse and Brendan Venter, you will be on track to being 'coach of the year'.

Mike Brearley is one of England's best known and most successful cricket captain; **Adrian Moorhouse** broke the world record in breast stroke five times and won an Olympic gold medal; and **Brendan Venter** was a member of the Springboks, South African Rugby Team, and subsequently played and coached at London Irish.

Order your copy now by visiting us online at www.cipd.co.uk/bookstore or call us on 0870 800 3366

Alison Hardingham is a business psychologist with more than twenty years' experience of coaching individuals and teams. She is a successful author and conference speaker.

2004	1 84398 075 4	Paperback	216 pages

The Chartered Institute of Personnel and Development is the leading publisher of books and reports for personnel and training professionals, students, and for all those concerned with the effective management and development of people at work.

Also from CIPD Publishing . . .

Learning and Development

4th Edition

Rosemary Harrison

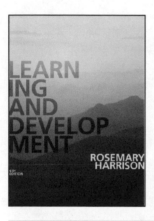

Learning and Development is the definitive textbook for all students of learning and development (L&D) issues. It provides a clear and detailed exposition of this increasingly important business subject, equipping students and practitioners alike with the tools to perform at both an operational and strategic level.

This book has been thoroughly revised to take into account the new CIPD Standard in L&D. It provides an invaluable framework for anyone studying the subject - combining the latest academic research and thinking with practical approaches that can be used in the workplace.

The text contains detailed sources of further information, and frequent questions and learning activities to enable readers to place theories firmly in a practical context. Each chapter has a clear overview and concise summary, providing ideal points for revision and reference.

Order your copy now online at www.cipd.co.uk/bookstore, or call us on 0870 800 3366

Rosemary Harrison has been the CIPD''s Chief Examiner, Employee Development/Learning and Development since 1996 and was formerly Director of the HRD Research Centre, University of Durham. She is a Chartered Fellow of the CIPD, Fellow of the Royal Society of Arts and Member of the Society of Authors, and is the author of many articles, chapters and texts on human resource management and development. She has a long record of consultancy and research in the strategic HRM and HRD fields, and has written about much of that work in her various publications.

| Published 2005 | 1 84398 050 9 | Paperback | 416 pages |

The Chartered Institute of Personnel and Development is the leading publisher of books and reports for personnel and training professionals, students, and for all those concerned with the effective management and development of people at work.

Also from CIPD Publishing . . .

Evaluating the ROI from Learning:

How to develop value-based training

Paul Kearns

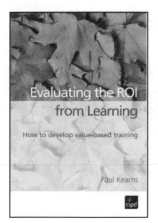

Want to add value to your organization through the choices you make? By evaluating the return on your investment in learning, you can add value to your organization.

Collect and understand the essential baseline measures that will help you to:
- work out your ROI;
- engage the learner;
- gain management commitment;
- build success into all training and development activities;
- prioritise resources to achieve the greatest value for your money; and
- enhance the credibility of the training team.

This book shows that effective evaluation isn't just about justifying your job, it's about making value-based choices that will improve and strengthen the impact of the training you provide.

Order your copy now online at www.cipd.co.uk/bookstore, or call us on 0870 800 3366

Paul Kearns is Director of PWL, an HR and training evaluation and measurement consultancy. He has worked in the field of HR, training, development and learning since 1978 and began specialising in training evaluation and ROI in 1991. He has a global reputation as both a consultant, facilitator, trainer and conference speaker. He has written several books on HR and training matters all with a focus on measuring benefits in terms of business results.

| Published 2005 | 1 84398 078 9 | Paperback | 176 pages |

The Chartered Institute of Personnel and Development is the leading publisher of books and reports for personnel and training professionals, students, and for all those concerned with the effective management and development of people at work.

Also from CIPD Publishing . . .

Creating a Learning and Development Strategy

2nd Edition

Andrew Mayo

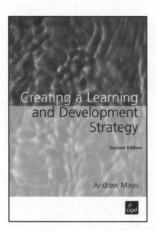

Learning and Development programmes must be intimately linked with your organisation's business strategy to create value. This books explains how to plan, create and implement a learning and development strategy that is aligned with your business' goals and objectives.

Through the use of stategic information and tools, along with practical examples, checklists and assignments, this text will help you to discover how to work with colleagues to align learning and development, as well as challenge business assumptions to clarify your organisation's needs and objectives.

Order your copy now online at www.cipd.co.uk/bookstore, or call us on 0870 800 3366

Andrew Mayo is Professor of Human Capital Management at Middlesex University Business School and Director of Mayo International Learning Ltd, a consultancy specialising in developing human capital. He is also Fellow and Programme Director for the Centre of Management Development at London Business School.

Published 2004	1 84398 056 8	Paperback	224 pages

The Chartered Institute of Personnel and Development is the leading publisher of books and reports for personnel and training professionals, students, and for all those concerned with the effective management and development of people at work.